MW01115673

FROM ANCIENT WISDOM TO MODERN UNDERSTANDING

A HISTORICAL SURVEY OF SYSTEMATIC THEOLOGY

From Ancient Wisdom to Modern Understanding

A Historical Survey of Systematic Theology

J. NEIL LIPSCOMB

Practical Primers on Systematic Theology

FROM ANCIENT WISDOM TO MODERN UNDERSTANDING: A HISTORICAL SURVEY OF SYSTEMATIC THEOLOGY

Copyright © 2023 by J. Neil Lipscomb

All rights reserved.

No part of this work may be reproduced or transmitted in any form or by any means, electronic or mechanical, including photocopying and recording, or by any information storage or retrieval system, except as may be expressly permitted by the 1976 Copyright Act or by written permission of the publisher, except for brief quotations in printed reviews.

ISBN 979-886-392-731-2

Scripture quotations taken from the (LSB®) Legacy Standard Bible®, Copyright © 2021 by The Lockman Foundation. Used by permission. All rights reserved. Managed in partnership with Three Sixteen Publishing Inc. LSBible.org and 316publishing.com.

Second Edition, 2024

14 15 16 17 18 19 20 21 22 23—10 9 8 7 6 5 4 3 2 1
PRINTED IN THE UNITED STATES OF AMERICA

TABLE OF CONTENTS

ACKNOWLEDGEMENTS

As anyone who has written a book well knows, such an endeavor is never a single effort, and this is particularly true with this, my first book. In attempting to heed the biblical injunction to pay "honor to whom honor is owed" (Rom. 13:7), I would like to single out the following friends and family for their specific help in this project.

First, to Robert S. Whitworth, forever known affectionately as "Chaplain Bob," who graciously loved an unlovable, patiently witnessed to me, and spent years discipling me. Everything I aspire to do and be I first saw modeled in this man of God.

Second, to pastor and professor Josh Philpot, and to pastor Chris Engelsma, both for their encouragement and feedback, and for their help in locating hard-to-find information.

Third, to a special group of friends: Joshua Beaver, Daniel McAdams, Jennifer Law, and Sabrina Cady. Their wonderful sense of humor, quick wit, love of Scripture, firm stance on biblical truth, vibrant faith in the Lord Jesus, and warm fellowship and friendship has been a godsend. Special thanks, too, to pastor Luke Morrison for volunteering as a reader, and for his encouragement. I also appreciate the outstanding copyediting and constructive criticisms offered by James Quiggle.

Fourth, to Dennis, professional philosopher and my father, for decades of stimulating conversations and encouragement, and for countless books purchased. Above all, I am grateful for the manner in which my Dad has modeled steadfast, unconditional love from the beginning.

Finally, but most importantly, I would be remiss to not acknowledge the Lord Jesus, who loved me and gave Himself for me when I did not love Him. Among the countless blessings of being made a new creation (cf. 2 Cor. 5:17), the Lord took someone who once hated both God and academics, and turned him into some whose first book is this, a survey of the history of systematic theology. Truly, Yahweh's ways and thoughts are not our own (Isa. 55:8-9).

ABBREVIATIONS

General

AD—*anno Domini* (in the year of [our] Lord)
BC—before Christ
ca.—*circa*, about, approximately
cf.—confer, compare
chap., chaps.—chapter(s)
comp.—compiled, compilation, compiler
ed.—edition
e.g.—*exempli gratia*, for example
et al.—*et alii*, and others
etc.—*et cetera*, and the rest
Gk.—Greek
Heb.—Hebrew
ibid.—*ibidem*, in the same place
i.e.—*id est*, that is
lit.—literal, literally
n., nn.—note(s)
NT—New Testament
OT—Old Testament
par., pars.—paragraph(s)
pl.—plural
q.v.—*quod vide*, which see
s.v.—*sub verbo*, under the word
trans.—translation, translator, translated
vol., vols.—volume(s)
vs.—versus

Resources

For full bibliographical information, see the Bibliography. When cited, superscripted numbers (e.g., *EDT*^{2}, *EDT*^{3}) indicate subsequent editions of that particular work (thus, lack of a superscripted number indicates a first edition).

BCDTT = *Baker Compact Dictionary of Theological Terms*
BECA = *Baker Encyclopedia of Christian Apologetics*
CamDCT = *Cambridge Dictionary of Christian Theology*
CDCT = *Concise Dictionary of Christian Theology*
CDTT = *Concise Dictionary of Theological Terms*

CEPR = *Concise Encyclopedia of the Philosophy of Religion*

DHT = *Dictionary of Historical Theology*

EAC = *Encyclopedia of Ancient Christianity*

ECT = *Encyclopedia of Christian Theology*

EDT = *Evangelical Dictionary of Theology*

EDWR = *Evangelical Dictionary of World Religions*

GDT = *Global Dictionary of Theology*

HOT = *A Handbook of Theology*

MHT = *Moody Handbook of Theology*, rev. and exp.

NDT = *New Dictionary of Theology*

NHCT = *New Handbook of Christian Theology*

ODCC = *Oxford Dictionary of the Christian Church*

WDT = *Wycliffe Dictionary of Theology*

WDTT = *Westminster Dictionary of Theological Terms*

Abbreviations of Books of the Bible

Old Testament

Gen—Genesis
Ex—Exodus
Lev—Leviticus
Num—Numbers
Deut—Deuteronomy
Josh—Joshua
Judg—Judges
Ruth—Ruth
1–2 Sam—1–2 Samuel
1–2 Kgs—1–2 Kings
1–2 Chr—1–2 Chronicles
Ezra—Ezra
Neh—Nehemiah
Esth—Esther
Job—Job
Ps, Pss (pl.)—Psalms
Prov—Proverbs
Eccl—Ecclesiastes
Song—Song of Solomon
Isa—Isaiah
Jer—Jeremiah
Lam—Lamentations
Ezek—Ezekiel
Dan—Daniel
Hos—Hosea
Joel—Joel
Amos—Amos
Obad—Obadiah
Jonah—Jonah
Mic—Micah

Nah—Nahum
Hab—Habakkuk
Zeph—Zephaniah
Hag—Haggai
Zech—Zechariah
Mal—Malachi

New Testament

Matt—Matthew
Mark—Mark
Luke—Luke
John—John
Acts—Acts
Rom—Romans
1–2 Cor—1–2 Corinthians
Gal—Galatians
Eph—Ephesians
Phil—Philippians
Col—Colossians
1–2 Thes—1–2 Thessalonians
1–2 Tim—1–2 Timothy
Titus—Titus
Phlm—Philemon
Heb—Hebrews
Jas—James
1–2 Pet—1–2 Peter
1–2–3 John—1–2–3 John
Jude—Jude
Rev—Revelation

SERIES PREFACE

"Practical Primers on Systematic Theology" is a series of books designed to provide readers with a comprehensive understanding of the major teachings of the Christian faith. A sound knowledge of biblical doctrine is essential for living a holy life that pleases and glorifies God. To this end, this series of primers will provide readers with a thorough overview of all the major loci of systematic theology, as well as issues germane to such. These primers are intended as a learning tool for both laypeople and scholars, providing a foundation for further study and reflection on the doctrines of Christianity.

Primers, as learning tools, are designed to provide a basic understanding of a subject. They are intended to be an introduction to a particular topic, and are meant to be accessible to those with little or no prior knowledge of the subject matter. The purpose of these particular primers is to provide readers with a comprehensive introduction to the discipline of systematic theology. Through their clear and concise writing, readers will gain an understanding of the key doctrines and themes of the Christian faith. Each primer in the series will provide readers with the foundational knowledge of systematic theology they need to gain a deeper understanding of Scripture.

Sound doctrine is vital for the Christian life. It provides a foundation for understanding the nature of God and our relationship to Him, and is essential for the growth and maturity of believers. It is also necessary for the pursuit of holiness and for glorifying God in our lives. This series will focus on providing readers with a solid understanding of the doctrines of

Christianity, so that they may learn how to apply biblical truths to their lives and ministry, and thus be better equipped to live a life that is pleasing to God. May the Practical Primers on Systematic Theology Series be an invaluable resource for those seeking a solid foundation in the principles of Christian doctrine. Our prayer is that the books in this series will help readers grow in their knowledge of the faith and equip them to live out God's Word in the world. The prayer of Augustine of Hippo (354–430) is our own:

> "O Lord the one God, God the Trinity, whatever I have said in these books that is of Thine, may they acknowledge who are Thine; if anything of my own, may it be pardoned both by Thee and by those who are Thine. Amen."[1]

[1] Augustine, *On the Trinity*, Book XV, Chapter 28, 51.

INTRODUCTION

TWO thousand years ago, the Lord Jesus fulfilled His promise to send another Helper (John 14:16; 15:26), and on the Day of Pentecost the Holy Spirit was poured out and the church (also promised by Jesus in Luke 24:49; Acts 1:4–5, 8) was birthed. God's special revelation[1] through the Lord Jesus and His apostles was inscripturated (2 Tim. 3:16–17; 2 Pet. 1:20–21), and eventually these writings were providentially collected into the biblical canon.[2] For the

---

[1] One of two categories of God's revelation or self–disclosure (the other being general, or natural, revelation), "special" revelation is God's disclosing of Himself at particular times and places through particular media, most notably in Scripture (2 Tim 3:16–17; 2 Pet 1:19–21) and ultimately and supremely in His Son, Jesus Christ (John 1:18; 5:3–37; 6:63; 14:10). A helpful work (written while he was still theologically conservative) is Clark H. Pinnock, *Biblical Revelation* (Chicago, IL: Moody, 1971). See also Colin Gunton, *A Brief Theology of Revelation* (Edinburgh, Scotland: T&T Clark, 1995); and Peter Jensen, *The Revelation of God,* Contours of Christian Theology (Downers Grove, IL: InterVarsity, 2002). Briefly, see *MHT*, 159–63; Rhyne Putnam, "Revelation," in *HOT*, 25–36.

[2] The canon of Scripture (from Gk. *kanōn*, "reed; measuring rod; standard of measure") refers to the collection of divinely inspired or God-breathed (2 Tim. 3:16–17; 2 Pet. 1:19–21) and thus inerrant and infallible books accepted by the church as authoritative for faith and practice. Two classic studies are R. Laird Harris, *Inspiration and Canonicity of the Bible* (Grand Rapids, MI: Zondervan, 1969); and F. F. Bruce, *The Canon of Scripture* (Downers Grove, IL: InterVarsity, 1988).

past two millennia, the Holy Spirit has gifted the body of Christ with teachers (Eph. 4:11), who have sought to faithfully equip the church with sound doctrine, preaching and teaching the whole counsel of God's Word (cf. Acts 20:27).

Despite those who would downplay if not reject doctrine—perhaps repeating the pious–sounding and altogether foolish mantra, "Just give me Jesus!"—the fact is, Scripture has much to say about the importance and necessity of doctrine. Adam Harwood (b. 1974) provides a helpful summary:

> The practice of providing a comprehensive explanation and defense of the Christian faith can be seen in the writings of the New Testament and throughout the history of the church. For example, Paul refers to church leaders instructing in "sound doctrine" (*hygiainousē didaskalia*, Titus 1:9) as well as refuting those who contradict sound doctrine. Similar instructions are seen in 1 Timothy 1:10; 2 Timothy 4:3; and Titus 2:1. Also, Paul refers to correctly handling "the message of truth" (*ton logon tēs alētheias*, 2 Tim 2:15) and names two teachers who swerved from the truth and ruined the faith of some people (2 Tim 2:18). Jesus said his "teaching" (*didachē*, John 7:16) was from the one who sent him, and the apostles were accused by the high priest of filling Jerusalem with their teaching (Acts 5:28). Jesus and the apostles taught people about God.[3]

Harwood continues, "Although the New Testament references to doctrine and teaching are not synonymous with postcanonical attempts to

---

[3] Adam Harwood, *Christian Theology: Biblical, Historical, Systematic* (Bellingham, WA: Lexham Academic, 2022), 2.

formulate and articulate the Christian faith, the former is the foundation of the latter."[4]

These "postcanonical attempts to formulate and articulate the Christian faith" have been variously denominated *doctrina sacra* (Augustine), *sacra scriptura*, *sacra eruditio*, *sacra pagina*, *sacra doctrina*, and, ultimately (due to the influence of the influence of John Scotus Eriugena, 810–77), as *theologia.* The word *theology* comes from the Greek word *theologia*, being a compound of *theos* ("God") and the suffix *–logia* ("word," "discourse," or "doctrine"); accordingly, *theology* is simply the *logos* concerning *theos*.[5]

This discourse concerning God—the program of study and the actual construction of systematic theology—is, or at least ought to be, *systematic*.[6] God is not the author of confusion (1 Cor. 14:33), and if it is God's will that in the church all things be done decently and in order (1

[4] *Ibid*, 3. Hence, as Kevin Vanhoozer observes, "Theology is as old as the proclamation, explication and application of the Scriptures as the Word of God." Vanhoozer, "Systematic Theology," in *NDT*², 885.

[5] The earliest known occurrence of the word *theologia* is in Plato, *Politeia* II 379a.5–6 (written *ca.* 375 BC), in a passage questioning the pedagogical use of mythology. Cf. Aristotle, *Metaph.* 10, 7, 4; 11, 6, 4; and Lactantius, *De Ira Dei*, 11. Veli–Matti Kärkkäinen (b. 1958) clarifies, "In pre–Christian usage, the term 'theology' appeared in three different types, namely, as 'mythical' theology of the poets concerning the deities, as 'political' theology of public life, and as 'natural' theology as the inquiry into the nature of the deities." Veli-Matti Kärkkäinen, *Christ and Reconciliation* (Grand Rapids, MI: Eerdmans, 2013) ePub: Introduction: A Methodological Vision in a New Key, Location 21.

[6] The English word *systematic* is a mid-seventeenth century term and another compound Greek word (*sustēmatikos*), being derived ultimately from *syn* ("together" or "with") and *histanai* ("to set up together," "combine," or "to cause to stand"). Thus, "Systematic" describes the parameters of the material—a structured development of the conversation concerning God and His works.

Cor. 14:46; cf. 14:2, 34), then thinking and teaching about eternal truth should also be systematic, coherent, and orderly. The cover of this work, with its imaginary cathedral, is meant to capture this truth. The great French Thomist philosopher Étienne Gilson (1884–1978) once described the apex of scholastic theology, Thomas Aquinas' unfinished yet massive *Summa Theologicae* (1266–73; 1,500,000 words), as "a cathedral of the mind" (Fr. *Cathédrale de la pensée*"; lit. a cathedral of thought or ideas).[7] Building cathedrals—whether literal edifices of worship or systems of theology—requires a tremendous amount of planning, organization, and effort to execute.[8]

For evangelicals,[9] systematic theology is a systematic study of what the Bible teaches concerning any given subject. More fully, systematic

---

[7] The Gilson reference describing the medieval schoolmen as building a "cathedral of the mind" (Fr. "cathédrale de la pensée") is from Étienne Gilson, *La philosophie au moyen âge* (Paris: Payot & Co., 1922), 56: "…nous verrons apparaître les Sommes qui sont, au moyen âge, les cathédrale de la pensée." Many follow Alister E. McGrath, *Christian Theology: An Introduction*, 5th ed. (Malden, MA: Wiley-Blackwell, 2011), 128, and also his *Historical Theology: An Introduction to the History of Christian Thought*, 2nd ed. (Malden, MA: Wiley-Blackwell, 2013), 4–5, in referring to this description from Gilson, without citing the primary source.

[8] For a fascinating work of historical fiction that depicts cathedral building in the Middle Ages, see Ken Follett's *Pillars of the Earth* (New York, NY: William Morey, 1989). See similarly Ben Hopkins, *Cathedral* (New York, NY: Europa, 2021).

[9] In American Protestantism, *evangelical* (from Gk., *euangelion*, "good news") is a designation for one who places particular emphasis on the authority of the Bible, the gospel, evangelism, and the need for personal conversion. According to the "Bebbington Quadrilateral," historian David W. Bebbington's (b. 1949) four distinguishing characteristics of evangelicalism, an evangelical affirms the following: (1) *conversionism* (the need for personal faith in the gospel and a resultant changed life); (2) *activism* (living the gospel through missional endeavors and social involvement); (3) *biblicism* (trust in Scripture as true and

theology is the comprehensive and methodical study of God, His nature, and His relationship with His creation. This discipline seeks to coherently organize and present the diverse elements of Christian theology, drawing from the authoritative source of the Bible and incorporating insights from relevant secondary sources (better: resources) such as tradition, reason, experience, and community. Systematic theology employs sound grammatical-historical exegesis, respects the historical development of doctrine within the church, and restates these truths in a manner that is understandable and applicable to contemporary audiences. The ultimate goal of systematic theology is to strengthen and satisfy believers in their relationship with God, promote a unified understanding of divine

---

the ultimate authority); and (4) *crucicentrism* (stress on the cross of Christ as the only means of accomplishing salvation). Bebbington, *Evangelicalism in Modern Britain: A History from the 1730s to the 1980s* (London: Unwin Hymna, 1989), 1–17. Adding to Bebbington's four criteria, John G. Stackhouse adds a fifth criterion—namely, transdenominationalism. Stackhouse, "Evangelical Theology Should Be Evangelical," in *Evangelical Futures: A Conversation on Theological Method,* ed. John G. Stackhouse Jr. (Grand Rapids, MI: Baker, 2000), 42, and more fully in "Generic Evangelicalism," in *Four Views on the Spectrum of Evangelicalism*, ed. Andrew David Naselli and Collin Hansen (Grand Rapids, MI: Zondervan, 2011), 116–42. Bebbington has criticized Stackhouse in "About the Definition of Evangelicalism . . .," Review of *Four Views on the Spectrum of Evangelicalism*, ed. Andrew David Naselli and Collin Hansen, in *Evangelical Studies Bulletin* 83 (Fall 2012), 1–6. Timothy Larsen (b. 1967) has crafted his own five-fold definition, which he relates his colleagues have referred to as "the Larsen Pentagon." Larsen, "Defining and Locating Evangelicalism," in Timothy Larsen and Daniel J. Treier, eds., *The Cambridge Companion to Evangelical Theology,* Cambridge Companions to Religion (New York, NY: Cambridge University, 2007), 1 (the whole essay spans 1–14). See further Derek J. Tidball, *Who Are the Evangelicals?* (London: Marshall Pickering, 1994); Thomas J. Kidd, *Who Is an Evangelical? The History of a Movement in Crisis* (New Haven, CT: Yale University, 2019). See also H. Wayne House, "Evangelicals," *EDWR*, 184–88.

revelation, and apply these truths to the full scope of human life and thought, ultimately bringing praise and glory to God's name.

The phrase "systematic theology" originated in the sixteenth century with the work of the German Calvinist theologian and philosopher, Bartholomäus Keckermann (1572–1609),[10] and gained prominence during the period of Protestant scholasticism, although materially the concept certainly can be traced back to Christianity's beginnings and, indeed, in Scripture itself.[11] In 1727, the German Lutheran theologian Johann Franz Buddeus (1667–1729) reasoned that a theological proposition may be called "systematic" if: 1) it addressed the subject matter in a comprehensive manner, and 2) explained, proved, and confirmed its content in detail.[12]

The systematic approach to theology has its roots in the works of early church fathers like Irenaeus of Lyons (*ca.* 130–*ca.* 200), Origen (*ca.* 185–*ca.* 254), and Augustine (*ca.* 354–*ca.* 430), who sought to present a

---

[10] According to Harwood, *Christian Theology,* 4; citing Bartholomäus Keckermann, *Systema Sacrosanctae Theologiae, tribus libris adornatum* (Hanoviae: Apud Guilielmum Antonium, 1602). *Contra* Norman R. Gulley, *Systematic Theology*, 4 vols. (Berrien Springs, MI: Andrews University, 2003–16), 1:139, who asserts that "the term 'systematic theology' was not used until early in the eighteenth century." For more on Keckermann, known particularly for his *Analytic Method,* see Joseph S. Freedman, "The Career and Writings of Bartholomew Keckermann (d. 1609)," *Proceedings of the American Philosophical Society* 141 (1997), 305–64. See also Wolfhart Pannenberg, *Theology and the Philosophy of Science* (Louisville, KY: Westminster John Knox, 1976), 231–41.

[11] Harwood, *Christian Theology,* 2.

[12] Wolfhart Pannenberg, *Systematic Theology,* 3 vols., trans. Geoffrey W. Bromiley (Grand Rapids, MI: Eerdmans, 1991) 1:18; citing J. Buddeus, *Isagoge historica–theologica ad theologiam universam singulasque eius partes* (Leipzig, 1727), 303.

coherent account of Christian doctrine. However, it was during the Middle Ages (600–1500), with theologians like John of Damascus (*ca.* 652–*ca.* 750) and Thomas Aquinas (1224–74), that the systematic approach became more prominent. As practiced today, systematic theology is a discipline which addresses theological topics one by one (e.g., God, Humanity, Sin, Salvation) and attempts to summarize all the biblical teaching on each particular subject (see appendix 4). Sometimes called *dogmatic theology* (or, less commonly, *constructive theology*),[13] the goal is to present the major themes (i.e. doctrines) of the Christian faith in an organized and ordered manner, based upon the biblical witness.

To illustrate, consider the following sample definitions of "systematic theology" from a number of prominent contemporary scholars:

- James Leo Garrett, Jr. (1925–2020): "Systematic theology is the orderly exposition of the doctrines of Christianity as its formulator in the context of his or her confessional tradition understands them, according to an integrated and interrelated method, using the Bible,

---

[13] "Constructive theology" connotes an understanding of theology as a discourse that is both constructed and engaged in ongoing construction. A major difference between *constructive* and *systematic* theology is that the latter seeks to develop a system, providing a comprehensive framework for theological topics; constructive theology, on the other hand, rejects closed systematic frameworks in favor of more open-ended reflections and on-going construction. See further William R. Barr, ed., *Constructive Christian Theology in the Worldwide Church* (Grand Rapids, MI: Eerdmans, 1997); Rebecca S. Chopp and Mark Lewis Taylor, eds., *Reconstructing Christian Theology* (Minneapolis, MN: Fortress, 1994); Serene Jones and Paul Lakeland, eds., *Constructive Theology: A Contemporary Approach to Classical Themes* (Minneapolis, MN: Fortress, 2005); and Joerg Rieger, *God and the Excluded: Visions and Blindspots In Contemporary Theology* (Minneapolis, MN: Fortress, 2001); Jason A. Wyman, *Constructing Constructive Theology: An Introductory Sketch* (Minneapolis, MN: Fortress, 2017).

the Christian tradition, Christian experience, and possibly other sources and hopefully of the idiom of those to whom it is addressed."[14]

- Gordon R. Lewis (1926–2016) and Bruce A. Demarest (1935–2021): "Systematic theology... aims to produce normative guidelines to spiritual reality for the present generation; it organizes the material of divine revelation topically and logically, developing a coherent and comprehensive world view and way of life."[15]

- Millard J. Erickson (b. 1932): "A good preliminary or basic definition of theology is the study or science of God." Erickson continues, "Yet more needs to be said to indicate what this science does. So we propose a more complete definition of theology: the discipline that strives to give a coherent statement to the doctrines of the Christian faith, based primarily upon the Scriptures, placed in the context of culture in general, worded in a contemporary idiom, and related to the issues of life."[16]

- John MacArthur (b. 1939) and Richard Mayhue (b. 1944): "Christian theology is the study of the divine revelation in the Bible. It has God

---

[14] James Leo Garrett, Jr., *Systematic Theology: Biblical, Systematic, and Historical*, 2 vols. (1993–95; reprint, Eugene, OR: Wipf & Stock, 2014), 1:8.

[15] Gordon R. Lewis and Bruce A. Demarest, *Integrative Theology: Historical, Biblical, Systematic, Apologetic, Practical,* 3 vols. (Grand Rapids, MI: Zondervan, 1987–94), 1:23.

[16] Millard J. Erickson, *Christian Theology*, 3rd ed. (Grand Rapids, MI: Baker Academic, 2013), 8.

for its perpetual centerpiece, God's Word as its source, and godliness as its aim."[17]

- Wayne Grudem (b. 1948): "Systematic theology is any study that answers the question, 'What does the Bible teach us today?' about any given topic."[18]

- Adam Harwood (b. 1974): "systematic theology is the study of God, his ways, and his world, as revealed in the Bible and creation, affirmed by the church, and restated for contemporary audience."[19]

The history of systematic theology is a captivating expedition through the corridors of time, an exploration of the profound journey of Christian thought and reflection over the course of two millennia. From the baptismal confessions in the earliest days of the ancient church to the monumental *Summae* and *Sentences* of Scholastic theology and the vibrant resurgence of recent times, the development of this discipline bears witness to the ceaseless quest of Christians to comprehend and articulate the truths of the faith in a manner that is biblically faithful, logically consistent, historically attested, existentially relevant, doxologically oriented, and missionally engaged.[20]

Throughout the chapters of this book, we will embark on a succinct yet comprehensive survey of the developments, key thinkers, and their

---

[17] John MacArthur and Richard Mayhue, eds., *Biblical Doctrine: A Systematic Summary of Bible Truth* (Wheaton, IL: Crossway, 2017), 34.

[18] Wayne Grudem, *Systematic Theology: An Introduction to Biblical Doctrine*, 2nd ed. (Grand Rapids, MI: Zondervan, 2020), 1.

[19] Harwood, *Christian Theology*, 4.

[20] Adapted from MacArthur and Mayhue, *Biblical Doctrine,* 36; and *BCDTT*, s.v. "exclusivism," 78.

writings as they have indelibly shaped the path of systematic theology. From the towering figures of the early church fathers to the intellectual giants of medieval Scholasticism, from the bold Reformers to the deep and thoughtful theologians of the modern era, each generation has woven threads into the rich tapestry of the Christian tradition, imbuing it with depth and diversity.

Yet, the development of systematic theology is not a solitary endeavor detached from the currents of history, culture, and broader intellectual landscapes. It is intricately entwined with the ebb and flow of human events, drawing inspiration and wrestling with challenges arising from the social, political, and philosophical contexts in which it arises. It is a *living* discipline, both shaped by and shaping the world in which it exists.

Far from being a mere academic pursuit, systematic theology has played a vital role in molding the contours of the Christian faith, offering a framework to comprehend the nature of God and our relationship with Him. It has been instrumental in shaping our perspectives on the world and our place in it. In recent years, a renewed interest in systematic theology has emerged, accompanied by the establishment of professional groups and the burgeoning field of analytical theology.[21] These developments have brought forth fresh perspectives and profound insights, ushering in a golden age of accessible texts that cater to a broad

---

[21] Analytic theology is a theological method that draws on the tools and methods of analytic philosophy to clarify and analyze theological concepts. This approach values precision, rigor, and clarity in the formulation and defense of theological claims. See further Oliver D. Crisp and Michael C. Rea, eds., *Analytic Theology: New Essays in the Philosophy of Religion* (Oxford: Oxford University, 2009); Thomas J. McCall, *An Invitation to Analytic Christian Theology* (Downers Grove, IL: IVP Academic, 2015); William J. Wood, *Analytic Theology and the Academic Study of Religion* (Oxford: Oxford University, 2021).

readership, enabling a deeper understanding of the Christian faith and fostering a more meaningful faithful and fruitful walk with the Lord.

In attempting to canvas such a rich and variegated subject spanning nearly two thousand years, it will be helpful to organize the material based on the four periods of historical theology (according to the typical approach to periodization): (1) Early Church (New Testament–600); (2) Medieval Church (600–1500); (3) Reformation and Post–Reformation Church (1500–1750); (4) Modern Church (1750–Present).[22] Note that contributions come from both individuals and the corporate church (via creeds, confessions, catechisms, and councils), though the former will be

---

[22] Gregg R. Allison, *Historical Theology: An Introduction to Christian Doctrine* (Grand Rapids, MI: Zondervan, 2011), 12n. 3; cf. "Chapter 1: Introduction to Historical Theology," 23–34. In organizing the history of systematic theology, Malcolm B. Yarnell, III—whose discussion I closely follow—terms the "four major historical periods that have significantly shaped the way scholars engage in systematic theology (although the term itself is a modern one)" as "the Patristic period, the Middle Ages, the Reformation and the modern period." Yarnell, "Systematic theology, history of," in *NDT*^{2}, 886. Similarly Paul Enns, *Moody Handbook of Theology,* rev. ed. (Chicago, IL: Moody, 2008), 440: (1) ancient theology (1st cent.–AD 490), (2) medieval theology (590–1517), (3) Reformation theology (1517–1750), (4) modern theology (1750–present). See also Bruce Riley Ashford and Keith Whitfield, "Theological Method: An Introduction to the Task of Theology," in *A Theology for the Church,* rev. ed., ed. Daniel L. Akin (Nashville, TN: Broadman and Holman Academic, 2017), 17–39. There are alternative schemas, as in Philip Schaff (1819–93), who distinguishes "six principal periods: the Patristic, the Mediæval–Scholastic, the Reformatory, the Protestant–Scholastic, the Rationalistic, and the modern Evangelical." Schaff, *Theological Propædeutic: A General Introduction to the Study of Theology, Exegetical, Historical, Systematic, and Practical, Including Encyclopædia, Methodology, and Bibliography* (1894; reprint, Eugene, OR: Wipf & Stock, 2007), 364.

given primary consideration here.[23] These periods may be summarized thusly, corresponding to their respective chapters in this work:[24]

Early Church (1st–6th Century): This period begins with the life of Jesus and the apostles, and includes the spread of Christianity throughout the Roman Empire. The early centuries of Christianity were marked by theological debates and controversies that shaped the understanding of key doctrines, leading to the Councils of Nicaea (325) and Chalcedon (451), which formulated crucial statements concerning the nature of Christ. Further, the early church witnessed the rise of monasticism, and the Christianization of the Roman Empire. Key figures include Irenaeus, Origen, Athanasius, the Cappadocian fathers, and Augustine. To study this period, primary sources like the New Testament, the writings of the Church Fathers, and historical accounts like Eusebius' *Ecclesiastical History* are essential.

---

[23] See the helpful surveys by Gerald Bray, "Systematic Theology, History of," in *NDT,* 671–72; and Yarnell, "Systematic theology, history of," in *NDT*², 886–89. See also Alister E. McGrath, *Theology: The Basics*, 4th ed. (Oxford: Wiley-Blackwell, 2018) xiii–xxv; M. James Sawyer, *The Survivor's Guide to Theology* (2006; reprint, Eugene, OR: Wipf & Stock, 2016) 224–33; and Anthony C. Thiselton, *Approaching the Study of Theology: An Introduction to Key Thinkers, Concepts, Methods and Debates* (Downers Grove: InterVarsity, 2018) 12–31. In–depth studies include Bengt Hägglund, *History of Theology,* 4th rev. ed., trans. Gene J. Lund (St. Louis, MO: Concordia, 2007); Yves M. J. Congar, *A History of Theology* (Garden City, NY: Doubleday, 1968); William C. Placher, and Derek R. Nelson. *A History of Christian Theology: An Introduction,* 2nd ed. (Louisville, KY: Westminster John Knox, 2013); G. R. Evans, *The Beginnings of Theology as an Academic Discipline* (Oxford: Clarendon, 1980).

[24] See James E. Bradley and Ricard A. Muller's helpful volume, *Church History: An Introduction to Research Methods and Resources,* 2nd ed. (Grand Rapids, MI: Eerdmans, 2016).

Middle Ages (7th–15th Century): This period saw the growth of monasticism, the development of the papacy, and the split between the Eastern Orthodox and Western Catholic churches (Great Schism, 1054). Additionally, there was the launching of the Crusades, and the rise of Scholasticism and intellectual renewal. Key figures include John of Damascus, Peter Abelard, Peter Lombard, Thomas Aquinas, and Gabriel Biel. Primary sources include the writings of these figures, as well as Church councils and historical accounts.

Reformation and Post–Reformation Church (16th–18th Century): This period was marked by significant theological disputes that led to the split between the Catholic Church and Protestant reformers. The Reformation and its aftermath was followed by the Catholic counter-Reformation, the expansion of Christianity through missionary endeavors, religious conflicts and religious wars. Key figures include Martin Luther, John Calvin, Martin Chemnitz, and Francis Turretin. To study this period, one should read the writings of these the Reformers and Protestant thinkers, as well as the Council of Trent's response to the Reformation.

Modern and Postmodern Era (18th Century–Present): This period includes the rise of denominations, the spread of Christianity globally, and the interaction between Christianity and modern thought. Key movements include the Enlightenment, the Great Awakenings, the rise of biblical criticism and the historical-critical method, the advent of modernity and postmodernity, the growing emphasis on ecumenism and interfaith dialogue, and Vatican II. Key figures include Friedrich D. E. Schleiermacher, Charles Hodge, Karl Barth, Carl F. H. Henry, Donald G. Bloesch, and Millard J. Erickson. Primary sources include the writings of key theologians, church documents, and historical accounts.

Additionally, Chapters 5 and 6 present a lengthy two-part collection of brief biographical sketches of key theologians and scholars, from Peter Abelard to Huldrych Zwingli. Where applicable, significant writings are noted, particularly in the field of systematic theology.

Finally, a number of appendices provide material germane to the history of systematic theology. The first appendix provides a chronological listing of important events in Christian history; the second discusses the difference types of church councils, and then lists (again chronologically) key examples with summary descriptions; the third appendix lists notable Christian theologians chronologically by century of birth; finally, the fourth appendix briefly summarizes the major loci typically addressed in contemporary systematic theology. A full bibliography is provided, with entries grouped under six headings: (1) standard reference works, (2) church history, (3) history of doctrine, (4) primary systematic theologies, (5) articles and chapters, and (6) monographs.

CHAPTER ONE: THE EARLY CHURCH (NEW TESTAMENT–600)

THE early church period, also known as the post–apostolic period, covers the time from the end of the New Testament period to around AD 600. This was a period of profound theological development, a captivating narrative of faith, growth, and transformation. From its humble beginnings as a small Jewish sect in the first century AD, Christianity rapidly spread throughout the Roman Empire and beyond, encountering numerous challenges and triumphs along the way. This era was marked by the growth of the nascent Christian faith, the emergence of key doctrines in the midst of a number of theological controversies, the formation of the biblical canon, and the establishment of ecclesiastical structures, and institutionalization, all of which have left an indelible imprint on the landscape of systematic theology.

1. The Birth and Early Expansion of Christianity

Christianity emerged in the first century AD with the life, teachings, death, and resurrection of Jesus Christ. The apostles, particularly Peter and Paul, played a pivotal role in spreading the message of Christ, establishing communities of believers, and laying the foundation for the early church. Despite persecution and opposition, Christianity experienced remarkable growth, aided by the *Pax Romana*, the common Greek language, and the Roman road network.

2. Theological Controversies and Doctrinal Development

The early centuries of Christianity were marked by theological debates and controversies that shaped the understanding of key doctrines. The Gnostic heresies, which sought to merge Christian teachings with Greek philosophy, posed a significant challenge. In response, early Church Fathers such as Irenaeus and Tertullian defended orthodox Christian beliefs, emphasizing the importance of apostolic tradition and the authority of Scripture. The formulation of creeds, such as the Apostles' Creed, provided a concise summary of essential Christian beliefs.

3. Persecution and Martyrdom

Christianity faced intermittent periods of persecution, particularly under Roman emperors who viewed it as a threat to the established order. The persecutions, such as those under Nero and Diocletian, resulted in the martyrdom of countless Christians.[1] However, these acts of persecution also served to strengthen the faith and resolve of believers, inspiring others to embrace Christianity.

4. The Councils and the Formation of Orthodoxy

To address theological controversies and establish doctrinal unity, several ecumenical councils were convened. The Council of Nicaea in AD 325, for instance, addressed the Arian controversy and affirmed the orthodox belief in the divinity of Christ. The Council of Constantinople in AD 381

---

[1] On these persecutions, see further James Corke-Webster, "The Roman Persecutions," in *The Wiley-Blackwell Companion to Christian Martyrdom* (Malden, MA: Wiley-Blackwell, 2020), 31–50.

further clarified the nature of the Holy Spirit. These councils played a crucial role in defining and establishing the boundaries of orthodoxy, while simultaneously combating heresies.

5. The Rise of Monasticism and the Spread of Christianity

The first Christian monks appeared in Egypt and Syria in the third century. The fourth and fifth centuries witnessed the rise of monasticism, with figures like Anthony of Egypt and Pachomius establishing communities of monks who sought to live a life of asceticism and devotion to God. Monasticism became a powerful force in preserving and spreading Christianity, as monastic communities served as centers of learning, piety, and missionary activity. Monks and missionaries, such as Patrick in Ireland, and Cyril and Methodius in Eastern Europe, played a vital role in the expansion of Christianity beyond the Roman Empire.

6. The Christianization of the Roman Empire

The fourth century saw a significant turning point in the history of Christianity with the conversion of Emperor Constantine to Christianity. This marked the beginning of the Christianization of the Roman Empire, as subsequent emperors issued edicts granting religious freedom and support to Christians. Christianity became the dominant religion within the empire, leading to the construction of grand basilicas and the integration of Christian symbols and practices into Roman society.

Summary of the Times

The first 600 years of Christianity were a period of immense growth, theological development, and institutionalization. From its humble beginnings, Christianity spread throughout the Roman Empire and beyond, encountering theological controversies, persecution, and triumphs along the way. The formulation of creeds, the convening of councils, and the rise of monasticism all contributed to the establishment of orthodoxy and the shaping of a distinct Christian identity. The Christianization of the Roman Empire marked a significant milestone forever altering the course of history. The early centuries of Christianity laid the foundation for the subsequent development of the faith, leaving a lasting legacy that continues to shape the beliefs and practices of Christians worldwide. Being a period of vibrant theological activity, the people, writings, and events of the early church era laid the foundation for and shaped the contours of systematic theology, providing a rich heritage upon which subsequent generations of theologians have built.

The Development of Systematic Theology in the Early Church Period

As Kevin Vanhoozer (b. 1957) observes, "Theology is as old as the proclamation, explication and application of the Scriptures as the Word of God."[2] The formation of the canon of Scripture[3] was therefore a crucial

---

[2] Kevin J. Vanhoozer, "Systematic Theology," in *NDT*², 885. Sydney Ahlstrom (1919–84) memorably opined, "Christian theology is a series of footnotes to St. Paul." Ahlstrom, *Theology in America* (Indianapolis, IN: Bobbs–Merrill, 1967), 23.

[3] The canon of Scripture (from Gk. *kanōn*, "reed; measuring rod; standard of measure") is the collection of divinely inspired and thus inerrant and infallible books accepted by the church as supremely authoritative for faith and practice. Ancient Judaism accepted the present thirty-nine OT books as canonical; early Christians came to accept the books of the present NT in addition to the Jewish canon. Later, Roman Catholicism would officially declare in favor of the canonicity of the same, in addition to most of the Apocrypha. A classic study remains R. Laird Harris, *Inspiration and Canonicity of the Bible* (Grand Rapids, MI: Zondervan, 1969).

development in the history of Christian theology. The process of establishing a canon of authoritative texts was a gradual one that took place over several centuries, as the early church sought to identify and affirm the authoritative writings of the prophets and apostles. The canonization of these texts was a key step in the development of Christian theology, as it established a clear set of authoritative sources for the faith and practice of Christians. The providentially–guided inclusion of certain texts in the canon was based on a number of criteria, such as their apostolic origin, their widespread use and acceptance within the early church, and their consistency with other biblical writings.[4]

Systematic theology is rooted in creedal and catechetical expressions of Christian doctrine. Early creedal expressions, sometimes called the *regula fidei* (Lat. "rule of faith") and occasionally called a baptismal confession because such would be repeated by a person about to be baptized,[5] include the so–called Old Roman Symbol, which would in turn form the basis of the Apostles' Creed. The Old Roman Symbol (Lat. *Vetus Symbolum Romanum, ca.* 140) professes:

---

[4] For the canonical criteria (retroactively discerned), see F. F. Bruce, *The Canon of Scripture* (Downers Grove, IL: InterVarsity, 1988) 255–69; Lee Martin McDonald, *Formation of the Bible: The Story of the Church's Canon* (Peabody, MA: Hendrickson, 2012), 100–04. Briefly, see *MHT*, 174–77.

[5] See further V. Grosssi, "Regula Fidei," in *EAC*, 3:387; M. E. Osterhaven, "Rule of Faith," in *EDT*[3], 762. Discussing the *regula fidei*, Irenaeus claimed that the church, "although scattered throughout the whole world, yet, as if occupying but one house, carefully preserved [the faith]. . . . For, although the languages of the world are dissimilar, yet the import of the tradition is one and the same" (*Haer.* 1.10.2).

> I believe in God the Father almighty.
>
> And in Jesus Christ, his only Son, our Lord;
>
> Who was born by the Holy Spirit of the Virgin Mary;
>
> Was crucified under Pontius Pilate and was buried;
>
> The third day he rose from the dead;
>
> He ascended into heaven; and sits on the right hand of the Father;
>
> From thence he will come to judge the quick and the dead.
>
> And in the Holy Spirit,
>
> The Holy Church,
>
> the remission of sins,
>
> the resurrection of the flesh.[6]

---

[6] Text is drawn from Philip Schaff, *The Creeds of Christendom: With a History and Critical Notes*, 3 vols. (1877; reprint, Grand Rapids, MI: Baker, 1996), 1:21–2. See also J. N. D. Kelly, *Early Christian Creeds,* 2nd ed. (New York: D. McKay, 1961), 102. Concerning the precise wording of the Old Roman Symbol, there is some divergence in the forms preserved in Greek (e.g., of Marcellus of Ancyra) and Latin (e.g., of Tyrannius Rufinus), particularly with regard to the concluding clause, "life everlasting," which is present in Marcellus' Greek (ζωην αιώνιον) but not Rufinus' Latin. The Latin version of Nicetas of Remesiana, in his *Explanatio Symboli,* does include *vitam eternam* ("life everlasting"), as well as the phrase *communionem sanctorum* ("communion of the saints"), omitted by Marcellus and Rufinus. See further D. Larrimore Holland, "The Earliest Text of the Old Roman Symbol: A Debate with Hans Lietzmann and J. N. D. Kelly," *Church History* 34.3 (Sept. 1965), 262–81. The Old Roman Symbol was itself an expanded Trinitarian baptismal formula: "I believe in God the Father Almighty and in Jesus Christ His Son, our Lord, and in the Holy Spirit, the holy Church, and the resurrection of the flesh."

As far as catechesis for new Christian converts, an outstanding example of this systematic form is evident in the later *Catechetical Lectures* (*ca.* 348–50) of Cyril of Jerusalem (313–86). These lectures, or homilies, are a series of twenty-three addresses providing instruction to new converts to Christianity preparing for baptism and communion. For instance, in one place, Cyril helpfully discusses the role of creeds as summaries of biblical doctrine which believers ought to memorize:

> But in learning and professing the faith, acquire and hold on only to what has been delivered to you by the Church, which is firmly grounded in all the Scriptures. Now not all are able to read the Scriptures. Some are prevented from gaining such a knowledge by lack of learning, and others by a lack of free time. In order that the soul may not perish through ignorance, we summarize the whole doctrine of the faith in a few lines. I wish you both to commit this summary to memory when I recite it, and to rehearse it with all diligently among yourselves, not writing it down on paper, but engraving it on your hearts by committing it to memory. [...] This synthesis of faith was not made to be agreeable to human opinions, but to present the one teaching of the faith in its totality, in which what is of greatest importance is gathered together from all the Scriptures. And just as a mustard seed contains a great number of branches in its tiny grain, so also this summary of faith brings together in a few words the entire knowledge of the true religion which is contained in the Old and New [Testaments]. So take care, my brothers and sisters, and hold

> fast the traditions which you now receive, and write them on the table of your heart.[7]

From this same period came a widely accepted baptismal creed that was codified for general use through the ecumenical councils of Nicaea (325) and Constantinople (381), establishing boundaries between orthodoxy and heresy.[8] The creed known as the Nicene (or, more accurately, the Niceno–Constantinopolitan) Creed is the creed (from Lat. *credo*, "I believe") or statement of faith devised by the orthodox bishops in response to Arius at the first Council of Nicaea and later expanded by the Council of Constantinople.[9] The First Council of Nicaea, convened by the Roman emperor Constantine the Great (ruled AD 306–37), rejected the heresy known as Arianism, which denied the deity of Jesus Christ.[10] The Nicene Creed formally proclaimed the deity and equality of Jesus Christ, the Son of God, in the Trinity. Significantly, this creed affirms that Jesus Christ is "of the same substance" (Gk. *homoousios*) as the Father, while being a distinct being from Him. The final form of the Creed reads:

---

[7] Cyril of Jerusalem, *Catechesis*, V, 12.

[8] On how the ecumenical councils helped define orthodoxy, see Bradley Nassif, "How Was Orthodoxy Established in the Ecumenical Councils?," *Christian Research Journal* 40.6 (2017), 42–7.

[9] See Phillip Cary, *The Nicene Creed* (Bellingham, WA: Lexham, 2023).

[10] Arianism is a Christological heresy named after Arius (270–336), a priest in Alexandria, who denied the full deity of the Son of God, asserting instead that Christ is the highest of the created beings (and therefore ontologically subordinate to the Father) and is thus appropriately referred to as "god" but not *the* God. This view was rejected by the Council of Nicaea, which upheld the orthodox doctrine of the consubstantiality of the Father and the Son. Jehovah's Witnesses are modern-day Arians.

> We believe in one God, the Father Almighty, Maker of heaven and earth, and of all things visible and invisible.
>
> And in one Lord Jesus Christ, the only-begotten Son of God, begotten of the Father before all worlds (*æons*), Light of Light, very God of very God, begotten, not made, being of one substance with the Father; by whom all things were made; who for us men, and for our salvation, came down from heaven, and was incarnate by the Holy Ghost of the Virgin Mary, and was made man; he was crucified for us under Pontius Pilate, and suffered, and was buried, and the third day he rose again, according to the Scriptures, and ascended into heaven, and sitteth on the right hand of the Father; from thence he shall come again, with glory, to judge the quick and the dead; whose kingdom shall have no end.
>
> And in the Holy Ghost, the Lord and Giver of life, who proceedeth from the Father, who with the Father and the Son together is worshiped and glorified, who spake by the prophets. In one holy catholic and apostolic Church; we acknowledge one baptism for the remission of sins; we look for the resurrection of the dead, and the life of the world to come. Amen.[11]

An important document form the early church is the *Didache* (Gk. "Teaching"), also called *Teaching of the Twelve Apostles* (Gk. *Didachē*

[11] This text is drawn from Schaff, *Creeds of Christendom,* 28–9. Schaff, *in loc. cit.*, provides both the original and final forms of the Creed.

Kuriou dia dōdeka apostolōn).[12] The *Didache* is the oldest surviving Christian church order, and was probably written in Egypt or Syria in the second century AD. It presents a general program for instruction and initiation into the primitive church. Chapters 1–6 give ethical instruction concerning the "Two Ways," of life and of death, and reflect an early Christian adaptation of a Jewish pattern of teaching in order to prepare catechumens (candidates for Christian baptism). Chapters 7–15 discuss baptism, fasting, prayer, the Eucharist, how to receive and test traveling apostles and prophets, and the appointment of bishops and deacons. Chapter 16 considers the signs of the Second Coming of the Lord. For example, in the opening chapter the *Didache* speaks concerning the two ways:

> There are two ways, one of *life* and one of *death*. And there is a great difference between the two ways. On the one hand, then, the way of life is this. *First, you will love the God* who made you; *second, you will love your neighbor as yourself*. The way of life is this. *As many things as you might wish not to happen to you, likewise, do not do to another*. And concerning these matters, the teaching is this. *Speak well of the ones speaking badly of you, and*

---

[12] See briefly, "Didache," in *ODCC*³, 478–79, and W. Rordorf, "Didache," in *EAC*, 1:708–09, both with bibliography. For an excellent new translation, see William Varner's *The Apostolic Fathers: An Introduction and Translation* (New York: T&T Clark, 2023), 5–21. The *Didache* was known only through references in early Christian works until a Greek manuscript of it, written in 1056, was discovered in Istanbul in 1873 by Philotheos Bryennios (1833–1914), an Eastern Church theologian and metropolitan. Bryennios subsequently published *The Teaching of the Twelve Apostles* (1883), with valuable notes of his own. See Varner, *op. cit.*, 6–8, for details.

> *pray* for your enemies, and fast *for the ones persecuting you; for what merit is there if you love the ones loving you? Do not even the Gentiles do the same thing? You, on the other hand, love the ones hating you,* and you will not have an enemy. Abstain from fleshly and bodily desires. *If anyone should strike you on the right cheek, turn to him also the other, and you will be perfect; if anyone should press you into service for one mile, go with him two; if anyone should take away your cloak, give to him also your tunic; if anyone should take from you what is yours, do not ask for it back;* for you are not even able to do so. *To everyone asking you for anything, give it and do not ask for it back;* for to all the Father wishes to give from his own free gifts. Blessed is the one giving according to the commandment, for he is blameless. Woe to the one taking; for, on the one hand, if anyone having need takes, he will be blameless. On the other hand, the one not having need will stand trial why he received and for what use; and being in prison, he/she will be examined thoroughly concerning the things he has done, *and he will not come out from there until he pays back the last cent.* But also, concerning this, on the other hand, it has been said. "Let your alms sweat in your hands, until you know to whom you might give it."[13]

The *Didache* would subsequently form the basis of chapter 7 of the fourth-century *Apostolic Constitutions*, a collection of early Christian

---

[13] *Didache*, 1:1–6, in Varner, *Apostolic Fathers,* 15; I have italicized what Varner had originally bolded to alert the reader to possible biblical quotations.

ecclesiastical law.[14] So esteemed was this writing, that some early Christian writers even considered the *Didache* to be canonical.[15]

Irenaeus of Lyons (*ca.* 130–*ca.* 200) was a second-century bishop of Lugdunum (now Lyon, France) and writer who defended Christian orthodoxy against the heresies of Gnosticism. His work *Adversus haereses* ("Against Heresies," *ca.* 180), provides a comprehensive refutation of Gnostic teachings, particularly the followers of the Egyptian religious philosopher, Valentinus (*ca.* 100–*ca.* 160). The treatise is divided into five books and provides a comprehensive account of the doctrines and beliefs of these heretical groups, as well as Irenaeus' arguments against them. In the first two books, Irenaeus provides a detailed description of the heretical sects and their beliefs, along with occasional remarks on their absurdity and the truth they opposed. The remaining books are organized around the themes of God, Christ, and humanity, and focus on the proper interpretation of Scripture.

While noted patrologist Johannes Quasten (1900–87) pointed to Irenaeus as the first Christian theologian,[16] Origenes Adamantius (*ca.* 185–*ca.*

---

[14] See further "Apostolic Constitutions," in *ODCC*^{3} 90; and P. Nautin, "Apostolic Constitutions," in *EAC,* 1:197–98, both with bibliography.

[15] E.g., Clement of Alexandria (*ca.* AD 170) in *Strom.*, i.20.

[16] Johannes Quasten, *Patrology*, 3 vols. (1950; reprint, Westminster, MD: Christian Classics, 1983), 1:294: "In spite of his suspicious attitude toward speculative theology, Irenaeus deserves great credit for having been the first to formulate in dogmatic terms the entire Christian doctrine." Quasten is cited with approval by Gulley (*Systematic Theology*, 1:139), who specifically points to Irenaeus' five–volume *Adversus Haereses* (*Against Heresies*) as the first system of theology. Anthony Thiselton, however, has commented that Irenaeus' *Adversus Haereses* "can hardly be called 'systematic' theology." Thiselton,

254)—better known simply as Origen—is almost universally proclaimed as the first *systematic* theologian.[17] Although he never attempted a

---

Approaching the Study of Theology: An Introduction to Key Thinkers, Concepts, Methods and Debates (Downers Grove: IVP Academic, 2018), 72. Kevin Vanhoozer ("Systematic theology," in *NDT*², 886) seems to agree with Quasten *et al.*, based on his distinction between "hard" and "soft" theological systems:

> What we may term 'hard' theological systems enjoy a high degree of intelligibility vis–à–vis the intellectual framework of the day, but at a cost, namely, that the content of the Bible may be governed by a conceptual scheme—by some '-ism', like Platonism or existentialism—that ends up getting imposed upon the text.
>
> For Irenaeus, the 'whole' is more like a narrative than a system of geometry. Irenaeus's 'soft' system consisted simply in recognizing the distinction in unity of creation and redemp-tion and the typological connections that bind the history of Israel to the history of Jesus Christ. Such systematicity requires only that one take responsibility for the overall consistency of one's beliefs.

[17] See Joseph Wilson Trigg, *Origen: The Bible and Philosophy in the Third–Century Church* (Atlanta: John Knox, 1983), 87–129. Although Henri Crouzel (1919–2003), in *Origen: The Life and Thought of the First Great Theologian*, trans. A. S. Worral (Edinburgh: T&T Clark, 1989), 46 and 168, explicitly denies that Origen's *Peri Archon* is a systematic theology, this is apparently a minority dissent. See, e.g., Yarnell, "Systematic theology, history of," 887; cf. Bavinck, *Reformed Dogmatics,* 35; Sawyer, *Survivor's Guide to Theology*, 225; D. J. Treier, "Systematic Theology," in *EDT*³, 853–54. Éric Junod (b. 1941) comments, "The *Peri Archôn* defines and accomplishes a theological program that had no precedent or counterpart in the patristic era: that of developing, on the basis of symbols, on the faith of the Church, and on Scripture, a coherent doctrine of God, humanity, and the world." Junod, "Origen," in *EAC,* 1163. Concerning Irenaeus' status as a theologian, Everett Ferguson (b. 1933) has written:

> One can interpret Irenaeus as a "biblical theologian" for his emphasis on Scripture, creation, redemption and resurrection; or one can interpret him as a theologian of the developing Catholic tradition for his arguments from tradition, apostolic succession..., the importance of Rome, and Mary as the

complete systematization of doctrine, Origen's groundbreaking *Peri Archon* (or, in Rufinus' surviving Latin translation, *De Principiis—Concerning First Things* or *First Principles*) introduced his synthesis of ancient pagan philosophy and early Christian theology with the aim of producing a true corpus or "body" of Christian teaching, that is, a coherent and condensed exposition of Christian truth: *et unum ut diximus corpus efficiat exemplis et affirmationibus* (Lat., "a connected series and body of truths agreeably to the reason of all these things").[18] Here, Origen—described by the venerable Jerome as "a teacher second only to the great Apostle"[19]—treated in four books God and heavenly beings, the material world and human beings, free will and its consequences, and the interpretation of Scripture. Beginning with a Trinitarian exposition of the creed, Origen then proceeded to consider the doctrines of God, creation,

---

> new Eve. Since Scripture and tradition had the same content for Irenaeus (i.e., the gospel), biblical theology is the substance of his thought. The "Catholic" elements appear primarily as polemical arguments against the Gnostics and Marcion. Likewise, the doctrines he emphasizes are those challenged by heretics.

Ferguson, "Irenaeus," in *NDT*², 457.

[18] Origen, *Peri Archon*, Preface 10. His whole statement reads:

> Every one, therefore, must make use of elements and foundations of this sort, according to the precept, 'Enlighten yourselves with the light of knowledge,' [Hos 10:12 LXX] if he would desire to form a connected series and body of truths agreeably to the *reason* of all these things, that by dear and necessary statements he may ascertain the truth regarding each individual topic, and form, as we have said, one body of doctrine, by means of illustrations and arguments,—either those which he has discovered in holy Scripture, or which he has deduced by closely tracing out the consequences and following a correct method.

[19] Jerome, *Letter LXXX, From Rufinus to Macarius*, 1.

humanity and sin, as well as angels, Scripture, and eschatology. In one place, Origen lays out his view on the three ways of reading Scripture, using the imagery of "body, soul, and spirit":

> There are three ways in which the meaning of the Holy Scriptures should be inscribed on the soul of every Christian. First, the simpler sort are edified by what may be called the "body" of Scripture. This is the name I give to the immediate acceptance. Secondly, those who have made some progress are edified by, as it were, the "soul." Thirdly, the perfect [...] are edified by the "spiritual" Law, which contains the shadow of the good things to come. Thus just as a human being consists of body, soul, and spirit, so also does the Scripture which is the gift of God designed for human salvation. [...]
>
> Some parts of Scripture have no "body." In these parts, we must look only for the "soul" and "spirit." Perhaps this is the point of the description in John's gospel of the water-pots "for the purifying of the Jews, holding two or three measures" (John 2:6). The Word implies by this that the apostle calls the Jews in secret, so that they may be purified through the word of the Scripture which sometimes holds two measures, that is what one may call the "soul" and "spirit"; sometimes three, that is, the "body" as well. [...] The usefulness of the "body" is testified by the multitude of simple believers and is quite obvious. Paul gives us many examples of the "soul." [...] The spiritual interpretation belongs to people who are able to explain the way in which the worship of the "Jews after the flesh" (1 Corinthians 10:18) yields

> images and "shadows of heavenly things" (Hebrews 8:5) and how the "Law had the shadow of good things to come."[20]

After Origen, Firmianus Lactantius (*ca.* 260–*ca.* 330) composed a comprehensive apology (Gk. *apologia*, lit "defense") for the Christian faith, *Divinarum Institutionum Libri VII*, or the *Divinae institutiones* (306–13). Structured in seven books, the text covers a wide range of topics related to theology, philosophy, and morality. Lactantius presents arguments against pagan beliefs and defends the superiority of Christianity as the true faith. In one interesting passage, Lactantius discusses the implications of humanity being created in God's image (using the Latin word *simulacrum* in place of the more common *imago*), highlighting the inherent dignity of all people:

> I have spoken about what is due to God; now I shall speak about what is due to other people, although what is due to people still equally relates to God, since humanity is the image of God [*homo dei simulacrum est*]. The first duty of justice concerns God and binds us to him; the second concerns humanity. The name of the first is religion; the name of the second is mercy or humanity. Religion is a characteristic of the righteous and those who worship God. It alone is life. God made us naked and fragile in order to teach us wisdom. In particular he gave us this affection of piety in order that we might protect our fellow human beings, love them, cherish them, defend them against all dangers, and give them help. The strongest bond which unites us is humanity.

---

[20] Origen, *Peri Archon*, IV.ii.4–5.

> Anyone who breaks it is a criminal and a parricide. Now it was from the one human being that God created us all, so that we are all of the same blood, with the result that the greatest crime is to hate humanity or do them harm. That is why we are forbidden to develop or to encourage hatred. So if we are the work of the same God, what else are we but brothers and sisters? The bond which unites our souls is therefore stronger than that which unites our bodies. So Lucretius does not err when he declares:
>
> Finally, we are all the offspring of heavenly seed.
>
> To everyone that same one is Father.
>
> [...] We must therefore show humanity if we want to deserve the name of human beings. And showing humanity means loving our fellow human beings because they are human beings, just as we are ourselves.[21]

During this same period, theologians such as Athanasius (300–73) and the Cappadocian fathers—Basil of Caesarea (*ca.* 329–79), his brother Gregory of Nyssa (*ca.* 335–94), and their friend Gregory of Nazianzus (*ca.* 329–89)—engaged in lively debates and clarification of crucial theological concepts, particularly the relationship of the Son and the Holy Spirit to the Father.[22] The culmination of these discussions led to the

---

[21] Lactantius, *Divinae Institutiones*, VI, 10–11.

[22] Jaroslav Pelikan provides an excellent discussion of the contribution of the Cappadocians (and their contemporaries) to the development of Trinitarian language in *The Christian Tradition: A History of the Development of Doctrine,*

formulation of the previously quoted Niceno-Constantinopolitan Creed in 381, which became the central confession of the church's Trinitarian faith. Although this period of intense theological activity did not produce any comprehensive systematic compendia, Gregory of Nyssa made a significant contribution with his preliminary collection of theological topics in his *Catechetical Orations* (or, *Addresses on Religious Instruction*), intended for new converts. Gregory of Nazianzus, acclaimed "The Theologian," preached five celebrated *Theological Orations* against the Arians, in which he argued for the equality of the Father and the Son and the consubstantiality of the Spirit with the Father and the Son.

The preeminent theologian of the early church is unquestionably Augustine of Hippo (354–430), acknowledged as "the greatest of the Latin theologians of the early church, and one of the greatest Christian thinkers of all time."[23] While Augustine (who defined theology as *intellegimus de divinitate rationem sive sermonem*, "the rational

---

vol. 1, *The Emergence of the Catholic Tradition (100—600)* (Chicago, IL: University of Chicago, 1971) 211–25.

[23] Sara Parvis, "Augustine," in *NDT*², 82. In fact, Thiselton (*Approaching the Study of Theology,* 72) writes that, more than Irenaeus and Origen, Augustine "more clearly merits the title 'systematic theologian'...." Bavinck (*Reformed Dogmatics,* 37) has written:

> Though he did not produce a theological dogmatic system—the closest is his *Enchiridion: Handbook on Faith, Hope, and Love*, an interpretation of the principal truths of faith that follows the Apostles' Creed—no church father entered into all the problems of theology more deeply than Augustine. He was the first person who attempted clearly to account for all the theological issues that would later be treated in the prolegomena of dogmatic theology and who penetrated the ultimate psychological problems of the human person seeking to know God.

discussion respecting the deity")[24] did not write systematically, he did write comprehensively—indeed, according to Anthony Thiselton (b. 1937), Augustine "produced the largest body of Christian writings of the first millennium."[25] Of special note here are the voluminous writings comprising his anti-Pelagian corpus spanning 411–30 (e.g., *The Spirit and the Letter*) and his *De Trinitate* (*The Trinity*), a tour de force in fifteen books written over a span of some two decades (399–419). Of note, too, is Augustine's *De Doctrina Christiana* (*On Christian Doctrine*, 397); *Enchiridion* (*Handbook on Faith, Hope, and Love,* 421–23), a brief doctrinal handbook for believers; and his magnum opus, *De Civitate Dei Contra Paganos* (*City of God Against the Pagans*), a twenty–two book Christian philosophy of history which appeared in installments (416–22).[26] Philip Schaff (1819–93) wrote that Augustine "meditated and speculated profoundly and devoutly on almost every topic of faith and philosophy…. He ascended the highest heights and sounded the deepest

---

[24] Augustine, *City of God,* VIII.i.

[25] *CEPR,* s.v. "Augustine of Hippo," 21. Joanne McWilliam ("Augustine of Hippo," in *DHT,* 43) agrees: "Augustine's extant writings form the largest single corpus from the patristic age."

[26] Significant translations, in descending order of publication, include: *The City of God,* trans. William Babcock, Notes by Boniface Ramsey (Hyde Park, NY: New City, 2012); *The City of God against the Pagans,* trans. R. W. Dyson (New York: Cambridge University, 1998); *The City of God,* trans. Henry Bettenson (Harmondsworth, England: Penguin Books, 1972); *The City of God,* trans. Gerald G. Walsh, S. J., *et al.*, Introduction by Étienne Gilson (New York: Doubleday, 1958); *The City of God,* trans. Marcus Dods, Introduction by Thomas Merton (1971; reprint, New York: Random House, 1950); *The City of God,* trans. John Healey, Introduction by Ernest Barker (New York: E. P. Dutton, 1945); *Of the Citie of God,* trans. John Healey, Notes by Juan Luis Vives (London: George Eld, 1610).

depths of divine and human knowledge and of Christian experience."[27] To illustrate Augustine's contributions, consider a passage from his *De natura et gratia* (415) in which he discusses the complex nature of sin and its effect on human nature:

> Human nature was certainly originally created blameless and without any fault [*vitium*]; but the human nature by which each one of us is now born of Adam requires a physician, because it is not healthy. All the good things, which it has by its conception, life, senses, and mind, it has from God, its creator and maker. But the weakness which darkens and disables these good natural qualities, as a result of which that nature needs enlightenment and healing, did not come from the blameless maker but from original sin [*ex originali peccato*], which was committed by free will

[27] Schaff, *Theological Propædeutic,* 366; yet, cf. 368 where Schaff candidly notes some problems with Augustine. Most infamous is Augustine's misreading of Rom. 5:12 (which Schaff notes, *op. cit.*, 367n.), wherein Augustine misunderstood ἐφ' ᾧ πάντες ἥμαρτον (*eph hō pantes hēmarton*), following the Vulgate's mistranslation *in quo omnes peccaverunt,* as meaning "in whom [Adam] all sinned," while the Greek has "because all sinned." In other words, a bad reading of Rom. 5:12 led Augustine to conclude that all humans are as culpable (guilty) as Adam for *what Adam did*—all humanity sinned *in him.* As Millard Erickson (b. 1932) remarks, "Accordingly, his [Augustine's] understanding of the final clause in verse twelve was that we were actually 'in Adam,' and therefore Adam's sin was ours as well. But since his interpretation was based upon an inaccurate translation, we must investigate the clause more closely." Erickson, *Christian Theology*, 3rd ed. (Grand Rapids, MI: Baker Academic, 2013), 579. See the discussion in Harwood, *Christian theology,* 364–66 (cf. the entire discussion of original sin, spanning 353–85). Note that modern translations (e.g., HCSB, CSB, ESV, LEB, NRSV, NASB, NET, NIV, NKJV, LSB) render the phrase in question as "because all sinned."

> [*liberum arbitrium*]. For this reason our guilty nature is liable to a just penalty. For if we are now a new creature in Christ, we were still children of wrath by nature, like everyone else. But God, who is rich in mercy, on account of the great love with which He loved us, even when we were dead through our sins, raised us up to life with Christ, by whose grace we are saved. But this grace of Christ, without which neither infants nor grown persons can be saved, is not bestowed as a reward for merits, but is given freely [*gratis*], which is why it is called grace [*gratia*]. […]
>
> For this reason it is that those who are not made free by that blood (whether because they have not been able to hear, or because they were not willing to obey, or were not able to hear on account of their youth, and have not received the bath of regeneration which they might have done and through which they might have been saved) who are most justly condemned because they are not without sin, whether they derived from their origins or were acquired by evil actions. For all have sinned, whether in Adam or in themselves, and have fallen short of the glory of God (Romans 3:23).[28]

During the early church period, then, the following selection highlights some notable examples of comprehensive and systematic expressions of the Christian faith:[29]

---

[28] Augustine, *De natura et gratia,* iii, 3–iv, 4.

[29] The standard collection of the Greek and Latin texts of the Church Fathers is J. P. Migne's mid-19th century *Patrologia Graeca* (PG) and the *Patrologia*

- Unknown author, *The Didache* (*ca.* 110)
- *Old Roman Symbol* or *Creed* (*ca.* 140)
- Irenaeus (*ca.* 130–*ca.* 200), *Proof of the Apostolic Preaching* (180–99)
- Clement of Alexandria (*ca.* 150–*ca.* 215), *Stromata* (or *Stromateis, Miscellanies,* 208–11)
- Origen (*ca.* 184–*ca.* 254), *Peri Archon* (or, in Latin, *de Principiis*, *Concerning First Things* or *First Principles*, *ca.* 229)
- Firmianus Lactantius (*ca.* 260–*ca.* 330), *Divinarum Institutionum Libri VII* (or *Institutiones Divinae*, *ca.* 300–11)
- Cyril of Jerusalem (313–386), *Catechetical Lectures* (*ca.* 348–50)

Latina (PL). More recent critical editions, and gradually replacing Migne, are *Corpus Scriptorum Ecclesiasticorum Latinorum* (CSEL) and *Corpus Christianorum Series Latina* (CCL). The most important contemporary series is *Sources chrétiennes* (SC) (Paris: Editions du Cerf, 1950s–), with 600+ volumes published to date; it has the original text (either Greek or Latin) with a French translation on the facing page; volumes also include extensive introductions and notes. Also significant is the 500+ volume series, *Corpus Scriptorum Christianorum Orientalium* (CSCO), with texts preserved in the languages of the Christian East (Coptic, Syriac, Armenian, Georgian, Arabic, and Ethiopic) and a translation into a modern European language (usually English, French, or German). Important English–translation series with complete works include *Fathers of the Church*, 130+ volumes to date (Washington: Catholic University of America, 1948–); *Ancient Christian Writers*, 66 volumes to date (Westminster, MD: Newman/ New York: Paulist, 1946–); *Ante–Nicene Fathers*, 10 volumes (1867; reprint, Peabody, MA: Hendrickson, 1995); *Nicene and Post–Nicene Fathers*, 28 volumes (1886; reprint, Peabody, MA: Hendrickson, 1995); *Popular Patristics Series*, 60+ volumes to date, ed. John Behr (Crestwood, NY: St. Vladimir's Seminary, 1979–); and *Ancient Christian Texts*, 17 volumes to date (Downers Grove: InterVarsity, 2009–).

- *Nicene Creed* (325)
- Gregory of Nazianzus (*ca.* 335–*ca.* 390), *Five Theological Orations* (379–81)
- Gregory of Nyssa (*ca.* 335–395), *Catechetical Orations* (or, *Addresses on Religious Instruction, ca.* 383–86)
- Augustine (354–430), *Enchiridion ad Laurentium* (421–23); *De Trinitate* (*The Trinity*, 399–419); *De Civitate Dei* (*The City* of *God*, 413–26)
- *Niceno-Constantinopolitan Creed* (381)

CHAPTER TWO: THE MEDIEVAL CHURCH (600—1500)

THE era in European history known as the medieval period spans nearly a millennium, between antiquity (the end of the Roman Empire in the fifth century) and the Italian Renaissance (early sixteenth century).[1] The Renaissance (derived from the French word for "rebirth") was a period of immense cultural and literary change spanning the fifteenth through seventeenth centuries, during which people thought that their own age and the time of ancient Greece and Rome were advanced and civilized. They invented the term *Middle Ages*—meant as a term of derision—to refer to the period between themselves and the ancient world.[2] They saw the Middle Ages as a period of intellectual and cultural stagnation, characterized by the dominance of the Roman Catholic Church, feudalism, and a lack of scientific progress.

---

[1] Two standard reference works on the Medieval period include Rosamund McKitterick, ed., *The New Cambridge Medieval History*, 7 vols. (Cambridge: Cambridge University, 1996–2005); and Robert Fossier, ed., *The Cambridge Illustrated History of the Middle Ages*, 3 vols. (New York: Cambridge, 1986, 1992).

[2] The adjective *medieval* comes from the Latin words for this term, *medium* (middle) and *aevum* (age).

However, more recent scholarship has challenged this view, arguing that the Middle Ages were a time of significant intellectual and cultural achievements, as well of significant theological development. There were a number of key events, figures, and shifts in religious thought that characterized Christianity during this time, including the rise of the papacy, the spread of monasticism, the Crusades, the emergence of scholasticism, and the challenges posed by the Protestant Reformation.

1. The Rise of the Papacy and the Church's Influence

During the early Middle Ages, the papacy emerged as a central authority within the Christian Church. Popes such as Gregory the Great and Innocent III exerted significant influence over both religious and secular affairs. The papacy played a crucial role in the conversion of pagan tribes, the establishment of monastic orders, and the promotion of Christian doctrine. The institutional Church's power and wealth grew, leading to the construction of magnificent cathedrals and the development of a distinct ecclesiastical hierarchy.

2. Monasticism and the Preservation of Knowledge

Monasticism continued to flourish during this period, with monastic orders such as the Benedictines and the Cistercians playing a vital role in preserving knowledge, promoting education, and providing social services. Monasteries became centers of learning and culture, where manuscripts were copied and preserved, and where monks engaged in theological reflection and spiritual practices. Figures like John Cassian, Benedict of Nursia, and Bernard of Clairvaux exemplified the ideals of monastic life, and contributed to the spiritual and intellectual life of the Church. Their writings, including Cassian's *Conferences* and Benedict's

Rule, emphasized the importance of asceticism, prayer, and community life in the pursuit of Christian holiness.

3. The Crusades and Christian Expansion

The Crusades, a series of military campaigns launched by Western Christians, aimed to reclaim the Holy Land from Muslim control.[3] These expeditions had profound consequences for both Christianity and the wider world. While the Crusades were driven by a mix of religious fervor, political ambition, and economic interests, they also led to cultural exchanges, the spread of ideas, and the encounter with different religious traditions.[4] The Crusades left a lasting impact on Christian-Muslim relations and shaped the identity of Western Christianity.

4. Scholasticism and Intellectual Renewal

The period from the eleventh to the fourteenth century witnessed a revival of intellectual activity within Christianity known as scholasticism. Schoolmen such as Anselm of Canterbury, Peter Abelard, and Thomas Aquinas sought to reconcile faith and reason, drawing on the works of ancient philosophers and engaging in theological debates in the pursuit of settling questions concerning reality. Scholasticism emphasized the use of logic and rational inquiry to explore theological questions, leading to the development of systematic theology and the synthesis of Christian thought with Aristotelian (and Platonic) philosophy.

---

[3] See Anthony Levi, "Crusades," in *ECT*, 394–96.

[4] See George F. Maclear's classic study, *History of the Christian Mission in the Middle Ages* (London: MacMillan 1863).

5. Challenges and the Protestant Reformation

The late medieval period saw the emergence of various challenges to the established order of the Church. Criticisms of corruption, the sale of indulgences, and the perceived distance between the clergy and the laity led to calls for reform, all of which would lead ultimately to the Protestant Reformation. Initiated by figures such as Martin Luther, John Calvin, and Huldrych Zwingli, the Protestant Reformation would challenge the authority of the papacy, emphasize the primacy of Scripture, and promote the idea of salvation by grace alone, through faith alone, in Christ alone, to the glory of God alone.

Summary of the Times

The period from 600 to 1500 was a time of profound change and development in the history of Christianity. The rise of the papacy, the spread of monasticism, the Crusades, the intellectual renewal of scholasticism, the integration of classical philosophy with Christian thought, and the development of diverse theological perspectives, and the increasing call for reform all contributed to the development of Christian thought, practice, and institutional structures.[5] These centuries witnessed the consolidation of the Church's power, the preservation of knowledge, the expansion of Christianity, the integration of classical philosophy with Christian thought, and the emergence of new theological perspectives. The history of Christianity during this period reflects the complex interplay between faith, power, and cultural dynamics, leaving a lasting

---

[5] Despite these achievements, the Middle Ages were also marked by significant challenges, including war, famine, disease, and religious conflict. The term "Middle Ages" therefore encompasses a complex and multifaceted historical period that continues to be the subject of much debate and scholarship.

impact on the religious landscape of the world. The people, writings, and events of this era have significantly shaped the course of systematic theology, providing a foundation upon which subsequent generations of theologians have continued to build.

The Development of Systematic Theology in the Medieval Period

This period of history saw the first attempt at an exhaustive explanation of Christian doctrine by John of Damascus (*ca.* 652–*ca.* 750), in his *De Fide Orthodoxa* (*Exposition of the Orthodox Faith*).[6] John, the last of the Greek fathers, brought together the teaching of Scripture and the church Fathers[7] in one hundred chapters, organized according to theological

---

[6] Gerald Bray ("Systematic Theology, History of," in *NDT*^{2}, 671–72) asserts that the Damascene wrote the first systematic theology. English theologian and Byzantine specialist Andrew Louth (b. 1944), in *St. John Damascene: Tradition and Originality in Byzantine Theology* (Oxford: Oxford University, 2002), 85, denies that the Damascene's *De Fide Orthodoxa* is a systematic theology. Roman Catholic theologian and philosopher Emilio Brito (b. 1942) comments:

> Origen's *Peri Arkhon* or—perhaps more rightly so—Gregory of Nyssa's *Great Catechesis*… are generally considered to be the first attempts at a systematic articulation of the content of Christian faith. In the eighth century John of Damascus's *Expositio de fide orthodoxa*… is characterized even more clearly by fairly complete dogmatics. Even though he was undoubtedly more concerned with orthodoxy than with a deeper speculative examination, and even though his procedures in compiling somewhat offended the internal cohesion of the theological exposé, John of Damascus was a major witness to the evolution of theology.

Brito, "Dogmatic Theology," in *ECT,* 453.

[7] Those bearing the honorific title "church father" are those who (1) belong to an early period of the church, (2) who led a holy life, (3) whose writings are generally free from doctrinal error and contain an outstanding defense or explanation of Christian doctrine, and (4) whose writings have received

terms. The chapters, subsequently divided into four books, treat the doctrines of God, creation, and salvation in the first three books; the final book considers the doctrines of Christ's two natures, the sacraments, and eschatology. Not only is John's *De Fide Orthodoxa* a classic statement of Greek patristic theology, but David K. Clark (b. 1952) has noted that the Damascene's "fourfold pattern (prolegomena, theology, anthropology and soteriology, ecclesiology and eschatology)" "still influences some forms of theology today."[8] In one place, the Damascene discusses the deity of the Holy Spirit, affirming the unity of the Father, Son, and Holy Spirit while also noting their distinctive roles:

> In the same way, we believe in the Holy Spirit, the Lord and Giver of life, who proceeds from the Father and dwells in the Son; who is adored and glorified together with the Father and the Son as consubstantial and co-eternal with them; who is the true and authoritative Spirit of God and the source of wisdom and life and

---

ecclesiastical approval. They contributed a somewhat standardized set of Christian teachings to be taught to the inhabitants of the Roman Empire. The Western Fathers include Tertullian (*ca.* 160–*ca.* 220), Ambrose (*ca.* 339–97), Augustine (354–430), Gregory the Great (*ca.* 540–604), and Jerome (*ca.* 347–419); the Eastern Fathers include Clement of Alexandria (*ca.* 150–*ca.* 215), Justin Martyr (*ca.* 100–65), Origen (*ca.* 185–*ca.* 254), Athanasius (*ca.* 293–373), Basil (*ca.* 329–79), John Chrysostom (354–407), and Gregory of Nazianzus (*ca.* 329–89). See Michael A. G. Haykin, *Rediscovering the Church Fathers: Who They Were and How They Shaped the Church* (Wheaton: Crossway, 2011); Bryan M. Liftin, *Getting to Know the Church Fathers: An Evangelical Introduction* (Grand Rapids, MI: Baker Academic, 2016). For a fresh translation, see William Varner, *The Apostolic Fathers: An Introduction and Translation* (New York: T&T Clark, 2023).

[8] David K. Clark, *To Know and Love God: Method for Theology* (Wheaton, IL: Crossway, 2003), ePub: Chapter One: Concepts of Theology, Location 63.

sanctification; who is God together with the Father and the Son and is proclaimed as such; who is uncreated, complete, creative, almighty, all-working, infinite in power; who dominates all creation but is not dominated; who deifies but is not deified; who fills but is not filled; who is shared in but does not share; who sanctifies but is not sanctified; who, as receiving the intercessions of all, is the Intercessor; who is like the Father and the Son in all things; who proceeds from the Father and is communicated through the Son and is participated in by all creation; who through Himself creates and gives substance to all things and sanctifies and preserves them; who is distinctly subsistent and exists in His own Person indivisible and inseparable from the Father and the Son; who has all things whatsoever the Father and the Son have except being unbegotten and being begotten. For the Father is uncaused and unbegotten, because he is not from anything, but has his being from himself and does not have from any other anything whatsoever that he has. Rather, he himself is the principle and cause by which all things naturally exist as they do. And the Son is begotten of the Father, while the Holy Spirit is himself also of the Father—although not by begetting, but by procession. Now, we have learned that there is a difference between begetting and procession, but what the manner of this difference is we have not learned at all. However, the begetting of the Son and the procession of the Holy Spirit from the Father are simultaneous.[9]

[9] John of Damascus, *De fide orthodoxa*, I, 8.

Although rooted in the monastic and cathedral schools established under the first Carlovingian (or Carolingian) king of the Franks, Charlemagne (742–814),[10] it was with the rise of the universities (a new scientific institution) in the twelfth and early thirteenth centuries[11] that systematic theology became a sustained discipline—with an accompanying and deleterious emphasis on theology as a theoretical discipline (Lat. *scientia*).[12] Not coincidentally, disputes over various controversial doctrines initially dominated the landscape—particularly concerning the *filioque* clause,[13] the dual predestination (and supralapsarianism) of

---

[10] Instrumental in this was the English educator and scholar, Alcuin (735–84), who worked for the revival of palace schools.

[11] See Hastings Rashdall, *The Universities of Europe in the Middle Ages*, 3 vols. (1937; reprint, Oxford: Oxford University, 1987).

[12] As Harvie Conn (1933–99) remarked, "The practitioners of theology began to narrow—from believer to scholar, from lay people to clergy." Conn continues, "Theology as disciplined *scientia* became a technical and specialized scholarly undertaking; it was to be undertaken like any other pure science—systematically, rationally, and without the necessity of any accompanying faith in the supernatural character of its objects of study." Conn, "Theological Systems," in *EDWR,* 947–48. R. Albert Mohler, Jr., has remarked, "The transformation of theology into an academic discipline more associated with the university than the church has been one of the most lamentable developments of the last several centuries." Mohler, *The Pastor as Theologian* (Louisville, KY: Southern Baptist Theological Seminary, 2006), 4.

[13] The *Filioque* controversy refers to the disagreement between the medieval Eastern and Western churches over the inclusion of the term "filioque" (Lat., "and [from] the Son") in the Niceno-Constantinopolitan Creed at the Council of Toledo (589) as a description of the provider of the Holy Spirit, thereby expressing belief in the double procession of the Holy Spirit from the Father "and from the Son" (cf. Luke 24:49; John 15:26) By contrast, the Eastern Church maintained that the Holy Spirit proceeded only from the Father (John 15:26), and argued that this inclusion fundamentally altered the doctrine of the Trinity. The controversy culminated in the East–West Schism (1054) when each branch,

Gottschalk of Orbais (*ca.* 808–*ca.* 867),[14] and the Real Presence in the Eucharist (affirmed by Paschasius Radbertus, 785–865; opposed by Ratramnus, d. *ca.* 868).[15]

Anselm of Canterbury (*ca.* 1033–1109), the Italian theologian and archbishop became known as "the father of medieval scholasticism" for the speculative and dialectical character of his theology. In *Monologion* (1075–76), Anselm sets forth his cosmological argument for God's existence, examining the evidence that must belong to a being that is perfect. He argues that God must be the greatest conceivable being, and that existence is a necessary attribute of such a being. In *Proslogion* (1077–78), a continuation of *Monologion*, Anselm presents his ontological argument for God's existence, arguing that God is "that than which nothing greater can be conceived," and that such a being must exist

---

Roman Catholic and Eastern Orthodox, condemned the other. See H. B. Swete's classic study, *On the History of the Doctrine of the Procession of the Holy Spirit from the Apostolic Age to the Death of Charlemagne* (Cambridge: Cambridge University, 1876).

[14] In this, Gottschalk was following Isidore of Seville's (*ca.* 560–63) formulation: "There is a dual predestination, that of the elect at rest, that of the reprobates in death" (*Sentences* II. 6. 1). So contentious was the issue that, not only was Gottschalk condemned by several synods, including the Synod of Quierzy (858), but his refuter, John Duns Scotus (1255–1308), was also condemned at the Synod of Valence III (855). See Geoffrey W. Bromiley, *Historical Theology: An Introduction* (Grand Rapids, MI: Eerdmans, 1978), 165–70. See further Brian J. Matz, "Augustine in the Predestination Controversy of the Ninth Century: Part I: The Double Predestinarians Gottschalk of Orbias and Ratramnus of Corbie," *Augustinian Studies* 46.2 (2015), 155–84.

[15] See Bromiley, *Historical Theology*, 159–65. See further Gary Macy, *Treasures from the Storeroom: Medieval Religion and the Eucharist* (Collegeville, MN: Liturgical, 1999).

in reality, not just conceptually. *Cur Deus Homo* (*Why God Became Man*, 1094–98) is a theological treatise (widely considered one of the greatest work on the atonement ever written) Suggest change to in which Anselm explores the nature of the atonement and why it was necessary for God to become incarnate in order to save humanity. In a memorable passage, Anselm reflects upon God's compassion:

> But how are you merciful, yet at the same time impassible [*impassibilis*]? For if you are impassible, you do not feel sympathy. And if you do not feel sympathy, your heart is not miserable on account of its sympathy for the miserable. Yet this is what compassion is. Yet if you are not compassionate, where does such great comfort for the miserable come from? So how, O Lord, are you both compassionate and not compassionate, unless it is because you are compassionate in terms of our experience, and not in terms of your own being [*secundum te*]. You are truly compassionate in terms of our experience. Yet you are not so in terms of your own. For when you see us in our misery, we experience the effect of compassion; you, however, do not experience this feeling [*non sentis affectum*]. Therefore you are compassionate, in that you save the miserable and spare those who sin against you; and you are not compassionate, in that you are not affected by any sympathy for misery.[16]

Another important scholastic theologian is Peter Abelard (or Abailard, 1079–1142), the French philosopher, theologian, and logician. Known for

[16] Anselm of Canterbury, *Proslogion*, 8.

his contributions to scholasticism, his controversial views on theology, and his love affair with Héloïse, Abelard, one of the first to introduce the methods and ideas of Aristotle to Christianity, engaged in dialectical reasoning and explored theological and philosophical questions. His chief work, *Sic et Non* (*Yes and No,* composed probably *ca.* 1120–21), presents seemingly contradictory views from the fathers on a wide range of doctrines and practices. Abelard also wrote an *Introduction to Theology* (*Theologia Scholarium*, 1136) in three books. Abelard developed the concept of limbo, and introduced the moral influence theory of the atonement, the latter being illustrated in the following passage on the love of Christ in redemption:

> Love is increased by the faith which we have concerning Christ on account of the belief that God in Christ has united our human nature to himself, and that by suffering in that same nature he has demonstrated to us that supreme love (*in ipsa patiendo summam illam charitatem nobis exhibuisse*) of which Christ himself speaks: "Greater love has no one than this" (John 15:13). We are thus joined through his grace to him and our neighbor by an unbreakable bond of love. [...] Just as all have sinned, so they are justified without respect of person [*indifferenter*] by this supreme grace which has been made known to us by God. And this is what [Paul] declares: "For all have sinned, and all need the grace of God" (Romans 3:23), that is, they need to glorify the Lord as a matter of obligation. [...] Now it seems to us that we have been justified by the blood of Christ and reconciled to God in this way: through this singular act of grace made known in us (in that his Son has taken our nature on himself, and persevered in this

> nature, and taught us by both his word and his example, even to the point of death) he has more fully bound us to himself by love. As a result, our hearts should be set on fire by such a gift of divine grace, and true love should not hold back from suffering anything for his sake. [...] Therefore, our redemption through the suffering of Christ is that deeper love within us which not only frees us from slavery to sin, but also secures for us the true liberty of the children of God, in order that we might do all things out of love rather than out of fear—love for him who has shown us such grace that no greater can be found.[17]

Peter Lombard (*ca.* 1100–59), Italian theologian and bishop of Paris, was the first Western theologian to organize Christian doctrine into a comprehensive system. Drawing upon the recent translation of John of Damascus from Greek into Latin, Lombard organized his *Sententia in IV Libris Distinctae* (*Four Books of Sentences*) by arranging the subjects of the Damascene into a tighter format. He collected authoritative citations from the Fathers, and added his own arguments. In Book one, Lombard considered God as Trinity, proofs for God's existence, and the divine attributes. Book two assembled arguments regarding creation, angels, humanity, and sin. Book three considered the doctrines of Jesus Christ and the redemption of humanity. Book four contains Lombard's treatise on the sacraments (of which he concluded there were seven) and a treatise on eschatology. Lombard's *Sentences* earned for him the title *Magister Sententiarum* ("Master of the Sentences"). The *Sentences*, Aristotelian in orientation, remained *the* chief theological textbook in European

[17] Peter Abelard, *Expositio in Epistolam ad Romanos*, 2.

universities until the sixteenth century, being required reading for subsequent students, and did more than any other text to shape the discipline of medieval Scholastic theology. Significantly, in one place Peter offers his peculiar definition of a "sacrament," allowing him to reckon the seven that would in turn become definitive for the medieval church:

> A sacrament bears a likeness to the thing of which it is a sign. "For if sacraments did not have a likeness of the things whose sacraments they are, they would not properly be called sacraments" (Augustine). [...] Something can properly be called a sacrament if it is a sign of the grace of God and a form of invisible grace, so that it bears its image and exists as its cause. Sacraments were therefore instituted for the sake of sanctifying, as well as of signifying. [...] Those things which were instituted for the purpose of signifying alone are nothing more than signs, and are not sacraments, as in the case of the physical sacrifices and ceremonial observances of the Old Law, which were never able to make those who offered them righteous. [...] Now let us consider the sacraments of the New Law, which are baptism, confirmation, the bread of blessing (that is, the Eucharist), penance, extreme unction, ordination, and marriage. Some of these, such as baptism, provide a remedy against sin and confer the assistance of grace; others, such as marriage, are only a remedy; and others, such as the Eucharist and ordination, strengthen us with grace and power. [...] So why were these sacraments not instituted soon after the fall of humanity, since they convey righteousness and salvation? We reply that the

> sacraments of grace were not given before the coming of Christ, who is the giver of grace, in that they receive their virtue from his death and suffering.[18]

Many of the greatest Scholastic philosophers and theologians wrote commentaries on Lombard's *Sentences*, including Italian philosopher and theologian Thomas Aquinas (1225–74) in his *Scripta Super Libros Sententiarum* (*Writings on the Books of the Sentences*, *ca.* 1256), the Scottish theologian and philosopher John Duns Scotus (1266–1308) in two sets of *Commentaries on the Sentences*, and Gabriel Biel (*ca.* 1415–95) in his *Collectorium circa Quator Sententiarum* (*Collections around the Four Books of Sentences*). Not only did the coherent and comprehensive organization of Lombard's *Sentences* encourage theologians to write extensive commentaries on it as a means of expositing doctrine, but his structure still provides a typical, although by no means universally uniform, order for systematic theology: God, unity, Trinity; creation, angels, man, sin; Christology, redemption, virtues (or Christian life); sacraments (or ecclesiology), and eschatology. This pattern was followed by medieval dogmaticians such as Aquinas in his *Summa Theologiae* (*Summary of Theology*) and *Summa contra Gentiles* (*Summary against the Nations*), as well as by subsequent Protestant Scholastic theologians.

Medieval scholasticism reached its apex in Thomas Aquinas, called the "Angelic Doctor" (Lat. *Doctor Angelicus*). While he wrote dozens of texts of different kinds, Aquinas' greatest achievements are his two

---

[18] Peter Lombard, *Sententiarum libri quatuor*, IV.i.4, ii.1.

masterly compendia: the *Summa contra Gentiles* ("Gentiles" in the sense of "unbelievers"; 1259–64) and especially the unfinished yet massive *Summa Theologiae* (1266–73; 1,500,000 words). Aquinas' *Summa Theologiae*, begun in 1266 and uncompleted at his death in 1272, ranks as one of the greatest theological classics of all time.[19] Aquinas' *Summa Theologiae* covers in three volumes the whole field of systematics, being divided into (1) God and His works, (2) man in the image of God, and (3) Christ as the means of grace, and models the core pedagogical technique of the universities of his day—*quaestiones disputatae* (lit. "questions debated"). This technique takes up sides of an issue, articulated as a question, offer arguments for each side, and then evaluates the arguments and adjudicates. Using the *quaestione* format, the *Summa* is divided into four overall Parts (I, I–II, II–II, and III). Each Part is divided into Treatises (e.g., On the Creation, On Man, etc.). Each Treatise is divided into numbered "Questions," or general issues within the topic of the Treatise (e.g., "Of the Simplicity of God"). Finally, each Question is divided into numbered Articles, the basic thought-unit of the *Summa*. Each Article is framed in such a way that only two answers are possible: *yes* or *no* (e.g., "Whether God Is a Body?"). Each Article in turn has five structural parts: first, the question formulated in a *yes* or *no* format; then, a number of

[19] In the English and Latin edition of the Dominican Blackfriars, which contains the complete Latin text of the *Summa* with an English translation on facing pages, Aquinas' *Summa Theologiae* runs to sixty volumes. Commended by Pope Paul VI (1963), "By official appointment the *Summa* provides the framework for Catholic studies in systematic theology and for a classical Christian philosophy" (*Preface*, vol.1, xi). See Thomas Aquinas, *Summa Theologiae* (Cambridge: Blackfriars/New York: McGraw Hill, 1964–73). The English translation by the Blackfriars is generally reliable, although occasionally exhibiting a degree of interpretive freedom.

objections (usually three) to the answer to be given; third, Aquinas' own position, usually in an argument from authority; fourth, Aquinas then proves his own position; and fifth, each objection is addressed and answered.

In one place, Aquinas considers God's omnipotence (Lat. *omni-,* "all" and *potens,* "power") or all-encompassing power, His ability to do anything consistent with His own nature and all things that are proper objects of power, which attribute is His alone (Gen. 17:1; Ex 15:11-12; Deu. 3:24; Pss. 62:11; 65:6; 147:5; Jer. 32:17; Matt. 6:13; 19:26; Eph. 3:20; Rev. 19:6). Specifically, Aquinas considers the question, "Can God sin?," and whether answering in the negative contradicts God's omnipotence. Reasons Aquinas,

> It is commonly said that God is almighty. Yet it seems difficult to understand the reason for this, on account of the doubt about what is meant when it is said that "God can do 'everything.'" [...] If it is said that God is omnipotent because he can do everything possible to his power, the understanding of omnipotence is circular, doing nothing more than saying that God is omnipotent because he can do everything that he can do. [...] To sin is to fall short of a perfect action. Hence to be able to sin is to be able to be deficient in relation to an action, which cannot be reconciled with omnipotence. It is because God is omnipotent that he cannot sin. [...] Anything that implies a contradiction does not relate to the omnipotence of God. For the past not to have existed implies a contradiction. Thus to say Socrates is, and is not, seated is contradictory, and so also to say that he had, and had not, been

seated. To affirm that he had been seated is to affirm a past event; to affirm that he had not been seated is thus to affirm what was not the case.[20]

In addition to his magisterial *Summas,* Aquinas produced *On Being and Essence* (1242–43), *On Truth* (1256–59), *On Evil* (1263–68), *On Separate Substances* (1271), and up to eighty other works.[21] It would be misleading to emphasize his role as theologian at the expense of recognizing his genuine stature as a philosopher, and vice versa. Aquinas' system of thought, often called "Thomism," adapted Aristotelian philosophy to delineate between reason and faith.[22] According to

---

[20] Thomas Aquinas, *Summa Theologiae*, Ia, q. 25, aa. 3–4.

[21] The critical edition of Thomas Aquinas's writing is the so–called Leonine edition: *Sancti Thomae Aquinatis doctoris angelici Opera omnia iussu Leonis XIII.O.M. edita.,* cura et studio fratrum praedictorum (Rome: 1882–), 26 volumes to date. For a helpful selection of the major questions and articles from the Summa, see Frederick Christian Bauerschmidt, ed. and trans., *Holy Teaching: Introducing the Summa Theologiae of St. Thomas Aquinas* (Grand Rapids, MI: Eerdmans, 2005). For positive Evangelical assessments of Aquinas, see Norman L. Geisler, *Thomas Aquinas: An Evangelical Assessment* (1991; reprint, Eugene, OR: Wipf & Stock, 2003); *idem*, *Should Old Aquinas Be Forgotten?* (Charlotte, NC: Bastion Books, 2013).

[22] For an overview of the life and work of Aquinas, see Brian Davies and Eleanore Stump, eds., *The Oxford Handbook of Aquinas*, Oxford Handbooks on Religion (New York: Oxford University, 2012). On Thomism, see Jean-Pierre Torrell, "Thomism," in *ECT,* 1578–83; and Romanus Cessario, *A Short History of Thomism* (Washington, DC: Catholic University of America, 2005). Thomism is part of the "perennial philosophy" (Lat., *philosophia perennis*) contributed to by Socrates, Plato, Aristotle, Plotinus, Dionysius, Augustine, Boethius, Avicenna, Maimonides, and others. See Aldous Huxley's classic, *The Perennial Philosophy,* Harper Modern Classics (New York: Harper & Row, 2004). As an aside, while philosophy is clearly separate from and subordinate to theology, it exists in a symbiotic relationship with and in service to it. See further Diogenes

Aquinas, "sacred doctrine" is "partly speculative and partly practical; it transcends all others speculative and practical.... In both these respects this science surpasses other speculative sciences; in point of greater certitude, because other sciences derive their certitude from the natural light of human reason, which can err; whereas this derives its certitude from the light of the divine knowledge, which cannot be misled."[23]

The "golden age of scholasticism" during the thirteenth century was followed by the decline of medieval theology in the fourteenth and fifteenth centuries. The medieval English Franciscan friar, philosopher, and commentator on Peter Lombard's *Sentences*, William of Ockham (*ca.* 1280–1349), attacked the scholastic procedure of wedding Aristotelian philosophy to Christian theology, particularly as expressed in Thomism. According to Ockham, God is not known by rational inference, but by reception of divine revelation by faith. The metaphysical nominalism of Ockham and of his disciple, Gabriel Biel (1420–95), one of the last great scholastic theologians and one of the founders of the University of Tübingen, further disparaged reason's role in arriving at theological truth and asserted the power of human free will.[24]

While Christian mysticism found expression in the early church—being derived from Neoplatonism through the writings of Dionysius the

---

Allen, *Philosophy for Understanding Theology,* 2nd ed. (Louisville, KY: Westminster John Knox, 2007).

[23] Thomas Aquinas, *Summa Theologicae*, I, q. 1, a. 5.

[24] See Heiko A. Oberman, *The Harvest of Medieval Theology: Gabriel Biel and Late Medieval Nominalism*, 2nd ed. (1963; reprint, Grand Rapids MI: Baker Academic, 2012).

Areopagite, or Pseudo-Dionysius—with the gradual demise of speculative theology came the renewed medieval quest for God through mystical experience.[25] Johannes Eckhart (*ca.* 1260–1327), better known as Meister Eckhart, was the foremost mystic of Germany. Other important German mystics are Johannes Tauler (*ca.* 1300–61) and Heinrich Suso (1295–1366), followers of Eckhart and members of a group called the Friends of God. One of this group (likely Tauler) wrote the *Theologia Deutsch* (*German Theology*) that would influence Martin Luther. Prominent later figures include Thomas à Kempis (*ca.* 1380–1471), author of *Imitatio Christi* (*The Imitation of Christ*). English mystics of the fourteenth and fifteenth centuries include Margery Kempe (1373–1438), Richard Rolle (1300–49), Walter Hilton (1340–96), the anchoress Julian of Norwich (1342–1413), and the anonymous author of *The Cloud of Unknowing,* an influential treatise on mystic prayer.[26] Illustrative of this literature is Julian's "shewings" (or "revelations"), a record of sixteen personal revelations that she purportedly received in 1373. According to Julian's account of her own experience,

[25] See William Harmless' classic study, *Mystics* (New York: Oxford University, 2008). See further Steven Fanning, *Mystics of the Christian Tradition* (New York: Routledge, 2001); Amy Hollywood and Patricia Z. Beckman, eds., *The Cambridge Companion to Christian Mysticism* (Cambridge: Cambridge University, 2012); and Julia A. Lamm, ed., *The Wiley-Blackwell Companion to Christian Mysticism* (Oxford: Wiley-Blackwell, 2012).

[26] Notably, a number of the most distinguished Christian mystics have been women, notably Hildegard of Bingen (1098–1179), Catherine of Siena (1347–80), and Teresa of Ávila (1515–82). The 17th-century French mystic Jeanne Marie Bouvier de la Motte Guyon (1648–1717) introduced into France the mystical doctrine of quietism.

These revelations were shown to a simple and uneducated creature on the eighth of May 1373. Some time earlier she had asked three gifts from God: (i) to understand his passion; (ii) to suffer physically while still a young woman of thirty; and (iii) to have as God's gift three wounds.

With regard to the first I had thought I had already had some experience of the passion of Christ, but by his grace I wanted still more. I wanted to actually be there with Mary Magdalen and the others who loved him, and with my own eyes to see and know more of the physical suffering of our Saviour, and the compassion of our Lady and of those who there and then were loving him truly and watching his pains. I would be one of them and suffer with him. I had no desire for any other vision of God until after such time as I had died. The reason for this prayer was that I might more truly understand the passion of Christ.

The second came to me with much greater urgency. I quite sincerely wanted to be ill to the point of dying, so that I might receive the last rites of Holy Church, in the belief—shared by my friends—that I was in fact dying. In this illness I wanted to undergo all those spiritual and physical sufferings I should have were I really dying, and to know, moreover, the terror and assault of the demons—everything, except death itself! My intention was that I should be wholly cleansed thereby through the mercy of God, and that thereafter, because of that illness, I might live more worthily of him. Perhaps too I might even die a better death, for I was longing to be with my God. There was a condition with these two desires: "Lord, you know what I am wanting. If it is

> your will that I have it ... But if not, do not be cross, good Lord, for I want nothing but your will."
>
> As for the third, through the grace of God and the teaching of Holy Church, I developed a strong desire to receive three wounds, namely the wound of true contrition, the wound of genuine compassion, and the wound of sincere longing for God. There was no proviso attached to any part of this third prayer. I forgot all about the first two desires, but the third was with me continually.[27]

Among the many contributions to systematic theology from the medieval period, the following are a representative selection:[28]

---

[27] Julian of Norwich, *Revelations of Divine Love*, trans. Clifton Wolters (Harmondsworth: Penguin, 1966), 63–4.

[28] Helpful surveys of Medieval thought include: G. R. Evans, ed., *The Medieval Theologians: An Introduction to Theology in the Medieval Period* (Oxford: Blackwell, 2001); *idem*, *Philosophy and Theology in the Middle Ages* (New York: Routledge, 1994); *idem*, *Fifty Key Medieval Thinkers* (New York: Routledge, 2002); Brian Davies, ed., *Great Medieval Thinkers* series (New York: Oxford University, 2000–); Jaroslav Pelikan, *The Christian Tradition: A History of the Development of Doctrine*, 5 vol. (Chicago, IL: University of Chicago, 1974, 1978, 1984); Marcia L. Colish, *The Medieval Foundations of the Western Intellectual Tradition, 400–1400*, The Yale Intellectual History of the West (New Haven, CT: Yale University, 1997); Giulio D'Onofrio, ed., *History of Theology II: The Middle Ages* (Collegeville, MN: Liturgical, 2008); James Ginther, ed., *The Westminster Handbook to Medieval Theology*, Westminster Handbooks to Christian Theology (Louisville, KY: Westminster John Knox, 2009); Michael Haren, *Medieval Thought: The Western Intellectual Tradition from Antiquity to the Thirteenth Century*, 2nd ed. (Toronto: University of Toronto, 1992); B. B. Price, *Medieval Thought: An Introduction* (Cambridge, MA: Blackwell, 1992).

- John of Damascus (*ca.* 652–*ca.* 750), *De Fide Orthodoxa* (*Exposition of the Orthodox Faith, ca.* 730), and *The Fountain* of *Knowledge* (*ca.* 730)
- Symeon (or, Simeon) the New Theologian (949–1022), *Catecheses* (*ca.* 1000) and *Practical and Theological Chapters* (*ca.* 1005–22)
- Peter Abelard (1079–1142), *Sic et Non* (*Thus and Otherwise*, *ca.* 1123); *Introduction to Theology* (1136)
- Peter Lombard (*ca.* 1100–59), *Sententia in IV Libris Distinctae* or *Sententiarum Libri Quator* (*Four Book of Sentences,* 1157/58)
- William of Auvergne (Guillaume d'Auvergne, Guilielmus Alvernus, or William of Paris, *ca.* 1180–1290), *Magisterium Divinale et Sapientale* (*Teaching on God in the Mode of Wisdom*, 1223–40)
- Albertus Magnus (Albert the Great, 1193–1280), *Summa Theologiae sive De mirabilis scientia Dei* (*Summary of Theology Concerning the Wonderful Knowledge of God,* uncompleted)
- Bonaventure (1217–1274), *Breviloquium* (*Summary*, 1256/57)
- William of Auxerre (d. 1231), *Summa Aurea* (*The Golden Compendium*, Paris, 1500, 1518)
- Thomas Aquinas (1225–1274), *Summa contra Gentiles* (*Summary against the Nations*, 1261–64), and *Summa Theologiae* (*Summary of Theology*, 1265–73)
- Raymond Lull (Raymond Lully or Ramón Lull, *ca.* 1232–1316), *Ars Magna* (*The Great Art,* 1305–08)

- Gabriel Biel (*ca.* 1415–1495), *Collectorium circa Quator Sententiarum* (*Collections around the Four Books of Sentences,* completed by a follower in 1520)

CHAPTER THREE:
THE REFORMATION AND POST–REFORMATION CHURCH (1500—1750)

THE Reformation and post–Reformation church period covers the interval from around AD 1500 to 1750, a time of profound transformation and diversification in the history of Christianity. This era witnessed the birth and aftermath of the Protestant Reformation, the expansion of Christianity to new continents, and the intellectual and cultural shifts of the Enlightenment. Of particular note are the spread of Protestantism, the Catholic Counter-Reformation, various missionary endeavors, numerous religious conflicts, and the impact of Enlightenment thought on Christian theology and practice.

1. The Protestant Reformation and its Aftermath

The sixteenth century marked a significant turning point in Christian history with the Protestant Reformation, during which Protestantism emerged as a distinct branch of Christianity in Europe. It was sparked by a growing dissatisfaction with the practices and teachings of the Roman Catholic Church, particularly the sale of indulgences and the authority of the pope. Figures such as Martin Luther, John Calvin, and Huldrych Zwingli challenged the authority of the Catholic Church, emphasizing the primacy of Scripture, salvation by faith alone, and the priesthood of all believers. The Reformation led to the establishment of various Protestant denominations, including Lutheranism, Calvinism, and Anglicanism, and sparked religious conflicts that reshaped the religious and political landscape of Europe.

2. Catholic Counter-Reformation and Reform

In response to the Protestant Reformation, the Roman Catholic Church initiated a process of reform known as the Counter-Reformation. The Council of Trent (1545–1563) addressed doctrinal issues, reaffirmed Roman Catholic teachings, and implemented measures to combat corruption within the Church. New religious orders, such as the Jesuits, played a crucial role in promoting Roman Catholicism, engaging in missionary work, and establishing educational institutions. The Counter-Reformation revitalized Roman Catholicism and solidified its position as a major Christian tradition.

3. Expansion and Missionary Endeavors

The period from 1500 to 1750 witnessed the expansion of Christianity to new continents through missionary endeavors. European explorers and missionaries, such as Francis Xavier and Matteo Ricci, ventured to Asia, Africa, and the Americas, seeking to spread the Christian faith. These efforts resulted in the conversion of indigenous peoples, the establishment of Christian communities, and the blending of Christian beliefs with local cultures. Missionary work played a significant role in shaping the global reach of Christianity.

4. Religious Conflicts and Wars of Religion

The sixteenth and seventeenth centuries were marked by religious conflicts and wars of religion, fueled by the divisions between Roman Catholicism and Protestantism. The Thirty Years' War (1618–1648) stands as one of the most devastating conflicts, resulting in widespread destruction and loss of life.[1] These conflicts highlighted the deep religious divisions within Europe and led to the emergence of principles such as religious tolerance and the separation of church and state.

5. The Enlightenment and Christian Thought

The Enlightenment, an intellectual and cultural movement of the late seventeenth to early nineteenth centuries, had a profound impact on Christian thought and practice. Enlightenment thinkers, such as John Locke and Voltaire, challenged traditional religious beliefs, advocated for reason and scientific inquiry, and promoted religious tolerance. Christian theologians, such as Friedrich Schleiermacher, sought to reconcile Christian faith with Enlightenment ideals, leading to the emergence of liberal theology and a renewed emphasis on individual religious experience.

6. Revival Movements and Pietism

Amidst the intellectual and cultural changes of the Enlightenment, revival movements and pietism emerged as a response to what was perceived as a decline in religious fervor. Figures such as John Wesley and Jonathan Edwards led revivalist movements that emphasized personal conversion, spiritual renewal, and social reform. These movements revitalized Christian faith and played a significant role in shaping the religious landscape of Europe and North America.

---

[1] See especially Peter H. Wilson, *The Thirty Years War: Europe's Tragedy* (Cambridge, MA: Harvard University, 2009); and C. V. Wedgwood, *The Thirty Years War* (1938; reprint, New York: NYRB, 2005).

Summary of the Times

The period from 1500 to 1750 witnessed a dynamic and transformative era in the history of Christianity. The Protestant Reformation, Catholic Counter-Reformation, missionary endeavors, religious conflicts, and the impact of Enlightenment thought all contributed to the diversification and evolution of Christian theology, practice, and global reach. This period saw the emergence of new Christian denominations, the expansion of Christianity to new continents, and the engagement with intellectual and cultural shifts. The history of Christianity during this time reflects the complex interplay between religious, political, and intellectual forces, leaving a lasting impact on the religious landscape of the world, including systematic theology.

The Development of Systematic Theology in the Reformation and Post–Reformation Period

As R. T. Jones (1921–98) has remarked, "The Protestant Reformation produced a theology that was a massive reassertion of the centrality of God, the glory of his sovereignty, and the primacy of his grace in the salvation of humanity through Jesus Christ."[2]

The initial protest and eventual revolt against medieval theology by the Augustinian monk and Wittenberg professor, Martin Luther (1483–1546), was not concerned with the structure of systematic theology per se, but with its content. While Luther expressed himself in occasional

---

[2] R. T. Jones, "Reformation theology," *NDT*², 737. Good histories of the Reformation include Euan Cameron, *The European Reformation* (New York: Oxford University, 1991); Carter Lindberg, *The European Reformations*, 2nd ed. (Oxford: Wiley-Blackwell, 2009); and Diarmaid MacCulloch, *The Reformation: A History* (New York: Viking, 2004).

writings rather than systematic works,[3] he did produce a system of doctrine in both the *Long* (or *Great*) *Catechism* (mainly for students and priests) and a *Short Catechism* (mainly for children and lay people), both published in 1529, in which he followed the format of the Apostles' Creed, the Ten Commandments, the Lord's Prayer, and the sacraments.[4] (Previously, in 1520, Luther had published *A Short Form of the Ten Commandments... the Creed... and the Lord's Prayer.*) D. F. Wright (1937–2008) has observed that the *Long* and *Short Catechism* epitomized "the standard ingredients of subsequent Protestant catechisms."[5] Indeed, the catechism has been called "the heart of the Reformation."[6]

In *The Liberty of a Christian* (1520), Luther discusses the nature of justifying faith, using the imagery of marriage to illustrate both the

---

[3] After making a distinction between "a regular dogmatics and an irregular dogmatics," Karl Barth (1886–1968) lists Luther ("a typical irregular dogmatician") among those who wrote "irregular dogmatics," which roughly correlates to non–systematic theology, in distinction from Melanchthon and Calvin, who wrote "regular dogmatics." Barth, *Church Dogmatics*, 14 vols., trans. Geoffrey W. Bromiley and Thomas Forsyth Torrance (1975; reprint, Peabody, MA: Hendrickson, 2010), I/1, §7, 275–78.

[4] Significantly, Luther put the burden of catechizing on the parents, rather than the church: "If everything cannot be covered at once, let one point be taken up today, and tomorrow another. If parents and guardians will not take the trouble to do this, either themselves or through others, there never will be a catechism." Quoted in Johann M. Reu, *Dr. Martin Luther's Small Catechism: A History of Its Origin, Its Distribution and Its Use* (Chicago, IL: Wartburg, 1929), 13.

[5] D. F. Wright, "Catechisms," in *EDT*[3], 161.

[6] John Nordling, "The Catechism: The Heart of the Reformation," *Logia* 16.4 (2007), 5–13.

personal and legal aspects of faith and the believer's relationship to Christ:

> In the twelfth place, faith does not merely mean that the soul realizes that the divine word is full of all grace, free and holy; it also unites the soul with Christ [*voreynigt auch die seele mit Christo*], as a bride is united with her bridegroom. From such a marriage, as St Paul says (Ephesians 5:31–2), it follows that Christ and the soul become one body, so that they hold all things in common, whether for better or worse. This means that what Christ possesses belongs to the believing soul; and what the soul possesses, belongs to Christ. Thus Christ possesses all good things and holiness; these now belong to the soul. The soul possesses lots of vices and sin; these now belong to Christ. Here we have a happy exchange [*froelich wechtzel*] and struggle. Christ is God and a human being, who has never sinned and whose holiness is unconquerable, eternal, and almighty. So he makes the sin of the believing soul his own through its wedding ring [*braudtring*], which is faith, and acts as if he had done it [i.e., sin] himself, so that sin could be swallowed up in him. For his unconquerable righteousness is too strong for all sin, so that is made single and free [*ledig und frei*] from all its sins on account of its pledge, that is its faith, and can turn to the eternal righteousness of its bridegroom, Christ. Now is not this a happy business [*ein froehliche wirtschafft*]? Christ, the rich, noble, and holy bridegroom, takes in marriage this poor, contemptible, and sinful little prostitute [*das arm vorachte boetzes huerlein*], takes away all her evil, and bestows all his goodness upon her! It is no

> longer possible for sin to overwhelm her, for she is now found in Christ and is swallowed up by him, so that she possesses a rich righteousness in her bridegroom.[7]

Philip Melanchthon (1497–1560)—Luther's lieutenant and the chief architect of Lutheranism—was the first systematic theologian within the Protestant tradition. Melanchthon has been described as "One of the most erudite and intellectually powerful figures of his age,"[8] and his *Loci communes rerum theologicarum seu hypotyposes theologicae* (known more commonly as the *Loci communes*, the *Theological Commonplaces*) created not only the first dogmatic of the Lutheran Reformation, but also a new genre in theological literature.[9] Commenting on the *Sentences* of Peter Lombard and Paul's Epistle to the Romans, Melanchthon employed an ancient method, recommended by the Christian humanist Desiderius Erasmus (*ca.* 1466–1536), of noting the basic concepts—*topoi*, or *loci communes*—of a text in order to appropriate more fully its content.[10]

---

[7] Martin Luther, *The Liberty of a Christian*; in *D. Martin Luthers Werke: Kritische Gesamtausgabe*, vol. 7 (Weimar: Böhlaus, 1897), 25.26–26.9.

[8] "Melanchthon, Philipp," in *ODCC³,* 1066.

[9] As Richard Muller (b. 1948) has remarked, while, strictly speaking, it is true that "the literary genre of 'systematic theology' was unknown to the Reformation," nevertheless "the various forms of *Loci communes*, *Compendia*, *Institutiones*, and *Methodus* or *Corpus theologiae* found among the Protestants of the sixteenth and seventeenth centuries are the ancestors of modern theological system and were, in fact, the more or less systematic statements of theology for that time." Muller, *A Post–Reformation Reformed Dogmatics: The Rise and Development of Reformed Orthodoxy, ca. 1510 to 1725*, 2nd ed., 4 vols. (Grand Rapids, MI: Baker, 2003), vol.1, ePub: Section 1: The Study of Protestant Scholasticism, Location 79.

[10] Concerning *loci*, Bavinck (*Reformed Dogmatics*, 3) clarifies,

Melanchthon thereby addressed the *loci communes theologici de Deo* (theological topics concerning God), *de Scriptura* (concerning Scripture), *de creatione* (creation), *de homine* (humanity), *de peccato* (sin), *de Christo* (Christ), *de gratia* (grace, the doctrine of salvation), *de ecclesia* (the church), and *de novissimus* (eschatology, or last things).[11] Three editions of the *Loci communes* appeared before the end of the year of its initial release (1521) and eighteen editions by 1525, in addition to printings of a German translation. The last edition in 1558 was much enlarged and changed. Luther, with typical hyperbole, declared that the *Loci communes* deserved a place in the canon of Scriptures; the University of Cambridge in England later made it required reading; and Elizabeth I (1533–1603), queen of England and Ireland, virtually memorized it so she could converse about theology.

An outstanding example of Melanchthon's capabilities as a theologian can be seen in a lengthy passage wherein he discusses justification by faith, with particular concern for faith's relationship to good works:

This term, a translation of the Greek *τοποι* [*topoi*], comes from classical writers such as Cicero who used the term for the general rules or places where a rhetorician could find the arguments needed when treating any given topic. *Loci*, in other words, were the data bases, the proof–text barrels used by debaters as sources of material to bolster their arguments. For theologians seeking to serve the church, the *loci* were the places one could look for Scripture's own statements about a particular topic.

[11] Philip Melanchthon, *Loci Communes,* 1555 ed., trans. Clyde L. Manschreck (London: Oxford University, 1965). This is the English translation of the final and authoritative edition of this work, reprinted by Baker (1982) as *Melanchthon on Christian Doctrine*. See also Melanchton, "Loci Communes Theologici," in *Melanchthon and Bucer*, ed. Wilhelm Pauck. In *The Library of Christian Classics: Ichthus Edition* (Philadelphia: Westminster, 1979), 18–152.

For what cause is justification attributed to faith alone? I answer that since we are justified by the mercy of God alone, and faith is clearly the recognition of that mercy by whatever promise you apprehend it, justification is attributed to faith alone. Let those who marvel that justification is attributed to faith alone marvel also that justification is attributed only to the mercy of God, and not rather to human merits. For to trust in the divine mercy is to have no confidence in any of our own works. Anyone who denies that the saints are justified by faith insults the mercy of God. For since our justification is a work of divine mercy alone and is not a merit based on our own works, as Paul clearly teaches in Romans 11, justification must be attributed to faith alone: faith is that through which alone we receive the promised mercy.

So what about works that precede justification, works of the free will? All those who are of the cursed tree are cursed fruits. Although they are examples of the most beautiful virtues, comparable to the righteousness of Paul before his conversion, yet they are nothing but deceit and treachery on account of their having their source in an impure heart. Impurity of heart consists of ignorance of God, not fearing God, not trusting God, and not seeking after God, as we have shown above. For the flesh knows nothing but fleshly things, as it says in Romans 8:5: "Those who live according to the flesh set their minds on the things of the flesh." […] The philosophers list many such things in their definitions of the goal of what is good: one suggests "happiness," and another "lack of pain." It is clear that by nature human beings care nothing for the divine. They are neither terrified by the word of God, nor brought to life in faith. And what are the fruits of such a tree but sin?

But although the works that follow justification have their source in the Spirit of God who has taken hold of the hearts of those who are justified, because they are performed in a still impure flesh, the works themselves are also impure. Although justification has begun, it has not yet been brought to its conclusion. We have the first fruits of the Spirit, but not yet the whole harvest. We are still awaiting with groaning the redemption of our bodies, as we read in Romans 8:23. Therefore, because there is something unclean even in these works, they do not deserve the name of righteousness, and wherever you turn, whether to the works preceding justification, or to those which follow, there is no room for our merit. Therefore, justification must be a work of the mercy of God alone. This is what Paul says in Galatians 2:20: "And the life I now live in the flesh I live by faith in the Son of God, who loved me and gave himself for me." He does not say: "I live now in my good works," but "I live by faith in the mercy of God." Moreover, faith is the reason that those works which follow justification are not imputed as sin. This we shall discuss a little later.

Therefore, when justification is attributed to faith, it is attributed to the mercy of God; it is set apart from human efforts, works, and merits. The beginning and growth of righteousness are linked to the mercy of God so that the righteousness of the entire life is nothing else than faith. That is why the prophet Isaiah calls the Kingdom of Christ a kingdom of mercy: "And a throne will be

> established in steadfast love," etc. (Isaiah 16:5). For if we were justified by our own works, the kingdom would not be that of Christ, nor of mercy, but it would be our own—a kingdom of our own works. […] You will say: "so do we then merit nothing? For what reason, then, does Scripture use the word "reward" throughout?" I answer that there is a reward, and it is not because of any merit of ours; but because the Father promised, he has now laid himself under obligation to us and made himself a debtor to those who had deserved nothing at all. […] Paul says in Romans 6:23: "For the wages of sin is death, but the free gift of God is eternal life." He calls eternal life a "gift," not a "debt"—although as a matter of fact it is a debt because the Father has promised it and he has pledged it in faith.[12]

Huldrych (or, Ulrich) Zwingli (1484–1531) was the first of the Reformed theologians and leader of the Swiss reformation.[13] Initially a Roman Catholic—Zwingli was ordained a Catholic priest in 1506 by the bishop of Constance, and served parishes in the canton of Glarus (1506–16) and at the celebrated abbey of Einsiedeln (1516–18) before being appointed

---

[12] Philip Melanchthon, *Loci Communes* (1521); in *Melanchthons Werke in Auswahl*, ed. H. Engelland (Gütersloh: Bertelsmann Verlag, 1953), 2:106.22–110.11.

[13] On Zwingli, see W. P. Stephens, *The Theology of Huldrych Zwingli* (New York: Oxford University, 1986); idem., *Zwingli: An Introduction to His Thought* (New York: Oxford University, 1994); and Ulrich Gabler, *Huldrych Zwingli: His Life and Work*, trans. Ruth C. L. Gritsch (1986; reprint, London: T&T Clark, 1999).

(1518) *Leutpriester* ("people's priest") in the *Grossmünster* (Great Minster, or Cathedral) in Zürich—over time, as he studied Scripture and witnessed abuses within the Catholic Church, he began to question and challenge certain practices and teachings. From his humanistic background, including the influence of both the *via antiqua* (with its Aristotelian and Thomist presuppositions) and studying Erasmus's Greek New Testament, Zwingli wrestled with the issues of original sin, predestination (actually, to be precise, election), the work of Christ, the nature of the church, and the sacraments. He was a preacher and pastor in the city of Zürich, Switzerland (shepherding it to its declaration for reform in 1523), where he led the reformation movement. Succinct statements of Zwingli's theology are preserved in his *Sixty-Seven Theses* (1523), the *Ten Theses of Berne* (1528), and in *An Exposition of the Faith* (1529).[14] In *Von dem Touff* ("On Baptism"), published in German in 1525, Zwingli gives a lengthy discussion of baptism, stressing the symbolic nature of the ordinance and its function as a public profession of faith:

> Now [Christ] has left behind to us, his fellow members, two ceremonies, that is, two external things or signs: baptism and the thanksgiving or remembrance [*dancksagung oder widergedächtnus*], undoubtedly as a concession to our weakness. [...] By the first of these signs, baptism, we are initially marked off to God, as we shall see later. In the other, the Lord's Supper

[14] For Zwingli's writings, see Geoffrey W. Bromiley, ed., *Zwingli and Bullinger*, Library of Christian Classics (reprint of 1953 edition, Nashville, TN: Westminster John Knox, 1973).

or thanksgiving, we give thanks to God because he has redeemed us by his Son.

Before we speak about baptism, we must first identify the meaning of the word "sacrament." To us Germans, the word "sacrament" suggests something that has power to take away sin or to make us holy. But this is a serious error. For only Jesus Christ and no external thing can take away the sins of us Christians or make us holy. [...] As used in this context the word "sacrament" means a sign of commitment [*Pflichtszeichen*]. If a man sews on a white cross, he proclaims that he is a [Swiss] Confederate. And if he makes the pilgrimage to Nähenfels and gives God praise and thanksgiving for the victory delivered to our forefathers, he testifies from his heart that he is a Confederate.[15] Similarly the man who receives the mark of baptism is the one who is resolved to hear what God says to him, to learn the divine precepts and to live his life in accordance with them. And the man who, in the remembrance or supper, gives thanks to God in the congregation declares that he heartily rejoices in the death of Christ and thanks him for it. So I ask these quibblers that they allow the sacraments to be real sacraments, and that they do not describe them as signs [*zeichen*] which are identical with the things which they represent. For if they are the things which they represent, they are no longer signs: for the sign and the thing which is represented cannot be the same thing. Sacraments—as

---

[15] Zwingli is here referring to the annual pilgrimage to the battle site of Nähenfels—the "Näfelser Fahrtfeier"—which commemorated a major Swiss victory over the Austrians in April 1388.

> even the papists maintain—are simply the signs of holy things. Baptism is a sign which pledges us to the Lord Jesus Christ. The remembrance shows us that Christ suffered death for our sake. They are the signs and pledges [*zeichen und verpflichtungen*] of these holy things. You will find ample proof of this if you consider the pledge of circumcision and the thanksgiving of the Passover lamb.[16]

In the wake of the Reformation, subsequent systematic theologians initially followed a pattern established by specific catechisms tailored to their respective traditions. The *Heidelberg*, or *Palatinate*, *Catechism* (1563), was compiled in Heidelberg (in southwestern Germany), by German theologians Caspar Olevianus (1536–1587) and Zacharias Ursinus (1534–1583) at the request of the Elector Frederick III. The *Heidelberg Catechism,* which served as a comprehensive guide for many theologians of the time,[17] consists of one hundred and twenty-nine questions and answers, divided into three main parts. For example, questions 96–98 asks and answers concerning images of God:

> Question 96. What does God require in the next commandment?
>
> Answer: That we should not portray God in any way, nor worship him in any other manner than he has commanded in his Word.

[16] Huldrych Zwingli, *On Baptism*; in *Corpus Reformatorum: Huldreich Zwinglis sämtliche Werke* (Leipzig: Heinsius, 1927), 91:217.14–218.24.

[17] Today, the *Heidelberg Catechism* is one of the Three Forms of Unity, the doctrinal basis of many Reformed denominations originating from the Netherlands.

> Question 97. So should we not make any use of images?
>
> Answer: God cannot and should not be depicted in any way. As for creatures, although they may indeed be depicted, God forbids making use of or having any likeness of them, in order to worship them or to use them to serve him.
>
> Question 98. But should we allow pictures instead of books in churches, for the benefit of the unlearned?
>
> Answer: No. For we should not presume to be wiser than God, who does not want Christendom to be taught by means of dumb idols, but through the living preaching of his Word.

While figures like Luther, Melanchthon, and the Heidelberg theologians adhered to this catechetical form, the majority of Reformation systematic theologians diverged and adopted a scholastic model instead. Scholars such as Ulrich (Huldreich or Huldrych) Zwingli (1484–1531), Martin Bucer (1491–1551), and Peter Martyr Vermigli (1499–1562) made initial forays into formulating Reformation theology, laying the groundwork for the systematic theological tradition that would follow.

Among Reformation theologians, John Calvin (1509–64)—deemed the Aristotle and Thomas Aquinas of the Reformed Church[18]—exercised a

[18] See Philip Schaff, *History of the Christian Church,* 8 vols. (1910; reprint, Grand Rapids, MI: Eerdmans, 1962), 7:270–95. On Calvin, see Alasdair Heron, "Calvin, John," in *ECT,* 241–44; and R. S. Wallace, "Calvin, John," in *NDT*^{2}*,* 143–47. See further Bruce Gordon, *Calvin* (New Haven, CT: Yale University, 2009); Alister McGrath, *A Life of John Calvin: A Study in the Shaping of Western Culture* (Cambridge, MA: Blackwell, 1990); and Bernard Cottret, *Calvin: A Biography*, trans. M. Wallace MacDonald (Grand Rapids, MI: Eerdmans, 2000).

profound impact, and continues to do so. Calvin's theological treatises, commentaries, and sermons (some eight hundred in all) occupy fifty-nine quarto volumes.[19] His *Institutio Christianae Religionis* (*Institutes of the Christian Religion*), the final edition being the fruit of some three decades, has exercised the most influence.[20] Working through several revisions from 1536 to 1559, Calvin followed a four–book format based on the Apostles' Creed (while reflecting a Reformation emphasis). The first book deals with the knowledge of God, the second book addresses the knowledge of God the Redeemer in Christ, the third book focuses on the mode of obtaining the grace of Christ, and the fourth book discusses the external means or helps by which God leads us into communion with Christ. Calvin referred to his *Institutes* as his *Summa Pietatis* (*Summary of Piety*), and it is, unquestionably, an admirable example of theology as application. It has been said that "no system exceeds it in comprehensiveness, precision, lucidity, and literary elegance."[21] In the final version of the *Institutes* (1559), Calvin provides a helpful discussion of the nature of faith, the role of the Holy Spirit, and the reality of doubt:

---

[19] For Calvin's writings, see Wulfert DeGreef and Lyle D. Bierma, trans., *The Writings of John Calvin: An Introductory Guide* (Grand Rapids, MI: Baker, 1993); J. K. S. Reid, ed., *Calvin: Theological Treatises,* Library of Christian Classics (Philadelphia, PA: Westminster, 1954); and Joseph Haroutunian, ed., *Calvin: Commentaries,* Library of Christian Classics (Philadelphia, PA: Westminster, 1958).

[20] The English translation generally regarded as the standard is John T. McNeill, ed., *Calvin: Institutes of the Christian Religion*, 2 vol., Library of Christian Classics (Nashville, TN: Westminster John Knox, 1960).

[21] W. G. T. Shedd, *Dogmatic Theology*, 3 vols. (Grand Rapids, MI: Zondervan, n.d.), 1:5.

> Now we shall have a right definition of faith if we say that it is a steady and certain knowledge of the divine benevolence towards us [*divinae erga nos benevolentiae firmam certamque cognitionem*], which is founded upon the truth of the gracious promise of God in Christ, and is both revealed to our minds and sealed in our hearts [*revelatur mentibus nostris et cordibus obsignatur*] by the Holy Spirit. […] When we stress that faith ought to be certain and secure, we do not have in mind a certainty without doubt, or a security without any anxiety. Rather, we affirm that believers have a perpetual struggle with their own lack of faith, and are far from possessing a peaceful conscience, never interrupted by any disturbance. On the other hand, we want to deny that they may fall out of, or depart from, their confidence [*fiducia*] in the divine mercy, no matter how much they may be troubled.[22]

In another place, Calvin discusses the nature of predestination, setting forth the doctrine of double predestination, the belief that God not only selects individuals for eternal life but also chooses (or, at the very least, passes over—called preterition, from Lat. *praeter*, "beyond, past," and *praeteritus,* "that which is passed over") the remainder for eternal condemnation (cf. Rom. 9:18–22):

> The covenant of life is not preached equally to all people, and amongst those to whom it is preached, it does not meet with the same acceptance either constantly or in equal degree. In this diversity the unsearchable depths of God's judgment are made

[22] John Calvin, *Institutes of the Christian Religion*, III.ii,7.

known. For there is no doubt that this variety is subordinate to the will of God's eternal election. If it is clear that salvation is freely offered to some while others are barred from access to it, on account of God's pleasure, this raises some major and difficult questions. They can be explained only when election and predestination are rightly understood. Many find this a puzzling subject, in that it seems to be nothing less than capricious, that out of the human community some should be predestined to salvation, others to destruction. But it will become clear in the following discussion that such confusion is needless. In any case, the complexity of this matter makes known both the usefulness of this doctrine and also the very sweet fruit which it brings. We shall never be clearly persuaded, as we ought to be, that our salvation flows from God's free mercy until we come to know his eternal election, which casts light on God's grace by this comparison: he does not indiscriminately adopt all to the hope of salvation but gives to some what he denies to others. [...]

Predestination, by which God adopts some to the hope of life, and sentences others to eternal death, is denied by no one who wishes to be thought of as pious. But there are many, especially those who make foreknowledge its cause, who surround it with all kinds of petty objections. Both doctrines are indeed to be located within God, but subjecting one to the other is absurd. In attributing foreknowledge to God, we mean that all things always have been, and always will be, under God's eyes, so that there is nothing future or past to this knowledge, but all things are present—present in such a way that God not only conceives them

> through ideas, as we have before us those things which our minds remember, but God truly looks upon them and discerns them as things placed before God. And this foreknowledge is extended throughout the universe to every creature. We call predestination God's eternal decree, by which God determined what God willed to become of each human being. For all are not created in equal condition [*non enim pari conditione creantur omnes*]; but eternal life is foreordained for some, and eternal damnation for others. Therefore, as any person has been directed [*conditus*] to one or the other of these ends, we speak of him or her as predestined to life or to death.[23]

The successors to the early Reformers began to focus less on biblical interpretation and reformation, and more on preserving and expositing an established faith. With regard to content, Calvin's successor, Theodore Beza (1519–1605)—"the acknowledged champion of Genevan orthodoxy and chief spokesman for Reformed Protestantism"[24]—helped make predestination foundational for some post–Reformation Protestant systems. Among Beza's writings are the three-volume *Tractationes Theologicae* (*Theological Tractates*, 1570–82). In a letter to Calvin written in 1555, Beza forcefully defends the view that the cause of predestination—clearly distinguished from foreknowledge—lies in God's sovereignty:

> So if someone asks concerning the cause by which God should have decided from all eternity to elect some and to condemn

[23] Ibid., III.xxi.1, 5.

[24] I. McPhee, "Beza, Theodore," in *NDT*^{2}, 82.

others, I think that we must reply by saying that this is in order that God's immense power may be made known better. But if they then ask about the "material cause" (as they call it) of this eternal decree, then I have nothing to point to other than the will of God, who has just as much freedom [over the creation] as the potter, by which he can produce one vessel for honor, and the other for disgrace. If someone should ask why God should have predestined some people instead of others to salvation or destruction, I again point to the will of God, in whose power it lies not merely to produce some vessels for honor and others to disgrace from the same mass of clay, but also to express his own unique judgment in that distinction. So, in responding to these questions, I would not appeal to "secondary causes," among which number are included Christ and Adam, but rather to what follows on from this. The question does not concern the degree of election or reprobation, but their execution. There are ordained secondary causes for the execution of the divine counsel. A reason can be brought forward as to why and how we are elect—namely, that God, on account of his enormous love and as he sees us in Christ (to whom he determined to give us before all ages), was not able not to love us [*non potuit nos non amare*], so that we might be righteous and holy in him. But if it is asked what caused God to condemn some, I shall reply that the cause is to be located in the people themselves, in that they persist in corruption and sin, which merit the righteous hatred of God. Such people are thus rightly rejected and renounced by God. [...] So when we are said to be "elect in Christ before the creation of the world" (Ephesians 1:4), I understand this [...] to mean: God, when

> predestining us to election from all eternity, at the same time subordinated Christ to this decree [*simul huic decreto substravisse Christum*], in whom God might elect us, and call, justify and glorify the elect. On the other hand, when God predestined some to destruction, God at the same time appointed Adam, in whom those who had been corrupted might be hardened, so that God might declare his supreme power in them.[25]

With regard to form, with the rise of such Thomist theologians as Jerome Zanchi (1516–90), the style of systematic theology became scholastic. A comparison of Zanchi's eight-volume *Opera Theologica* (*Works of Theology,* 1803) with Aquinas' *Summa Theologiae* (*Summary of Theology*) demonstrates both a structural and philosophical correspondence. This trend with regard to logical structure and philosophical content would continue, and is still evident today.

Though the Fifth Lateran Council (1512–17), which had as one of its goals reform "of the head and of the parts," had expressed a desire for reform, it was the Protestant Reformation that finally forced Rome to reexamine and define its own doctrinal stance, and to address the theological and disciplinary issues raised by the Reformers. The Council of Trent (1545–63), called into session by Pope Paul III (1534–49), was a massive undertaking. According to F. Stuart Piggin, "So voluminous was the agenda that the council took eighteen years, spanning the reigns of five popes, to complete. Its sittings alone took over four years, and it produced a greater volume of legislation than the combined output of all

---

[25] Theodore Beza, Letter to John Calvin, July 29, 1555; in *Correspondance de Théodore de Bèze*, ed. H. Aubert (Geneva: Droz, 1960), 1:171.

the previous eighteen general councils recognized by the Catholic Church."[26] During the twenty-five sessions spanning three periods of the Council of Trent,[27] various topics were discussed and decrees were issued on matters such as the authority of Scripture (including the Apocrypha) and tradition (as coequal authorities), the authority of the Pope and the Magisterium (with the Roman Catholic Church being the authoritative determiner of the canon and interpreter of Scripture), original sin, the doctrine of justification by faith and subsequent works, the validity of the seven sacraments through which saving grace is mediated, and the veneration of saints and relics. Further, at the Council of Trent the dogma of transubstantiation and the practice of indulgences (though seeking to clarify their proper use and condemning abuses) were commended to the faithful.[28] In the decree *Cum hoc tempore* (sixteen chapters, comprising thirty-three canons) adopted during Trent's sixth session in 1547, Rome defined justification as both an event and a process, drawing on Augustine:

---

[26] F. S. Piggin, "Trent, Council of," *EDT*³, 895.

[27] As Piggin notes ("Trent, Council of," 895), "The council's history has three periods:

> 1. Sessions 1–10 (December 13, 1545, to June 2, 1547), during the pontificate of Paul III.
> 2. Sessions 11–16 (May 1, 1551, to April 28, 1552), under Julius III.
> 3. Sessions 17–25 (January 17, 1562, to December 4, 1563), under Pius IV."

To clarify: though the chronology of the Council spanned the reign of five popes over a period of two decades, the distinct sessions occurred during the reigns of three specific popes, as noted above.

[28] See J. H. Schroeder, ed. and trans., *The Canons and Decrees of the Council of Trent: English Translation* (Rockford, IL: TAN, 1978).

> The justification of the sinner may be briefly defined as a translation from that state in which a human being is born a child of the first Adam [*translatio ab eo statu in quo homo nascitur filius primi Adae*], to the state of grace and of the adoption of the sons of God through the second Adam, Jesus Christ our Savior [*in statum gratiae et adoptionis filiorum Dei per secundum Adam Iesum Christum Salvatore, nostrum*]. According to the gospel, this translation cannot come about except through the cleansing of regeneration, or a desire for this, as it is written, "No one can enter the kingdom of God without being born again of water and the Holy Spirit" (John 3:5).[29]

Later, during its thirteenth session (1551) in a decree comprising eleven canons, Rome definitively set forth its view of transubstantiation, the view that in the Eucharist (from the Gk. verb *eucharistēō*, "to give thanks," referring to the prayer of thanksgiving offered for the body and blood of Christ; see 1 Cor. 11:23-26) the bread and wine to be administered become, upon consecration by the priest, the actual body and blood of Jesus Christ, even though the external manifestations of the bread and wine—shape, color, flavor, and odor—remain:

> To begin with, the sacred Council teaches and confesses, openly and clearly, that in the noble sacrament of the holy Eucharist, after the consecration of the bread and wine, our Lord Jesus Christ, true God and human being, is truly, really, and substantially contained under the species of those sensible things.

---

[29] Council of Trent, Session VI, chapter 4; in *Enchiridion Symbolorum*, ed. H. Denzinger, 39th ed. (Freiburg im Breisgau: Herder, 2001), §1524.

For neither are these things mutually opposed to one another: that our Savior himself always sits at the right hand of the Father in heaven, according to the natural mode of existing; and that, nevertheless, he is, in many other places, sacramentally present to us in his own substance, by a manner of existing, which, though we cannot express it fully in words, yet we can, by understanding illuminated by faith, conceive that this is possible for God (as we ought most firmly to believe).

For thus all our forebears, as many as were in the true Church of Christ, who have treated of this most holy sacrament, have most openly professed, that our Redeemer instituted this truly admirable sacrament at the last supper; when, after the blessing of the bread and wine, he testified, in unambiguous and clear words, that he gave them his own true body and blood. These words were recorded by the holy Evangelists, and afterwards repeated by Saint Paul. For this reason, they carry with them that proper and most obvious meaning in which they were understood by the Fathers. It is totally unworthy that they should be distorted, by certain contentious and wicked people, into fictitious and imaginary figures of speech, whereby the reality of the flesh and blood of Christ is denied, contrary to the universal sense of the Church. [...] Because Christ our Redeemer declared that it was truly his body that he was offering under the species of bread, it has always been the belief of the Church of God, which this sacred council reaffirms, that by the consecration of the bread and wine a change takes place in which the entire substance of the bread becomes the substance of the body of Christ our Lord, and

> the whole substance of the wine becomes the substance of his blood. This change the holy Catholic Church has fittingly and correctly called "transubstantiation" [*quae conversio convenienter et proprie a sancta catholica Ecclesia transubstantiatio est appellata*].[30]

During this time, Lutheran orthodoxy would achieve its definitive form in the Formula of Concord (1577–80),[31] an authoritative, confessional

---

[30] Council of Trent, Session XIII, chapters 1, 4; in *Enchiridion Symbolorum*, ed. H. Denzinger, 39th ed. (Freiburg im Breisgau: Herder, 2001), §§1636–7, 1642.The major views of the Lord's Supper are: (1) *Transubstantiation*: the Roman Catholic understanding of the Eucharist, which holds that the bread and wine are changed in their substance (not appearance) into the literal body and blood of Christ; the Mass is thus a re-sacrifice of Christ. (2) *Consubstantiation*: the term popularly used to describe the Lutheran understanding of the nature of the Lord's Supper. Lutheranism holds that the elements are not transformed into the body and blood of Christ (as in transubstantiation), but that the body and blood of the risen Christ are "in, with, and under" the bread and wine in a special way. The Lutheran view necessitates holding to the ubiquity of Christ's human nature. (3) *Mystery Presence*: the Orthodox understanding of the Eucharist, which sees a real presence of Christ in the rite but refuses to speculate as to the nature of that presence, simply asserting it as beyond explanation and hence "mystery." (4) *Spiritual Presence*: The view of the Lord's Supper taught by Calvin that sees an actual spiritual feeding upon Christ at the Eucharist. (5) *Memorial View*: The understanding of the Lord's Supper propounded by Swiss Protestant theologian and leader of the Reformation in Switzerland, Huldreich Ulrich (or Huldreich) Zwingli (1484—1531), and characteristic of most American evangelicalism (particularly many free churches, e.g., Baptist and Bible churches). In contrast to the previous four views, which all affirm some sort of real presence, this view affirms that the Lord's Supper is simply to be understood as a memorial, a reminder of what Christ accomplished on the cross. There is no grace conveyed by the ordinance, nor is there a special spiritual presence of the risen Christ.

[31] See E. Lund, "Formula of Concord, in *NDT*[2], 345–46.

document that makes up the final section of the Lutheran *Corpus Doctrinae* (or *Body of Doctrine*), known as the Book of Concord (1580).[32] Written by a group of theologians, primarily the important and oft-overlooked German theologian Martin Chemnitz (1522–86) and the influential and significant Jakob Andreae (1528–90), to settle controversies within and without the Lutheran faith following the death of Martin Luther, the Formula of Concord has two parts: the Epitome and the Solid Declaration. The Epitome is a brief summary of the main points of the Formula of Concord, while the Solid Declaration is a more detailed explanation of these points. This expression of Lutheran orthodoxy would, in turn, be defended by such noted Lutheran Scholastics as Johannes Gerhard of Jena (1582–1637) in his massive twenty-three volume *Loci Communes Theologici* (*Theological Commonplaces,* 1610–22). Gerhard's work, in typical scholastic fashion, emphasized Aristotelian categories and terminology, and his *Loci* became the classic of Lutheran theology. Dogmatic texts with a decided scholastic bent were also produced by Johannes Andreas Quenstedt (1617–88) in his *Theologia Didactico–polemica Sive Systema Theologicum* (1685), Abraham Calovius (1612–86) and his twelve-volume *System of Theological Themes* (1655–77), David Hollaz (1648–1713) and his

[32] On which, see Friedrich Bente, *Historical Introductions to the Book of Concord* (1921; reprint, St Louis, MO: Concordia, 1965); Eugene F. Klug and Otto F. Stahlke, *Getting into the Formula of Concord* (St Louis, MO: Concordia, 1977). The Book of Concord includes the three ecumenical creeds (the Apostles' Creed, the Nicene Creed, and the Athanasian Creed); the Augsburg Confession and its *Apology*; Luther's *Smalcald Articles* and Melanchthon's *Treatise on the Power and Primacy of the Pope*; and Luther's *Large* and *Small Catechisms*.

Examen Theologicum Acroamaticum (1707), and Johann Wilhelm Baier (1647–95) in his *Compendium theologiae moralis* (1697).

Perhaps not surprisingly, the seventeenth century was an era of controversy for Reformed theology. The theologian and professor, Jacob Arminius (Dutch name Jakob Hermandszoon) of Leyden (1560–1609), challenged the extreme form of supralapsarianism championed by French Reformed theologian and pastor, Theodore Beza (1519–1605), leading to the development of Arminianism and the Remonstrant movement. He authored numerous writings, including *Declaration of Sentiments* (1608), *Examination of Perkins' Pamphlet*, *Public Disputations*, and (posthumously) *Seventy-Nine Private Disputations*. Arminius's followers published the *Five Articles of the Remonstrants* (1610) that, *inter alia,* limited the salvific decree to those whom God foresaw would trust Christ. After conferences held at The Hague (1611) and at Delft (1613) failed to settle the disagreement, the Synod of Dordrecht (or Dort, 1618–19) was called to settle the dispute, and decided in favor of the majority Reformed party, condemning Arminianism and issuing the Canons of Dort, also known as the 'Five Articles against the Remonstrants.' In direct response to the Remonstrants' five articles, the Canons of Dort discuss, under five headings, (1) divine predestination, (2) the death of Christ, (3) and (4) the extent to which all of humanity, after Adam's fall, is wholly affected by sin, and (5) the perseverance of the saints.[33]

Meanwhile, mainstream Calvinist orthodoxy found expression in a number of outstanding works, including William Ames' (1576–1633) *The Marrow of Theology* (1623), Johannes Wollebius' (1586–1629)

---

[33] See K. M. Kapic, "Dort, Canons of," in *NDT*^{2}, 267.

classic *Compendium of Christian Theology* (1626), Gisbert Voetius of Holland's (1589–1676) five-volume dogmatics, *Selected Theological Disputations* (1648–69), and Johannes Cocceius' (1602–69) trail-blazing *Summa doctrinae de foedere et testament Dei* (*The Doctrine of the Covenant and Testament of God,* 1648), wherein he ordered theology about the poles of the covenant of works and the covenant of grace. The Genevan-Italian Reformed scholastic theologian François Turrentini (Francis Turretin, 1623–87) produced the four-volume *Institutio Theologiae Elencticae* (*Institutes of Elenctic Theology,* 1679–85), organized in a question–and–answer format, which has exercised tremendous influence on Reformed theology, especially on nineteenth-century American Presbyterianism.[34] Meanwhile in France, Moise Amyraut (1596–1664) of the Saumur Academy published his *Apologia in Defense of the Reformed Religion* (1647) and the six-volume *Christian Ethics* (1652–60). In *A Short Treatise on Predestination and the Principal Arguments in Its Defense* (1634), he propounded the view that would come to be termed hypothetical universalism that stirred up dissent amongst the Reformers over the theme of election. Amyraut, in proposing a more moderate position in opposition to the strict Calvinism of Beza, sought to reconcile the universal scope of the Gospel with the particularism of election, was opposed by both the *Formula Consensus*

[34] Though Turretin's *Institutio Theologiae Elenchticae* was published in 1679–85 and reprinted in 1847, it was untranslated from the original Latin until George Musgrave Giger (1822–65) undertook the work in the mid-nineteenth century. Even then, his translation lay unpublished for over a century, until James T. Dennison (b. 1943) provided extensive editorial work. Only recently with the English publication of *Institutes of Elenctic Theology* has Turretin begun receiving the attention he deserves.

Helvetica (1675) and the *Formula's* principal author, Swiss theologian Johann Heinrich Heidegger (1633–98). Amongst Heidegger's writings are his masterful threefold theological curriculum: *Concise Marrow of Theology* (1696), *Medulla Theologiae Christianae* (*The Core of Christian Theology*, 1700), and the more advanced *Corpus Theologiae Christianae* (*The Body of Christian Theology*, 1700).

The Puritans were a group of English Protestants who emerged in the late sixteenth and seventeenth centuries. They sought to "purify" the Church of England from what they perceived as remnants of Roman Catholicism, advocating for simpler and more biblical forms of worship. Due to religious persecution in England, many Puritans emigrated to North America in the early seventeenth century, where they played a significant role in the founding of colonies, including the Plymouth Colony and the Massachusetts Bay Colony. The Puritans viewed theology practically as the act of living unto God, emphasized strict religious and moral codes, communal living, and a strong work ethic. The Puritans are known primarily for their excellent biblical commentaries and theological treatises on nearly every aspect of the faith. Leading Puritan theologians include Thomas Manton (1620–77) one of the most prolific puritans of the day, whose *Complete Works* (containing all his writings and treatises, along with nearly one thousand sermons) fill twenty-two volumes; John Owen (1616–83), author of *Theologoumena Pantodapa* (1661, published as *Biblical Theology: A History of Theology from Adam to Christ*); Stephen Charnock (1628–80), whose *Discourses Upon the Existence and Attributes of God* (1682) is still widely read; Jonathan Edwards (1703–58), especially his *Treatise Concerning Religious Affections* (1746) and *Freedom of the Will* (1754); and Samuel Hopkins' (1721–1803) *System of Doctrines* (1793). Their influence had a lasting impact on American culture and the development of American Protestantism.[35] One of Owens' most influential writings, *On the Mortification of Sin in Believers*, powerfully stresses that the way of sanctification, of mortifying sin, lies not in one's own strength, but in the power and resources of the indwelling Holy Spirit:

> The Holy Ghost works in us and upon us, as we are fit to be wrought in and upon; that is, so as to preserve our own liberty and free obedience. He works upon our understandings, wills, consciences, and affections, agreeably to their own natures; he works in us and with us, not against us or without us; so that his assistance is an encouragement as to the facilitating of the work, and no occasion of neglect as to the work itself. And, indeed, I might here bewail the endless, foolish labour of poor souls, who, being convinced of sin and not able to stand against the power of their convictions, do set themselves, by innumerable perplexing ways and duties, to keep down sin, but, being strangers to the Spirit of God, all in vain. They combat without victory, have war without peace, and are in slavery all their days. They spend their strength for that which is not bread, and their labour for that which profiteth not. This is the saddest warfare that any poor creature can be engaged in. A soul under the power of conviction from the law is pressed to fight against sin, but hath no strength

[35] See Patrick Collinson, "Puritanism," *ECT*, 1324–25; M. A. Noll, "Puritanism," *ECT*[3], 711–13; I. Breward, "Puritan theology," *NDT*[2], 719–22. An excellent reference work is John Coffey and Paul C. H. Lim, eds., *The Cambridge Companion to Puritanism* (Cambridge: Cambridge University, 2008).

> for the combat. They cannot but fight, and they can never conquer; they are like men thrust on the sword of enemies on purpose to be slain. The law drives them on, and sin beats them back. Sometimes they think, indeed, that they have foiled sin, when they have only raised a dust that they see it not; that is, they distemper their natural affections of fear, sorrow, and anguish, which makes them believe that sin is conquered when it is not touched. By that time they are cold, they must to battle again; and the lust which they thought to be slain appears to have had no wound.[36]

Though beginning in the late sixteenth century, eighteenth-century Europe saw the rise of the pietistic movement as a much-needed reaction to the dry and often sterile intellectualism of Protestant scholasticism. According to Dominique Bourel (b. 1952),

> Pietism emerged in reaction to Protestant orthodoxy; it wanted to recapture the momentum of early Christianity, as well as the initial impetus of the Reformation. It also presented itself as a decisive return to the Bible, for the purposes of meditation and mutual edification, as well as for science and knowledge. Lastly, it wanted to promote individuality and personal faith—or that of a small group of believers—in the face of church hierarchies....[37]

---

[36] John Owen, "On the Mortification of Sin in Believers," in John Owen, *Works*, 23 vols., ed. W. H. Goold (Edinburgh: Johnstone & Hunter, 1850–5), 3:17.

[37] Dominique Bourel, "Pietism," in *ECT,* 1242–43.

Further, as Bourel notes, "Pietism put its faith in the gap between doctrine, as expressed in the public confessional theology of the churches, and private faith."[38] Leading Pietists include the "Father of Pietism," Philip J. Spener (1635–1705), author of *Pia Desideria* (*Pious Desires*, 1675); the French mystic and philosopher, Pierre Poiret (1646–1719), in his *Theology of the Heart* (1690); the German Lutheran clergyman and Halle theologian, August Herman Francke (1663–1727), principally his *Manducatio ad Lectionem Scripturae Sacrae* (*Manual for the Reading of the Sacred Scriptures*, 1693), *Praelectiones Hermeneuticae* (*Lectures on Hermeneutics*, 1717), and *Lectiones Paraeneticae* (*Lessons on Paraenetics,* 1726–36); and the Lutheran clergyman, Greek-language scholar, and celebrated Wittenberg exegete, Johann Albrecht Bengel (1687–1752), whose *Gnomon Novi Testamenti* (*Exegetical Annotations on the New Testament*, 1742) remains one of the finest word-by-word expositions of the Greek Testament.

As the foregoing has shown, the two–and–a–half centuries of church history encompassing the Reformation and post–Reformation period were incredibly fertile, with the following comprising only a small sampling of important theologians and their works:[39]

---

[38] Ibid., 1243.

[39] Primary source translations and anthologies include: Carter Lindberg, *The European Reformations Sourcebook*, 2nd ed. (Oxford: Wiley-Blackwell, 2014); Gerald Bray, ed., *Documents of the English Reformation* (Minneapolis, MN: Fortress, 1994); Scott H. Hendrix, ed. and trans., *Early Protestant Spirituality, Classics of Western Spirituality* (New York: Paulist, 2009); Hans Hillerbrand, ed., *The Reformation: A Narrative Related by Contemporary Observers and Participants* (Grand Rapids, MI: Baker, 1978); Denis R. Janz & Shirley E. Jordan, ed., *A Reformation Reader: Primary Texts with Introductions*

- Ulrich (Huldreich or Huldrych) Zwingli (1484–1531), *Sixty–Seven Theses* (1523); *Commentary on True and False Religion* (1525); *An Exposition of the Faith* (1529)
- Guillaume (William) Farel (1489–1565), *Sommaire* (*Summary*, 1525)
- Philip Melanchthon (1497–1560), *Loci Communes Rerum Theologici* (*Theological Commonplaces*, 1521, revised in 1559, *Loci praecipui theologici*)
- Wolfgang Musculus (Müslen, 1497–1563), *Loci Communes Sacra Theologiae* (*Common Places of Sacred Theology*, 1567)
- Juan de Valdés (*ca.* 1498–1541), *Diálogo de Doctrina Cristiana* (*Dialogue Concerning Christian Doctrine*, 1529)
- Pietro Martire (Peter Martyr) Vermigli (1499–1562), *Loci Communes* (*Common Places*, 1576, 1583)
- John Calvin (1509–64), *Institutio Christianae Religionis* (*Institutes of the Christian Religion*, 1536–59)
- Girolamo (Jerome) Zanchi (1516–90), *Opera Theologica* (*Works of Theology*), 8 vols. (Geneva, 1803)
- Theodore Beza (1519–1605), *Tractationes Theologicae* (*Theological Tractates*). 3 vols. (1570–82)

(Minneapolis, MN: Fortress, 1999); Eric Lund, *Documents from the History of Lutheranism, 1517–1750* (Minneapolis, MN: Fortress, 2002); Robert S. Miola, ed., *Early Modern Catholicism: An Anthology of Primary Sources* (New York: Oxford University, 2007); John Baillie, John T. McNeill, and Henry P. Van Dusen, eds., *Library of Christian Classics* (Philadelphia: Westminster, 1950s).

- Martin Chemnitz (1522–86), *Examen Concilii Tridentini* (*Examination of the Council of Trent*). 4 vols. (1566–73); *Loci Theologici* (*Theological Topics*, 1591)
- David Chytraeus (1530–1600), *De Studio Theologicae* (*On the Study of Theology,* Wittenberg, 1562)
- Zacharias Ursinus (1534–83), *Summa Theologiae* (*Summary of Theology*, 1562)
- Caspar Olevianus (1536–87), *De substantia foederis gratuiti inter Deum et electos* (*Concerning the Nature of the Covenant of Grace between God and the Elect*, 1585)
- William Ames (1576–1633), *Technometria;*[40] (*Technometry*, Amstersdam–Leiden, 1632, 1633); *Medulla Theologiae* (*Marrow of Theology*, Franeker, 1623; Amsterdam, 1627, 1659); *The Marrow of Sacred Divinity* (1642)
- James Ussher (1581–1656), *A Body of Divinity, or, The Sum and Substance of Christian Religion* (1649)
- Johannes (John) Gerhard (1582–1637), *Loci Theologici* (*Theological Commonplaces*), 23 vols. (Jena, 1610–22); *Methodus Studii Theologici* (*Method of Theological Study,* Jena, 1654)
- Hugo Grotius (1583–1645), *De Veritate Religionis* Christianae (*The Truth of the* Christian *Religion*, 1627)
- Johannes Wollebius (1586–1629), *Compendium Theologiae Christianae* (*Compendium of Christian Theology*, 1626)

[40] To be precise, the full Latin title is *Technometria, omnium singularum artium fines addequate circumscribere* (*Technometry, adequately circumscribing the boundaries of all individual arts*).

- Johannes Cocceius (or Johannes Koch, 1603–69), *Summa doctrinae de foedere et testament Dei* (*The Doctrine of the Covenant and Testament of God*, 1648)
- Johann Musaeus (1613–81), *Introductio in Theologicam* (*Introduction to Theology,* Jena, 1679)
- John Owen (1613–83), *Theologoumena Pantodapa* (1661, published as *Biblical Theology: A History of Theology from Adam to Christ*)
- Abraham Calovius (also Calov or Kalov, 1612–86), *Systema Locorum Theologicorum* (*System of Theological Topics*), 12 vols. (Wittenberg, 1655–77)
- Richard Baxter (1615–91), *The Christian Directory* (1673); *Catholik Theologie* (1675); and *Methodus Theologiae Christianae* (*Method of Christian Theology*, 1681)
- Johannes Andreas Quenstedt (1617–88), *Theologia Didactico-polemica sive Systema Theologicae* (*Didactic–Polemic Theology and Systematic Theology*, Wittenberg, 1685)
- Thomas Watson (*ca.* 1620–86), *A Body of Divinity* (1692)
- Francis Turretin (François Turrentini, 1623–87), *Institutio Theologiae Elenchticae* (*Institutes of Elenctic Theology*). 4 vols. (3 parts, Geneva, 1679–85)
- Edward Fisher (fl. 1627–55), *The Marrow of Modern Divinity* (1645)
- Peter van Mastricht (1630–1706), *Theoretica–Practica Theologica* (*Theoretical–Practical Theology,* 1682–87)
- Johann Heinrich Heidegger (1633–98), *Concise Marrow of Theology* (1696), *Medulla Theologiae Christianae* (*Core of*

Christian Theology, 1700), and *Corpus Theologiae Christianae* (*Body of Christian Theology*, 1700)

- John Wiliam Baier (1647–95), *Compendium Theologiae Positivae* (*Compendium of Positive Theology*, 1685)
- Johann Franz Buddeus (or Budde, sometimes Johannes Franciscus Buddeus, 1667–1729), *Institutiones Theologiae Dogmatica* (*Institutes of Dogmatic Theology*, 1724)
- Jakobus Karpov (1699–1768), *Theologia Revelata Dogmatica* (*Theology of Revealed Dogmatics,* 1739)
- Samuel Hopkins (1721–1803), *System of Doctrines* (1793)

CHAPTER FOUR: THE MODERN AND POSTMODERN CHURCH (1750—PRESENT)

THE modern and postmodern church period covers the time from around AD 1750 to the present day, during which time Christianity has continued to evolve and adapt to the changing social, political, and cultural landscape. This era has been a complex interplay of challenges and opportunities. It has witnessed the Enlightenment and the rise of scientific inquiry challenging traditional religious beliefs and leading to the emergence of liberal Christianity. This period also saw significant social and cultural changes, which had a major impact on the Christian Church. The two World Wars, the Civil Rights movement, and the rise of secularism and consumerism all had an impact on the way Christianity was understood and practiced. This period also saw the emergence of new Christian movements, such as Pentecostalism, which became one of the fastest–growing Christian denominations in the world.

1. The Enlightenment and its Impact on Theology

The Enlightenment, an intellectual and cultural movement of the eighteenth century, had a profound influence on theological thought. Enlightenment thinkers, such as Immanuel Kant and Friedrich Schleiermacher, sought to reconcile faith and reason, emphasizing the importance of individual experience and the need for a more rational approach to theology. This led to the emergence of liberal theology and a shift towards a more subjective and experiential understanding of religious belief.

2. The Rise of Biblical Criticism and Historical-Critical Method
During this period, biblical criticism and the historical-critical method gained prominence. Scholars such as Julius Wellhausen and Rudolf Bultmann applied critical analysis to the Bible, seeking to understand its historical context, authorship, and literary development. This approach challenged and undermined traditional views of biblical inerrancy with its emphasis on Scripture as a human product influenced by human and cultural factors.

3. Theological Responses to Modernity and Postmodernity
The advent of modernity and postmodernity posed significant challenges to traditional Christian beliefs and practices. Theological movements such as neoorthodoxy, existentialism, and postliberalism emerged as responses to these cultural shifts. Figures like Karl Barth, Søren Kierkegaard, and Stanley Hauerwas sought to reassert the importance of faith, the transcendence of God, and the role of the church in a rapidly changing world.

4. Ecumenical Movements and Interfaith Dialogues
The modern and postmodern witnessed a growing emphasis on ecumenism and interfaith dialogue. The World Council of Churches, founded in 1948, sought to promote unity among Christian denominations and foster dialogue with other religious traditions. The founding of the World Council was attended by three hundred and fifty-one delegates representing one hundred and forty-seven denominations from forty-four

countries. The Second Vatican Council (1962–65) brought significant changes to the Roman Catholic Church in its attempt to renew and bring up to date (*aggiornamento*) all facets of Catholic faith and life, including a renewed focus on ecumenism and interreligious dialogue.

5. Theological Controversies and Debates

The modern and postmodern church has been marked by numerous theological controversies and debates. Issues such as the nature of biblical authority, the role of women in ministry, the acceptance of LGBTQ+ individuals, and the relationship between science and faith have sparked intense discussions and divisions within the church. These controversies have led to the formation of diverse theological perspectives and the reevaluation (and sometimes rejection) of traditional doctrines.

Summary of the Times

The period from AD 1750 through the present has been a time of immense theological exploration, diversity, and transformation within the church. The Enlightenment, biblical criticism, responses to modernity and postmodernity, ecumenism, theological controversies, and doctrinal formulation have all shaped the theological landscape of the modern and postmodern church. At the same time, there has been a growing emphasis on social justice and the role of the Church in addressing issues such as poverty, inequality, and environmental degradation. These developments reflect the ongoing engagement of the church with the cultural, intellectual, and social changes of the times.

Further, in recent decades, Christianity has faced new challenges in the form of secularization and the rise of non-religious worldviews. However, it continues to be a major global religion, with diverse expressions and traditions. The growth of Christianity in Africa and Asia has shifted the center of gravity of the faith away from its historical strongholds in Europe and North America. The history of systematic theology during this period is a testament to the dynamic nature of Christian thought and the ongoing quest for understanding and relevance in a rapidly evolving world.

The Development of Systematic Theology in the Modern and Postmodern Period

A number of major challenges have arisen in the modern period to confront systematic theology as codified in Protestant orthodoxy. Positively, Pietism (Ger. *Pietismus,* from Lat. *pius*, "holy")—described by Dominique Bourel (b. 1952) as "the most important movement of Protestant religious revival after the Reformation"[1]—developed in the seventeenth and eighteenth centuries in Europe in response to what its adherents saw as the intellectual and moral decline of Lutheranism, and is closely associated with Lutheran pastor Philipp Jakob Spener (1635–1705), particularly in his main work, *Pia Desideria* (*Pious Desires*, 1675).[2] To illustrate, Spener wrote that the "people must have impressed upon them and must accustom themselves to believing that it is by no

---

[1] Dominique Bourel, "Pietism," in *ECT,* 1242 (cf. 1242–45). See the helpful summary by Carl Diemer, "Pietism," in *The Popular Encyclopedia of Church History: The People, Places, and Events That Shaped Christianity*, ed. Ed Hinson and Dan Mitchell (Eugene, OR: Harvest House, 2013), 271–72, with bibliography. See further Roger E. Olson and Christian T. Collins Winn, *Reclaiming Pietism: Retrieving an Evangelical Tradition* (Grand Rapids, MI: Eerdmans, 2015).

[2] Philip Jacob Spener, *Pia desideria,* trans. Theodore G. Tappert (1964; reprint, Eugene, OR: Wipf & Stock, 2002).

means enough to have knowledge of the Christian faith, for Christianity consists rather of practice."[3]

Pietism emphasized a personal, heartfelt experience of faith, highlighting the need for individual spiritual renewal and moral reform, and arose as a heartfelt challenge to a dead orthodoxy and the perceived abstract, rigid structuring of theology. Originating in the seventeenth century among German Lutherans, Pietism would spread and eventually influence a variety of ethnic and denominational backgrounds, and contribute significantly to the founding of evangelicalism in the eighteenth-century. Notably, Pietism's influence inspired the Anglican priest John Wesley (1703–1791) to begin the Methodist movement, and Alexander Mack (1679–1735) to begin the Brethren (or Tunker) movement. In Wesley's sermon on justification (biblically, the act of God whereby He acquits the guilty, on the basis of Christ's substitutionary work, and then imputes Christ's righteousness to them, declaring them to be righteous), Wesley strongly rejected forensic justification (the doctrine that human beings are declared—not made—righteous by God in salvation [Rom. 4:3, 5, 9, 22], thereby viewing God as a judge who acquits a guilty party [Ps. 9:4]), viewing such as a morally untenable legal fiction:

> 4. Least of all does justification imply that God is deceived in those whom he justifies; that he thinks them to be what, in fact, they are not; that he accounts them to be otherwise than they are. It does by no means imply that God judges concerning us contrary to the real nature of things, that he esteems us better than we really are, or believes us righteous when we are unrighteous.

[3] Spener, *Pia Desideria,* § 3.

> Surely no. The judgement of the all-wise God is always according to truth. Neither can it ever consist with his unerring wisdom to think that I am innocent, to judge that I am righteous or holy, because another is so. He can no more, in this manner, confound me with Christ than with David or Abraham. Let any man to whom God hath given understanding weigh this without prejudice and he cannot but perceive that such a notion of justification is neither reconcilable to Reason or Scripture.
>
> 5. The plain scriptural notion of justification is pardon—the forgiveness of sins. It is that act of God the Father whereby, for the sake of the propitiation made by the blood of his Son, he "showeth forth his righteousness (or mercy) by the remission of sins that are past" (Romans 3: 25). This is the easy natural account of it given by St Paul throughout this whole Epistle.[4]

Pietism would play a pivotal role in shaping modern evangelicalism, with its emphasis on personal conversion and the importance of spiritual renewal. Its direct influence continues to be felt well into the twenty-first century.

Negatively, and in direct opposition to Pietism, this period of history witnessed the comprehensive challenge to Christian theology in the form of the optimistic rationalism that sprang from the Enlightenment.[5]

---

[4] John Wesley, Sermon V: "Justification by Faith," in John Wesley, *Sermons on Several Occasions* (London: G. Whitfield, 1746), 1:81–101.

[5] The term "Enlightenment" has been traced to the preface of French scientist and man of letters, Bernard Le Bovier de Fontenelle's (1657–1757) three-volume work, *History of the Renewal of the Royal Academy of Sciences* (1708, 1717, 1722), where it referred to the anticipated progress in the natural sciences, and

Immanuel Kant (1724–1804) formulated a classic definition of "the Enlightenment" (Fr. *siècle des Lumieres*; Ger. *Aufklärung*) as "man's exodus from his self–incurred tutelage... [by learning] to use your own understanding."[6] This so–called age of reason emphasized the role and powers of reason above and against the traditional sources of knowledge and authority, such as revelation (e.g., Scripture) and religion (e.g., church).[7] The Enlightenment, particularly with its antisupernaturalistic philosophies, sparked a challenge to and confrontation with Christianity. Rationalism continues to exercise a profoundly deleterious effect upon both the content and structure of systematic theology.[8]

From the Enlightenment sprang modernity (eighteenth to mid–twentieth centuries), which was marked by five characteristics:

Fontenelle's expectation of seeing "a century that will become more enlightened day by day." Over time, the term came to encompass advancements in the arts, particularly in philosophy.

[6] Immanuel Kant, *Philosophical Writings*, ed. Ernst Behler (1784; reprint, New York: Continuum, 1986), 263.

[7] Reinhold Niebuhr (1892–1971) offers a comprehensive account of the emergence of the rise of unbelief as "Enlightenment" in chapters I–IV of the first volume of his influential work, *The Nature and Destiny of Man*, 2 vols. (New York: Charles Scribner's Sons, 1941, 1964). Harold O. J. Brown (1933–2007) provides a valuable update to this narrative in his book, *Heresies: Heresy and Orthodoxy in the History of the Church* (1984; reprint, Peabody, MA: Hendrickson, 2000), specifically in chapter 19, titled "The Heresy of the Enlightenment." Brown's analysis serves to augment and refine the understanding of the unfolding story.

[8] See further G. R. Habermas, "Rationalism," *EDT*³ 721–23; S. N. Williams, "Rationalism," *NDT*², 730–32; D. Garb, "rationalism," *CDP*², 771–72.

> (1) the search for an unshakable foundation for universal, objective knowledge; (2) unquestioning trust in reason, science, and technology; (3) human autonomy, expressed in the rejection of divine revelation and religious authority; (4) loss of the supernatural, with a turn towards naturalism; and (5) belief in the unstoppable progress of humanity.[9]

The modernist-fundamentalist controversy of the late nineteenth and early twentieth centuries pitted traditionalists against those embracing modern thought. Fundamentalists defended biblical inerrancy and literal interpretation, while modernists sought to adapt Christianity to align with reason and science. Debates over issues like biblical authority and evolution fueled tensions. Out of this came *The Fundamentals*, a twelve-volume collection of ninety essays that sought to defend traditional doctrines, published between 1910 and 1915.[10] The controversy had a lasting impact on American Christianity, shaping theological perspectives and leading to the formation of new Bible colleges and new denominations.

Previously, Friedrich D. E. Schleiermacher (1768–1834)—"a German Protestant theologian commonly thought to be the founding father of liberal Protestantism"[11] and sometimes acclaimed the greatest theologian between Calvin and Barth—had attempted to reconcile Christianity with

---

[9] *BCDTT*, s.v. "modernism/modernity," 138. See further S. R. Holmes, "Modernity," *NDT*², 585–86.

[10] R. A. Torrey, ed., *The Fundamentals: A Testimony to the Truth* (reprint; Grand Rapids, MI: Baker, 1917).

[11] John B. Webster, "Schleiermacher, Friedrich Daniel Ernst," in *NDT*², 811.

modernity, particularly in his *On Religion: Speeches to Its Cultured Despisers* (1799, trans. 1893). According to Schleiermacher, "Christian doctrines are accounts of the Christian religious affections set forth in speech," and "Dogmatic Theology is the science which systematizes the doctrine prevalent in a Christian Church at a given time."[12] At the end of his *The Christian Faith* Schleiermacher sets forth his doctrine of the Trinity, which he intended to serve as a "coping-stone" (Ger. *als den Schlußstein*) to his work (and, indeed, to Christian theology as a whole):

> An essential element of our exposition […] has been the doctrine of the union of the Divine Essence with human nature, both in the personality of Christ and in the common Spirit of the Church; therewith the whole view of Christianity set forth in our Church teaching stands and falls. For unless the being of God in Christ is assumed, the idea of redemption could not be thus concentrated in His Person. And unless there were such a union also in the common Spirit of the Church, the Church could not thus be the Bearer and Perpetuator of the redemption through Christ. Now these exactly are the essential elements in the doctrine of the Trinity, which, it is clear, only established itself in defence of the position that in Christ there was present nothing less than the Divine Essence, which also indwells the Christian Church as its common Spirit, and that we take these expressions in no reduced or sheerly artificial sense, and know nothing of any special higher essences, subordinate deities (as it were) present in Christ and the

[12] Friedrich D. E. Schleiermacher, *The Christian Faith*, ed. and trans. H. R. McIntosh and J. S. Steward (Edinburgh: T&T Clark, 1928), §§ 15, 19.

Holy Spirit. The doctrine of the Trinity has no origin but this; and at first it had no other aim than to equate as definitely as possible the Divine Essence considered as thus united to human nature with the Divine Essence in itself. This is the less doubtful that those Christian sects which interpret the doctrine of redemption differently are also necessarily without the doctrine of the Trinity—they have no point of belief to which it could be attached—which could not possibly be the case if even in Catholic doctrine there existed at least some other points than this to which the attachment could be made. It is equally clear from this why those divergent sects which are chiefly distinguishable by their denial of the Trinity are not thereby forced into still other divergences in the doctrine of God and the divine attributes, as must have been the case if the doctrine of the Trinity were rooted in a special view of the nature of the Supreme Being as such. But on the other hand, they are forced to set up a different theory of the person of Christ, and hence also of the human need for redemption and of the value of redemption. In virtue of this connexion, we rightly regard the doctrine of the Trinity, in so far as it is a deposit of these elements, as the coping-stone of Christian doctrine [*als den Schlußstein der christlichen Lehre*], and this equating with each other of the divine in each of these two unions, as also of both with the Divine Essence in itself, as what is essential in the doctrine of the Trinity.[13]

[13] Friedrich Schleiermacher, *The Christian Faith*, trans. M. R. Mackintosh and J. S. Stewart (Edinburgh: T&T Clark, 1928), 738–39.

The adjective "liberal" was first applied to the heirs of Schleiermacher—most notably Albrecht Ritschl (1822–89) and Adolf von Harnack (1851–1930)—who sought to rearticulate the Christian faith in a way which appealed to the modern age. Under the influence of Schleiermacher and as a leader in the so-called New Theology,[14] the Baptist minister and theologian William Newton Clarke (1841–1912) wrote *An Outline of Theology* (1898), America's first systematic theology from a liberal perspective. Ritschl, the German antimetaphysical theologian heavily influenced by Kant's *Critique of Practical Reason* (1781), would, in his three-volume *The Christian Doctrine of Justification and Reconciliation* (1870–74), reject as "fact" the traditional doctrines of Christ's incarnation and resurrection, original sin, and forensic justification. His theory of "moral value" focused on the gradual realization of the kingdom of God via actualization of the ethic of Jesus. Ritschl would profoundly influence

[14] Not to be confused with the 20th-century Roman Catholic theological renew movement known as *Nouvelle Théologie* (French, lit., "new theology," also called ressourcement theology). *New Theology*—also termed *Evangelical Liberalism* or *Progressive Orthodoxy*—was part of the larger late nineteenth and early twentieth-century Protestant liberalism/modernism movements (*ca.* 1870s–1930s) that sought to preserve the Christian faith by adjusting traditional Christianity to developments in modern culture. New Theology thinkers attempted a synthesis between the old faith and the new scientific thought, hoping to preserve the main lines of Christian orthodoxy in an expression deemed more suitable (and palatable) for modern times. The movement's most popular representatives were the preachers Henry Ward Beecher (1813–87), Phillips Brooks (1835–93), Lyman Abbott (1835–1922) and Harry Emerson Fosdick (1878–1969). Its theologians—whose work generally escaped public awareness—included George Harris (1844–1922), William Newton Clarke (1841–1912), Theodore Munger (1813–1910), William Adams Brown (1865–1943), A. C. Knudson (1873–1953) and Eugene W. Lyman (1872–1948). Evangelical liberalism's more thoughtful social critics were Washington Gladden (1836–1918) and Walter Rauschenbusch (1861–1918).

the social gospel in America, itself rooted in such works as *Themes for the Protestant Clergy* (1851) by the theologian, industrialist, and philanthropist Stephen Colwell (1800–71). Among Ritschl's disciples are counted the Lutheran German theologian Johann G. W. Herrmann (1846–1922), who outlined his moralistic theology in *The Communion of the Christian With God* (1886) and a posthumous *Systematic Theology* (1925), and the German church historian Harnack, in his seven-volume *History of Dogma* (1894–99) and in his popular series of lectures *What Is Christianity?* (1901). Baptist clergyman Walter Rauschenbusch (1861–1918), the author of *A Theology for the Social Gospel* (1917), was an influential Ritschlian theologian in America, who argued that the gospel was not a message of personal salvation but rather the ethic of Jesus' love that would transform society through resolving social evils.

The effects of theological liberalism were significant and far-reaching. Positively, the movement emphasized the importance of social justice and reform, and theological liberals were often at the forefront of movements for civil rights, women's suffrage, and other social causes. Negatively, however, theological liberalism also led to significant divisions within the church, with traditionalists rejecting the liberal reinterpretation of doctrine and calling for a return to more orthodox teachings. Among the many destructive effects of theological liberalism are the obfuscation and perverting of the gospel, loss of doctrinal clarity, and an overemphasis on ethics and social justice.[15] The rise of theological liberalism also contributed to the decline of mainline Protestant denominations in the

[15] The best critical analysis of liberalism remains J. Gresham Machen's classic, *Christianity and Liberalism*, new ed. (1923; reprint, Grand Rapids, MI: Eerdmans, 2009).

twentieth century, as many Christians left these churches in search of more conservative or evangelical congregations.[16] Liberalism has in turn spawned a complex and seemingly endless variety of theologies catering to various publics, ranging from existentialism to liberation theology.[17]

From the modern period, the twentieth century theological scene was dominated by the "Three Bs"—Barth, Brunner, and Bultmann. Perhaps no work is more significant than *Church Dogmatics* (Ger. *Die Kirchliche Dogmatik*), the four–volume theological summa and magnum opus of Swiss Protestant theologian Karl Barth (1886–1968).[18] Barth's theology

---

[16] Fundamentalism is a religious movement that emerged in the United States in the early twentieth century as a response to the perceived threat of theological liberalism and the cultural changes that accompanied modernity. The movement took its name from a series of essays called "The Fundamentals" that were published in the early 1900s. These essays, written by conservative Protestant theologians, emphasized the importance of biblical inerrancy, the divinity of Christ, and other traditional Christian doctrines. The authors of the essays sought to defend orthodox Christianity against the perceived threat of theological liberalism, which they believed was undermining the faith.

[17] For helpful surveys, see Karl Barth, *Protestant Theology in the Nineteenth Century: Its Background and History*, trans. Brian Cozens and John Bowden (Grand Rapids, MI: Eerdmans, 2002); Hendrikus Berkhof, *Two Hundred Years of Theology: Report of a Personal Journey* (Grand Rapids, MI: Eerdmans, 1989); David Ford, ed., *The Modern Theologians: An Introduction to Christian Theology in the Twentieth Century*, 2nd ed. (Oxford: Blackwell, 1997); Kelly M. Kapic and Bruce L. McCormack, eds., *Mapping Modern Theology: A Thematic and Historical Introduction* (Grand Rapids, MI: Baker Academic, 2012); Helmut Thielicke, *Modern Faith and Thought* (Grand Rapids, MI: Eerdmans, 1990); Claude Welch, *Protestant Thought in the Nineteenth Century*, 2 vols. (1972; reprint, New Haven, CT: Yale University, 1985).

[18] Ironically, though trained in Swiss and German universities in the classic (Ritschlian) liberalism of the day, and for a time being a modified advocate of such liberalism, the events related to the German War effort (1914–18) and his own study of Scripture, especially the book of Romans, led to his rejection of

of revelation, also known as dialectic theology, had a significant impact on the field of systematic theology.[19] Though he wrote over five hundred books, articles, and papers, Barth is best–known for his *Church Dogmatics*. Widely regarded as one of the most important theological works of the century, it represents the pinnacle of Barth's achievement as a theologian. Barth published the *Church Dogmatics* I/1 (the first part-volume of the *Dogmatics,* hereafter abbreviated CD) in 1932 and continued working on it until his death in 1968, by which time it was 6 million words long in twelve part–volumes (or some 10,000 densely packed pages). By way of comparison, Barth's *Church Dogmatics* is larger than Thomas's *Summa Theologica* and nine times the size of Calvin's *Institutes*. The *Church Dogmatics* is divided into five volumes: the "Doctrine of the Word of God" (CD I), the "Doctrine of God" (CD II), the "Doctrine of Creation" (CD III), the unfinished "Doctrine of

---

liberal theology. The position Barth came to espouse is termed neoorthodoxy. C. A. Baxter comments:

> This title is applied to a twentieth-century development in theology, which is 'orthodox' inasmuch as it emphasizes key themes of Reformed theology, but 'neo-', i.e. 'new', inasmuch as it has taken serious account of contemporary cultural and theological developments. It originated with continental theologians: Barth, Brunner, Bultmann and Friedrich Gogarten, but others have become associated with it such as Aulén, Nygren, Tillich, C. H. Dodd, Richardson, J. Baillie, D. M. Baillie, Reinhold Niebuhr and H. Richard Niebuhr. It was in no sense an organized movement, and precise definitions or boundaries are impossible.

Baxter, "Neo-orthodoxy," in *NDT*², 608. For critical evaluation, see especially Charles C. Ryrie, *Neoorthodoxy: What It Is and What It Does* (Chicago, IL: Moody, 1956).

[19] See further Geoffrey W. Bromiley, *Introduction to the Theology of Karl Barth* (Grand Rapids, MI: Eerdmans, 1979).

Reconciliation" (CD IV) and the unwritten "Doctrine of Redemption" (CD V). The material published as the *Church Dogmatics* was originally delivered in lecture format to students at Bonn (1932) and then Basel (1935–1962), with his final incomplete volume (IV.4) produced in 1967 outside the realm of academia. According to Barth, "As a theological discipline dogmatics [i.e., systematic theology] is the scientific self–examination of the Christian Church with respect to the context of its distinctive talk about God."[20] Elsewhere, Barth wrote: "Theology is science seeking the knowledge of the Word of God spoken in God's work—science learning in the school of the Holy Scripture, which witnesses to the Word of God; science laboring in the quest for truth, which is inescapably required of the community that is called by the Word of God."[21] And in an important lecture given to the Free Protestant Theological Faculty at Paris, Barth issued a powerful protest against any temptation to professionalize theology:

> Of all the sciences which stir the head and heart, theology is the fairest. It is closest to human reality, and gives us the clearest view of the truth after which all science quests. It best illustrates the time-honored and profound word: "Fakultät". It is a landscape, like the landscape of Umbria or Tuscany, in which distant perspectives are always clear. Theology is a masterpiece, as well-planned and yet as bizarre as the cathedrals of Cologne and Milan. What a miserable lot of theologians—and what

[20] Karl Barth, *Church Dogmatics,* 12 vols., trans. G. T. Thompson (Edinburgh: T&T Clark, 1936), 1.1:4.

[21] Karl Barth, *Evangelical Theology*: *An Introduction* (Grand Rapids, MI: Eerdmans, 1963), 49–50.

miserable periods there have been in the history of theology—when they have not realized this! [...] The task which is laid upon theology, and which it should and can fulfil, is its service in the Church, to the Lord of the Church. It has its definite function in the Church's liturgy, that is, in the various phases of the Church's expression; in every reverend proclamation of the gospel, or in every proclaiming reverence, in which the Church listens and attends to God. Theology does not exist in a vacuum, nor in any arbitrarily selected field, but in that province between baptism and confirmation, in the realm between the Scriptures and their exposition and proclamation. Theology is, like all other functions of the Church, uniquely based upon the fact that God has spoken to humanity and that humanity may hear his Word through grace. Theology is an act of repentant humility, which is presented to humanity through this fact. This act exists in the fact that in theology the Church seeks again and again to examine itself critically as it asks itself what it means and implies to be a Church among humanity. [...]

The task of theology consists in again and again reminding the people in the Church, both preachers and congregations, that the life and work of the Church are under the authority of the gospel and the law, that God should be heard. [...] It has to be a watchman so as to carefully observe that constant threatening and invasive error to which the life of the Church is in danger, because it is composed of fallible, erring, sinful people. [...] Theology is not a private subject for theologians only. Nor is it a private subject for professors. Fortunately, there have always

> been pastors who have understood more about theology than most professors. Nor is theology a private subject of study for pastors. Fortunately, there have repeatedly been congregation members, and often whole congregations, who have pursued theology energetically while their pastors were theological infants or barbarians. Theology is a matter for the Church.[22]

Somewhat to the left of Barth on the theological spectrum was his colleague H. Emil Brunner (1889–1966), a Swiss Reformed dialectical theologian and prominent figure in the neoorthodox movement. Author of at least three hundred and ninety-six books and scholarly journal articles (of which at least twenty-three books have been translated into English), including the three-volume *Dogmatics* (1946–60), Brunner sought to bridge the gap between liberal theology and traditional orthodoxy, looking for a path between Barth and Rudolf Karl Bultmann (1884–1976). While abandoning liberalism, Brunner nevertheless also fell short of orthodoxy. In one interesting example of his thought drawn from his *Truth as Encounter*, and clearly writing under the influence of Jewish thinker Martin Buber's (1878–1965) "personalist" philosophy as expressed in his best-known work, *I and Thou* (*Ich und Du*, 1927), Brunner stresses the personal nature of God's revelation:

> The self-revelation of God is no object, but wholly the doing and self-giving of a subject—or, better expressed, a Person. A Person who is revealing himself, a Person who demands and offers Lordship and fellowship with himself, is the most radical

[22] Karl Barth, "Theology," in *God in Action*, trans. E. G. Homrighausen and Karl J. Ernst (Edinburgh: T&T Clark, 1936), 39–57.

antithesis to everything that could be called object or objective. Likewise, the personal act of trust is something quite other than subjectivity—that subjectivity which can become actual only when it is over against an object, that subjectivity which appropriates what is foreign to it. If we were to speak of appropriation in this context, it could be only of such a kind as when man gives himself to God to be owned by him. But if we know as believers, we recognize what is meant here, that that which happens in revelation and faith cannot be pushed into the framework of truth and knowledge of truth without its becoming in that way something quite different. Yet in the Bible what we have been talking about is just what is called truth. [...] This Biblical "truth" is as different from what otherwise is called truth as this personal encounter and the double-sided self-giving and its resulting fellowship are different from the comprehension of facts by means of reasoning. This is not to say that there do not also exist between both this Biblical and the general rational conception of truth positive relations outside of these differences. [...] The concern of the Bible is personal correspondence as it is realized in the correlation between the Word of God and faith; and, contrariwise, such an understanding of the concept of the Word of God and faith as is yielded by reflection about the fundamental Biblical category of personal correspondence.

> Through it the Biblical conception of truth is determined and differentiated from every other understanding of truth.[23]

Notable as well is German Jesuit theologian and philosopher, Karl Rahner (1904–84).[24] A professor at Innsbruck and Münster, Rahner played a significant role in the development of Catholic theology in the twentieth century. His works include *Foundations of Christian Faith* (1976) and the massive fourteen-volume *Theological Investigations* (1974–76). Rahner, ranked by some on a par with Barth, propounds a system of transcendental Thomism, which is a reinterpretation of Aquinas guided by insights from Immanuel Kant, Martin Heidegger, and the Belgian Jesuit Joseph Maréchal (d. 1944). Central to Rahner's theology is the "supernatural existential," the dynamic impulse that drives the person toward the immediate presence of God. Since all people—including adherents of other religions and even atheists—are subconsciously oriented toward the Absolute, the entire world is an "anonymous Christianity."[25] As Rahner puts it, "anyone who has let himself be taken hold of by this grace [of the Father in his Son] can be called with every right an 'anonymous Christian.'"[26]

---

[23] Emil Brunner, *Truth as Encounter*, 2nd ed., trans. Amandus Loos and David Cairns (London: SCM, 1964), 109.

[24] See the summary by W. Corduan, "Rahner, Karl," in *EDT*³, 717–18.

[25] Karl Rahner, *Theological Investigations*, 21 vols. (New York, Seabury, 1947–88), 5:115–34.

[26] Ibid., *Theological Reflections*, 6:395.

As the modern and postmodern period has witnessed an explosion of texts, at this juncture it will be helpful to identify several more or less conservative systematic theologies of the last hundred years or so.

Representing Presbyterian theologians in America, Charles Hodge (1797–1878) was a leading figure in nineteenth-century Reformed theology. He served as a professor at Princeton Theological Seminary for five decades, and his three-volume *Systematic Theology* (1871–73) defended the Calvinism of the old Princeton school and is a standard text in Reformed circles. A. A. Hodge (1823–86), the son of Charles Hodge, was a theologian and educator who followed in his father's footsteps and became a professor at Princeton Theological Seminary. His work focused on defending Reformed theology and addressing contemporary theological challenges. He authored the widely used *Outlines of Theology* (1878). William G. T. Shedd (1820–94) was also a theologian and professor. Among his many works, his multi-volume *Dogmatic Theology* (1889) provided a systematic exposition of Reformed theology and engaged with theological controversies of his time. B. B. Warfield (1851–1921), who succeeded A. A. Hodge at Princeton, though not writing a systematic theology (he believed that Hodges' *Systematic Theology* could not be improved upon) nevertheless penned scores of books and essays on biblical and systematic theology subjects that continue to be widely read and highly valued.

On the Continent, Dutch theologian, statesman, and journalist, Abraham Kuyper (1837–1920), played a significant role in the development of Reformed theology and was a key figure in the formation of the Anti-Revolutionary Party in the Netherlands, where he founded the Free University at Amsterdam (1880). Among his better-known works is

Principles of Sacred Theology (1898). Herman Bavinck (1854–1921) was a Dutch Reformed theologian and professor at Kampen and then the Free University of Amsterdam. His four-volume *Reformed Dogmatics* (*Gereformeerde Dogmatiek*), also available in a one-volume English synopsis as *Our Reasonable Faith* (1956), is considered a classic in Reformed theology. Bavinck's writings contributed to the development of neo-Calvinism. G. C. Berkouwer (1903–96), another Dutch Reformed theologian and professor at the Free University of Amsterdam, authored the thirteen-volume series *Studies in Dogmatics* (1949–67), though he appears to have gradually adopted a relational neoorthodox understanding of revelation. Dutch Reformed theologian Hendrikus Berkhof (1914–95), professor at the University of Leiden, wrote *Christian Faith* (1973; trans. 1979), in which he interacts in depth with the world of critical theological scholarship.

Back in America, the Dutch-American Reformed theologian Louis Berkhof (1873–1957), professor at Calvin Theological Seminary, authored the succinct and widely read *Systematic Theology* (1941). J. Oliver Buswell, Jr. (1895–1977), Presbyterian theologian and educator who served as president of both president of Wheaton College and Covenant College, wrote the two-volume *Systematic Theology of the Christian Religion* (1962–65), notable for its extensive exegetical sections and for advocating a premillennial position. Donald G. Bloesch (1928–2010) was an evangelical theologian and professor at the University of Dubuque Theological Seminary. His works, such as his two-volume *Essentials of Evangelical Theology* (1978–79) and the seven-volume *Christian Foundations* (1992–2004), sought to articulate "a Catholic Evangelicalism" that takes issue with both fundamentalism and liberalism. Morton H. Smith (1923–2013), author of the two-volume *Systematic Theology* (1994), was an American Presbyterian scholar who taught at Belhaven College and Reformed Theological Seminary, and was a professor at Greenville Presbyterian Theological Seminary. Robert L. Reymond (1923–2013) was a professor at Covenant Theological Seminary and later at Knox Theological Seminary. His *A New Systematic Theology of the Christian Faith* (1998) is considered a contemporary and comprehensive statement of classic Reformed faith. Michael Horton (b. 1964) is an American Reformed theologian and professor at Westminster Seminary California, and the author of the philosophically-informed *The Christian Faith: A Systematic Theology for Pilgrims on the Way* (2011). John M. Frame (b. 1939), another American Reformed theologian and professor, taught at Reformed Theological Seminary Orlando. Among his many writings are the richly biblical *Systematic Theology: An Introduction to Christian Belief* (2013), which presents Frame's unique triperspectivalism (also known as multiperspectivalism).[27] Finally, British Reformed theologian and Union School of Theology professor Robert Letham (b. 1947), has also published the excellent and comprehensive *Systematic Theology* (2019). Deviating from the traditional loci method, Letham's work begins with the Trinity *ad intra* and continues the Trinitarian motif as the works of God *ad extra* are

[27] This epistemological approach is advocated by Calvinist philosophers Frame and Vern S. Poythress (b. 1946). Triperspectivalism suggests that in every act of knowing, the knower is in constant contact with three things or "perspectives": the knowing subject himself, the object of knowledge, and the standard or criteria by which knowledge is attained. See further Vern Poythress, *Symphonic Theology: The Validity of Multiple Preservatives in Theology* (Grand Rapids, MI: Zondervan, 1987).

organized and discussed, broadly speaking, around the persons of the Trinity.

In the Lutheran tradition, the German-American theologian Franz (Francis) August Otto Pieper (1852–1931) was a prominent figure in the Lutheran Church–Missouri Synod, and his four-volume (three volumes plus index) *Christian Dogmatics* (1917–24; trans. 1950–57) provides a modern classic systematic exposition of Lutheran theology. John Theodore Mueller (1885–1967) prepared a one-volume condensation of Pieper bearing the same title, *Christian Dogmatics* (1934/55). A noteworthy modern dogmatics is German theologian Helmut Thielicke's (1908–1986) broadly evangelical three-volume *The Evangelical Faith* (1968–78; trans. 1974–82), guided by the salutary premise that "the value of dogmatics depends upon whether it can be preached."

Representing the Wesleyan-Arminian tradition, English Methodist theologian William Burt Pope's (1822–1903) *A Compendium of Christian Theology: Being Analytical Outlines of a Course of Theological Study, Biblical, Dogmatic, Historical* (1875–76) provided a comprehensive treatment of Methodist theology and engaged with theological controversies of his time. Methodist theologian John Miley (1813–95) produced the thorough two-volume *Systematic Theology* (1892–94). W. T. Purkiser (1910–1992) served as the president of Nazarene Theological Seminary, and wrote *Exploring Our Christian Faith* (1960). Writing from a Nazarene standpoint, H. Orton Wiley (1877–1961), president of Asbury Theological Seminary, prepared the scholarly three-volume *Christian Theology* (1940–43). The two-volume work edited by Charles W. Carter, *A Contemporary Wesleyan Theology: Biblical, Systematic, and Practical* (1983), presents a collection of twenty-four essays on major doctrinal themes by several scholars representing a wide range of conservative Wesleyan denominations expounding the main features of Wesleyan belief. Jack Cottrell (1938–2022), professor at Cincinnati Bible Seminary and writing from within the Christian Church/Churches of Christ, produced the three-volume *Doctrine of God* series: volume one: *What the Bible Says about God the Creator* (1983), volume two: *What the Bible Says about God the Ruler* (1984), and volume three: *What the Bible Says about God the Redeemer* (1987). J. Kenneth Grider (1921–2006), an American theologian and professor at Nazarene Theological Seminary, wrote his of *A Wesleyan–Holiness Theology* (1994) for clergy and laypeople. Thomas C. Oden (1931–2016) was an American Methodist theologian and professor at Drew University, and author of the historically rich three-volume *Systematic Theology* (2006), condensed into one volume as *Classic Christianity: A Systematic Theology* (2009). With an emphasis on ancient Christian tradition, Oden seeks to provide a consensus view of the faith.

Among the Baptists, theologian A. H. Strong (1836–1921), president and professor of theology at Rochester Theological Seminary, wrote the often-reprinted *Systematic Theology: A Compendium Designed for the Use of Theological Students* (1886, final ed. 1907), widely used in Baptist circles for most of the twentieth century. The Southern Baptist theologian Edgar Y. Mullins (1860–1928), former president of the Southern Baptist Theological Seminary, wrote the nontechnical and accessible *The Christian Religion in Its Doctrinal Expression* (1917), which sought to mediate between Calvinism and Arminianism. Carl F. H. Henry (1913–2003), an American evangelical theologian, leading figure in the mid-twentieth-century evangelical movement and co-founder of *Christianity*

Today, produced the incisive and penetrating six-volume opus *God, Revelation and Authority* (1976–83). While not a systematic theology per se, Henry masterfully covers the limited areas of prolegomena, revelation, and the Godhead, interacting with hundreds of other scholarly positions. Dale Moody (1915–92), professor at the Southern Baptist Theological Seminary, authored the scholarly and comprehensive *The Word of Truth: A Summary of Christian Doctrine Based on Biblical Revelation* (1981), which attempts to bring together insights from various disciplines. Gordon R. Lewis (1917–1991) and Bruce A. Demarest (1935–2021) were American theologians and professors at Denver Seminary, who produced the novel three-volume *Integrative Theology* (1987–94). They propose a six-step process, which in turn forms the basis for each chapter: the problem; historical hypotheses; biblical teaching; systematic formulation; apologetic interaction; and relevance for life and ministry. James Leo Garrett, Jr. (1925–2020), an American Baptist theologian, taught at Southern Baptist Theological Seminary, Baylor University, and at Southwestern Baptist Theological Seminary. He was a leading figure in Baptist theology and church history, and the author of the meticulously footnoted two-volume *Systematic Theology: Biblical, Historical, and Evangelical* (1990–95). Millard J. Erickson (b. 1932), an American theologian and professor who has taught at Baylor University and Western Seminary, is known for his prodigious work in systematic theology. His *Christian Theology* (3rd ed., 2013) replaced Strong's as a widely used textbook in evangelical seminaries and provides a comprehensive overview of Christian doctrine. It has been abridged by Erickson's former student, L. Arnold Hustad, as *Introducing Christian Doctrine* (1983; 3rd. ed., 2015). Daniel L. Akin (b. 1957), president of Southeastern Baptist Theological Seminary, has edited the important volume, *A Theology for the Church* (2007; rev. ed. 2014), with contributions from a number of significant Baptist theologians. Wayne Grudem (b. 1948), professor at Phoenix Seminary, authored the best-selling *Systematic Theology: An Introduction to Biblical Doctrine* (1994; 2nd ed., 2020), known for its clear language and emphasis on the biblical basis for each doctrine. Robert Duncan Culver (1916–2015), was an American theologian and professor at Wheaton College, and the author of the large *Systematic Theology: Biblical and Historical* (2005). Christopher W. Morgan (b. 1971), professor at California Baptist University, and Robert A Peterson (b. 1948), professor at Covenant Theological Seminary, have written the excellent volume, *Christian Theology: The Biblical Story and Our Faith* (2020). Adam Harwood (b. 1974), professor at New Orleans Baptist Theological Seminary, has written the popular *Christian Theology: Biblical, Historical, Systematic* (2022). Harwood seeks to offer a fresh synthesis of essential Christian doctrine in accessible language.

The Anglican tradition has until recently made only minor contributions in modern times to systematic theology. Despite its title, Arthur C. Headlam's (1862–1947) *Christian Theology* (1934) covers only revelation and theology proper. American Episcopalian theologian and priest, Francis Joseph Hall (1857–1932), produced *Introduction to Dogmatic Theology* (1907). The conservative Anglican W. H. Griffth Thomas (1861–1924), principal of Wycliffe Hall, Oxford, has provided a theological exposition of the Thirty-Nine Articles of the Church of England in *The Principles of Theology: An Introduction to the Thirty-Nine Articles* (5th ed., 1930). Irish theologian Edward Arthur Litton (1813–97) wrote *Introduction to Dogmatic Theology* (1960). More recently, the English-born Canadian theologian J. I. Packer (1926–2020), a prominent figure in Reformed theology and evangelicalism, wrote *Concise Theology: A Guide to Historic Christian Beliefs* (1993) in his typically accessible style. Gerald L. Bray (b. 1948), a British theologian and church historian, has made significant contributions to the study of Reformation theology and the history of Christianity, most recently with his *God Is Love: A Biblical and Systematic Theology* (2012). Michael F. Bird (b. 1974) is an Australian Anglican priest, theologian, New Testament scholar, and professor at Ridley College. His popular *Evangelical Theology: A Biblical and Systematic Introduction* evinces a Gospel-centered ethos, and has the strength of being a systematic theology written by a biblical scholar (2013).

Within the broad evangelical movement, Lewis Sperry Chafer (1871–1952), one of the founders of Dallas Theological Seminary, provided the classic exposition of the older dispensationalism (from a modified Calvinist perspective) in his eight-volume *Systematic Theology* (1947–48). A number of recent reformulations of and contributions from the dispensationalist position bear mention. Canadian-born American theologian Henry C. Thiessen's (1883–1947) *Lectures in Systematic Theology* (1949; rev. ed. 1979) is a nontechnical work written from a moderate dispensational point of view. The revised edition by Vernon D. Doerksen is more Calvinistic than the original. Charles C. Ryrie (1925–2016), professor at Dallas Theological Seminary and later president of the Philadelphia College of Bible, penned the clearly written and accessible *Basic Theology* (1986). Norman L. Geisler (1932–2019), an American systematic theologian, apologist, and philosopher, made scholarly contributions (as author, coauthor, or editor of over ninety books and hundreds of articles) to the subjects of systematic theology, most notably with his four-volume *Systematic Theology* (2002–05). Nathan D. Holsteen (b. 1961) and Michael J. Svigel (b. 1973) are both professors at Dallas Theological Seminary, and have edited the accessible three-volume *Exploring Christian Theology* (2014–15). The well-known American pastor and theologian John MacArthur (b. 1939), and theologian and professor Richard Mayhue (b. 1944), both at The Master's Seminary, have edited the volume *Biblical Doctrine: A Systematic Summary of Bible Truth* (2017), which seeks to present a clear and coherent account of the Christian faith that is rooted in the biblical witness. Rolland D. McCune (1934–2019), an American theologian who served as a professor and president at Detroit Baptist Theological Seminary, produced the three-volume *A Systematic Theology of Biblical Christianity* (2008–10).

And finally, for the charismatic/Pentecostal (or Renewal) movement, J. Rodman Williams (1918–2008) was an American Pentecostal theologian who taught at Regent University, and who wrote the three-volume *Renewal Theology: Systematic Theology from a Charismatic Perspective* (1988–92). Pentecostal theologian, historian, and educator William W. Menzies (1931–2011), along with prominent Pentecostal theologian Stanley M. Horton (1916–2014), authored *Bible Doctrines: A Pentecostal Perspective* (1993). Horton authored his own *Systematic Theology* (rev. ed. 1994).

Beyond these contributions to mainline evangelical systematic theology texts, a number of new perspectives have challenged traditional systematic theology. One of these includes theologies of existentialism and symbol. Philosophical theologian Paul Tillich's (1886–1965) theology focused on the "ground of being" and the symbolic interpretation of Christian doctrine. Seeking to forge a middle way between supernaturalism and naturalism with his "existential-ontological theism," Tillich's theology of existentialism had a significant impact on the field of systematic theology. Indeed, Tillich's mystical system of Being-Itself, set forth in his three-volume *Systematic Theology* (1951–63), would later encourage the so-called secular theology and the death-of-God movement.[28]

In recent years, the field of systematic theology has become increasingly diverse, with various perspectives and approaches being represented, including feminist theology, liberation theology, and postmodern theology.[29] These theologies focus on marginalized groups and their experiences, and challenge traditional systematic theology and its methodologies. According to the liberationists,[30] such as Gustavo

---

[28] See further David H. Freeman, *Tillich* (Philadelphia, PA: Presbyterian & Reformed, 1962). For a critique of Tillich, see Kenneth Hamilton, *The System and the Gospel: A Critique of Paul Tillich* (Grand Rapids, MI: Eerdmans, 1963).

[29] For which, see Bernard Ramm, *A Handbook of Contemporary Theology* (Grand Rapids, MI: Eerdmans, 1966); Dean William Ferm, *Contemporary American Theologies: A Critical Survey* (New York: Seabury, 1981). See further Kelly M. Kapic and Bruce L. McCormack, eds., *Mapping Modern Theology: A Thematic and Historical Introduction* (Grand Rapids, MI: Baker Academic, 2012); Roger E. Olson, *The Journey of Modern Theology: From Reconstruction to Deconstruction* (Downers Grove, IL: IVP Academic, 2013).

[30] See S. Escobar, "Liberation Theology," *NDT*², 518–22; John Milbank, "Liberation Theology," *ECT,* 913–15; J. E. Stam and R. S. Goizueta, "Liberation Theology," *GDT,* 486–92; M. Stewart, "Process Theology," *EDWR*, 395–98; and D. D. Webster, "Liberation Theology," *EDT,* 635–38. See further Harvie M. Conn, "Theologies of Liberation: An Overview" and "Theologies of Liberation,"

Gutierrez (b. 1928), professor of theology in Lima, Peru, and author of the so-called Magna Carta of liberation theology, *A Theology of Liberation: History, Politics, and Salvation* (1971), theology consists not in meditative reflection on supernaturally revealed truths but in praxis, namely, involvement in the plight of the poor and powerless of this world. Much of liberation theology—as expressed, e.g., by José Miguez Bonino (b.1924), a Methodist professor of theology in Buenos Aires, Argentina, and the Uruguayan Jesuit priest, Juan Luis Segundo (1925–96)—is indebted to the Marxist critique of society and its program of violent revolution. Black theologians[31] such as James Cone (b. 1938), professor of theology at Union Theological Seminary in New York City, undertake a similar program from the Black American perspective, particularly in Cone's *A Black Theology of Liberation* (1970) and *God of the Oppressed* (1975). In a similar vein, feminist theologies emerged in the early 1960s and 1970s to address the alleged oppression of women in Western culture. Some notable authors and their contributions include Georgia Harkness (1891–1974), *Women in Church and Society* (1971); Mary Daly (1928–2010), *Beyond God the Father* (1973); Phyllis Trible (b. 1932), *God and the Rhetoric of Sexuality* (1978); and Elisabeth Schüssler Fiorenza (b. 1938), *In Memory of Her: A Feminist Theological Reconstruction of Christian Origin* (1983).

Another recent development comes from process theology (also known as neoclassical theology). Theologies of process were derived from the

in *Tensions in Contemporary Theology,* ed. Stanley N. Gundry and Alan F. Johnson (Chicago, IL: Moody, 1976), 327–434.

[31] F. L. Ware, See "Black Theology," *GDT*, 111–18.

theistic metaphysics developed in the 1920s and 1930s by philosophers Alfred North Whitehead (1861–1947) in *Process and Reality* (1929) and Charles Hartshorne (1897–2000) in *Man's Vision of God and the Problem of Theism* (1941) and *The Divine Relativity* (1948). Process theology—so-called because this system holds that that reality is a process of becoming, rather than being a static universe of objects or substances—emphasizes the dynamic nature of God and the universe. In process theology, God is a special kind of energy event constantly growing and continually being shaped by relations with other actual occasions, with every actual being possessing at least some self-determination.[32] The main features of process theology have been outlined by John B. Cobb, Jr. (b. 1925), in *A Christian Natural Theology* (1965), as well as by Norman Pittenger (1905–1997) in *God in Process* (1967) and *The Divine Triunity* (1977).

Process theology in turn has contributed to the rise of open theism (also called neotheism, or free-will theism), the theological perspective that views God as limited by the future and not possessing exhaustive foreknowledge. As one model of nondeterminism, in this system God's foreknowledge is limited by the uncertainties inherent in creating humanity with truly free will where even He does not know what free human agents will choose to do. In other words, God's knowledge of the future is not exhaustive or predetermined, but rather God interacts with humanity in a dynamic and responsive manner. Thus, open theists reject

---

32 See André Gounelle, "Process Theology," *ECT,* 1287–88; and T. Bradshaw, "Process theology," *NDT*^{2}, 707–09; see further Norman L. Geisler, "Process Theology," in *Tensions in Contemporary Theology*, ed. Stanley N. Gundry and Alan F. Johnson (Chicago, IL: Moody, 1976), 237–84.

God's classical attributes (such as omniscience, omnipotence, omnipresence, and immutability). Some of open theism's main proponents include Canadian evangelical theologian Clark Pinnock (1937–2010) in *Most Moved Mover: A Theology of God's Openness* (2001), American theologian and Hendrix College professor John E. Sanders (b. 1956) in *The God Who Risks: A Theology of Providence* (1998), and American theologian Gregory A. Boyd (b. 1957) in *God of the Possible: A Biblical Introduction to the Open View of God* (2001).[33]

Furthermore, in the twenty-first century, a number of developments have exercised a very real influence on systematic theology. For one, there has been an increasing interest in interdisciplinary approaches to theology, drawing on fields such as philosophy, sociology, and literary theory to provide new perspectives on traditional theological topics. Similarly, there has been a growing awareness of the need to take into account the perspectives and contributions of theologians from around the world, particularly from the Global South, in order to develop a more inclusive

---

[33] Critiques of open theism include the following: James E. Dolezal, *All That Is in God: Evangelical Theology and the Challenge of Classical Christian Theism* (Grand Rapids, MI: Reformation Heritage, 2017); idem, *God without Parts: Divine Simplicity and the Metaphysics of God's Absoluteness* (Eugene, OR: Pickwick, 2011); Norman L. Geisler, *Creating God in the Image of Man? The New Open View of God—Neotheism's Dangerous Drift* (Minneapolis, MN: Bethany House, 1997); idem., and H. Wayne House, *The Battle for God: Responding to the Challenge of Neotheism* (Grand Rapids, MI: Kregel, 2001); John Piper, Justin Taylor, and Paul Kjoss Helseth, eds., *Beyond the Bounds: Open Theism and the Undermining of Biblical Christianity* (Wheaton, IL: Crossway, 2003); Bruce Ware, *God's Lesser Glory: The Diminished God of Open Theism* (Wheaton, IL: Crossway, 2001); and Douglas Wilson, ed., *Bound Only Once: The Failure of Open Theism* (Moscow, ID: Canon, 2001). See, helpfully, Robert L. Thomas, "The Hermeneutics of Open Theism" *The Master's Seminary Journal* 12 (2001), 179–202.

and diverse theology. Additionally, there has been an increasing concern for the environment and the impact of human activities on the planet, leading to the development of ecological theology, which addresses the relationship between humanity and the environment from a theological perspective. And finally, the rise of the internet and social media has led to new forms of communication and new opportunities for theology to engage with the public and new developments in digital theology which includes a study of the impact of digital technologies on religious practices, beliefs, and communities.

Overall, the field of systematic theology has undergone significant changes in the modern period, with new perspectives and approaches being introduced that challenge traditional understandings and expressions of Christian doctrine. The future prospects and challenges for systematic theology are likely to be shaped by a number of factors, including changing societal and cultural contexts, advances in science and technology, and the ongoing development of new theological perspectives and approaches.

Summing up the modern period, Bruce Riley Ashford (b. 1974) and Keith Whitfield (b. 1974) have remarked, "The modern period is marked by a dizzying diversity of theological paradigms, each with their attendant theological methods."[34] Nevertheless, evangelical orthodox theologies have continued to maintain a presence, and continue apace. As Scott Swain (b. 1972) has observed,

[34] Ashford and Whitfield, "Theological Method: An Introduction to the Task of Theology," 32.

> Though it has not arrived at its former glory, systematic theology has witnessed something of a revival over the past several decades. Due in part to institutional centers such as the Research Institute for Systematic Theology at King's College, London in the 1990s, journals like the *International Journal of Systematic Theology*, and the efforts of leading theologians in the field both to publish and to supervise at a doctoral level high quality academic work, systematic theology today enjoys some degree of prominence as an academic discipline in the English–speaking world. The recent spate of stand–alone and multivolume systematic theologies, which are beginning to appear in print, bodes well for the future of the discipline.[35]

Notable examples of systematic theology from the deluge of literature available in the modern period include the following works, which survey will be confined to books either in English or translated into English, written by single authors.[36]

---

[35] Scott R. Swain, "Theology as Dogmatics," in *The Task of Dogmatics: Explorations in Theological Method,* ed. Oliver D. Crisp and Fred Sanders (Grand Rapids, MI: Zondervan, 2017), ePub: Chapter 2: Dogmatics as Systematic Theology, Location 106. See further Gabriel Fackre, "The Revival of Systematic Theology: An Overview." *Interpretation* 49.3 (1995), 229–41.

[36] Good surveys include: Jaroslav Pelikan, *Christian Doctrine and Modern Culture,* vol. 5 *of The Christian Tradition: A of Development of Doctrine* (Chicago, IL: University of Chicago, 1989); Ed L. Miller & Stanley Grenz, eds., *Fortress Introduction to Contemporary Theologies* (Minneapolis: Fortress, 1998); Gareth Jones, *The Blackwell Companion to Modern Theology,* Blackwell Companions to Religion (Oxford: Blackwell, 2004); David F. Ford and Rachel Muers, eds., *The Modern Theologians: An Introduction to Christian Theology since 1918*, 3rd ed. (Oxford: Blackwell, 2005); James C. Livingston, *Modern Christian Thought*, 2 vols., 2nd ed. (Minneapolis: Fortress, 2006); Phillip

- John Gill (1697–1771), *A Complete Body of Doctrinal and Practical Divinity*. 2 vols. (1767–70)
- Timothy Dwight (1753–1811), *Theology: Explained and Defended.* 5 vols. (1818–19)
- John Dick (1764–1833), *Lectures in Theology. 4 vols.* (1834)
- Friedrich D. E. Schleiermacher (1768–1834), *Brief Outline of the Study of Theology* (1811; trans. 1850); *The Christian Faith* (1821–22, and revised 1831–32; trans. 1948)
- Thomas Chalmers (1780–1847), *Theological Institutes* (1843–47)
- Richard Watson (1781–1833), *Theological Institutes, or, A View of the Evidences, Doctrines, Morals, and Institutions of Christianity* (1823)
- John L. Dagg (1794–1884), *Manual of Theology* (1858)
- Charles Hodge (1797–1878), *Systematic Theology*. 3 vols. (1871–73)
- Samuel Wakefield (1799–1895), *A Complete System of Christian Theology; or, a Concise, Comprehensive, and Systematic View of the Evidences, Doctrines, Morals, and Institutions of Christianity* (1862)
- Johann Tobias Beck (1804–1878), *Outlines of Christian Doctrine* (1879)
- Isaac August Dorner (1809–1884), *A System of Christian Doctrine*. 4 vols. (1879–81)

Kennedy, *Twentieth–Century Theologians: A New Introduction to the Modern Christian Thought* (London: I. B. Tauris, 2010).

- Miner Raymond (1811–1897), *Systematic Theology. 3 vols.* (1877–79)
- Edward Arthur Litton (1813–1897), *Introduction to Dogmatic Theology* (1882–92)
- John Miley (1813–1895), *Systematic Theology*. 2 vols. (1892, 1894)
- Robert Lewis Dabney (1820–1898), *Systematic Theology* (1878)
- Heinrich Heppe (1820–1879), *Reformed Dogmatics: Set Out and Illustrated From the Sources* (1861)
- William G. T. Shedd (1820–1894), *Dogmatic Theology* (1889)
- William Burt Pope (1822–1903), *A Compendium of Christian Theology: Being Analytical Outlines of a Course of Theological Study, Biblical, Dogmatic, Historical. 3 vols.* (1875–76)
- A. A. Hodge (1823–1886), *Outlines of Theology* (1878)
- James Petigru Boyce (1827–1888), *Abstract of Systematic Theology* (1887)
- A. H. Strong (1836–1921), *Systematic Theology: A Compendium Designed for the Use of Theological Students* (final edition, 1907)
- Abraham Kuyper (1837–1920), *Principles of Sacred Theology* (1898)
- Francis Pieper (1852–1931), *Christian Dogmatics*. 4 vols. (1950–57)
- E. Y. Mullins (1860–1928), *The Christian Religion in Its Doctrinal Expression* (1917)
- Geerhardus Vos (1862–1949), *Gereformeerde Dogmatiek.* 5 vols. (trans. *Reformed Dogmatics*, 2012–16)

- Lewis Sperry Chafer (1871–1952), *Systematic Theology,* 8 vols. (1947–48)
- H. Orton Wiley (1877–1961), *Christian Theology*. 3 vols. (1940–43)
- Ernest S. Williams (1885–1981), *Systematic Theology. 3 vols.* (1953)
- Henry Clarence Thiessen (1883–1947), *Lectures in Systematic Theology* (1949; rev. ed. 1979)
- Karl Barth (1886–1968), *Die Kirchliche Dogmatic,* 14 vols. (trans. *Church Dogmatics*, 1932–67); *Fides Quarens Intellectuam* (1960)
- H. Emil Brunner (1889–1966), *Dogmatics. 3 vols.* (trans. 1950–62)
- James Oliver Buswell, Jr. (1895–1977), *A Systematic Theology of the Christian Religion*. 2 vols. (1962–63)
- Karl Rahner (1904–1984), *Foundations of Christian Faith: An Introduction to the Idea of Christianity* (New York, 1978); *Theological Investigations*, 23 vols. (London, 1961–81)
- Hans Urs von Balthasar (1905–1988), *The Glory of the Lord: A Theological Aesthetics*, 7 vols. (1983–90); *Theo–drama*. 5 vols. (1988–98); *Theo–logic*. 3 vols. (2001–05).
- Helmut Thielicke (1908–1988), *The Evangelical Faith*. 3 vols. (trans. 1974–82)
- Paul Tillich (1886–1965), *Systematic Theology. 3 vols.* (1951–63)[37]

---

[37] In actuality, Tillich's *Systematic Theology* is a misnamed work, as it is a philosophical treatise on ontology and not, properly speaking, a systematic

- Carl F. H. Henry (1913–2003), *God, Revelation, and Authority*, 6 vols. (1976–83)
- Robert Duncan Culver (1916–2015), *Systematic Theology: Biblical and Historical* (2005)
- J. Rodman Williams, (1918–2008), *Renewal Theology: Systematic Theology from a Charismatic Perspective*. 3 vols. (1988–1992)
- Morton H. Smith (1923–2013), *Systematic Theology. 2 vols.* (1994)
- Robert L. Reymond (1923–2013), *A New Systematic Theology of the Christian Faith* (1998)
- James William McClendon, Jr. (1924–2020), *Systematic Theology*. 3 vols. (1986–2000)
- James Leo Garrett, Jr. (1925–2020), *Systematic Theology: Biblical, Systematic, and Historical. 2 vols.* (1990, 1995)
- Charles C. Ryrie (1925–2016), *Basic Theology: A Popular Systematic Guide to Understanding Biblical Truth* (1986)
- Donald G. Bloesch (1928–2010), *Essentials of Evangelical Theology. 2 vols.* (1978–79); and *Christian Foundations*, 7 vols. (1992–2004)
- Hans Küng (1928–2021), *On Being a Christian* (1977)
- Wolfhart Pannenberg (1928–2014), *Basic Questions in Theology*. 3 vols. (trans. 1970–73); *Systematic Theology*. 2 vols. (1988–93; trans. 1991, 1994)

---

presentation of Christian doctrine. Sawyer (*Survivor's Guide to Theology,* 233) agrees.

- French L. Arrington (b. 1931), *Christian Doctrine: A Pentecostal Perspective*. 3 vols. (1992–94)
- Thomas C. Oden (1931–2016), *Systematic Theology*. 3 vols. (2006); condensed into one volume as *Classic Christianity: A Systematic Theology* (2009)
- Millard J. Erickson (b. 1932), *Christian Theology,* 3rd ed. (2013); *Introducing Christian Theology*, 3rd ed. (2015)
- Norman L. Geisler (1932–2019), *Systematic Theology*. 4 vols. (2002–05); condensed into one volume as *Systematic Theology in One Volume* (2011)
- Norman R. Gulley (b. 1933), *Systematic Theology. 4 vols.* (2003–16)
- Rolland McCune (1934–2019), *A Systematic Theology of Biblical Christianity. 3 vols.* (2009–10)
- Daniel L. Migliore (b. 1935), *Faith Seeking Understanding: An Introduction to the Christian Faith* (1991)
- Anthony C. Thiselton (b. 1937), *Systematic Theology* (2015)
- John M. Frame (b. 1939), *Salvation Belongs to the Lord: An Introduction to Systematic Theology* (2006); *Systematic Theology: An Introduction to Christian Belief* (2013)
- Douglas F. Kelly (b. 1943) *Systematic Theology. 3 vols.* (2008–21)
- Robert Letham (b. 1947), *Systematic Theology* (2019)
- Gerald Bray (b. 1948), *God Is Love: A Biblical and Systematic Theology* (2012)
- Wayne Grudem (b. 1948), *Systematic Theology: An Introduction to Biblical Doctrine,* 2nd ed. (2020)

- Stanley J. Grenz (1950–2005), *Theology for the Community of God* (2000)
- Frank Macchia (b. 1952), *Introduction to Theology: Declaring the Wonders of God* (2023); *Tongues of Fire: A Systematic Theology of the Christian Faith* (2023)
- Alister E. McGrath (b. 1953), *Christian Theology* (3rd ed., 2001); *A Scientific Theology,* 1: *Nature*; Vol. 2: *Reality*; Vol. 3: *Theory* (2001–03); *Theology: The Basics* (4th ed., 2018)
- Michael S. Horton (b. 1964), *The Christian Faith: A Systematic Theology for Pilgrims on the Way* (2011)
- Daniel J. Treier (b. 1972), *Introducing Evangelical Theology* (2019)
- Michael F. Bird (b. 1974), *Evangelical Theology: A Biblical and Systematic Introduction* (2013)
- Adam Harwood (b. 1974), *Christian Theology: Biblical, Historical, Systematic* (2022)
- John C. Peckham (b. 1981), *God With Us: An Introduction to Adventist Theology* (2023)[38]

---

[38] As of this writing, a number of prominent theologians are in the process of writing systematic theologies, including Malcolm B. Yarnell III (b. 1962), Matthew Barrett (b. 1982), Kevin Vanhoozer (b. 1957), and Steven J. Wellum (b. 1961).

CHAPTER FIVE: BIOGRAPHICAL SKETCHES OF KEY THEOLOGIANS, PART I

THE study of systematic theology is not merely an exploration of abstract ideas and doctrines, but also an engagement with the minds that have influenced and shaped Christian faith and practice. As with "Appendix 3: Notable Theologians," inclusion in this chapter does not indicate agreement with an individual, although this chapter is limited in scope and generally more focused on orthodox writers. The point here is to briefly introduce the scholars who have had (for better or worse) a significant impact on Christianity in general, and systematic theology in particular. [1]

---

[1] In addition to the standard reference works (e.g., *ODCC*^{3}, *NDT*, *NDT*^{2}, *EDT*, *ECT*), the following are particularly helpful: John Bowden, *Who's Who in Theology* (London: SCM, 1991); Patrick W. Carey and Joseph T. Lienhard, eds., *Biographical Dictionary of Christian Theologians* (Greenwood, CT: Greenwood, 2000); G. R. Evans, ed., *The First Theologians: An Introduction to the Theology of the Early Church* (Oxford: Blackwell, 2004); *idem*, ed., *The Medieval Theologians: An Introduction to the Medieval Period* (Oxford: Blackwell, 2005); David F. Ford and Rachel Muers, eds., *The Modern Theologians: An Introduction to the Christian Faith in the Twentieth Century,* 2nd ed. (Oxford: Blackwell, 1997); Philip Kennedy, *Twentieth–Century Theologians: A New Introduction to Christian Thought* (New York: I. B. Tauris, 2010); Donald M. Lewis, ed., *The Blackwell Dictionary of Evangelical Biography: 1730—1860,* 2 vols. (Oxford: Blackwell, 1995); Carter Lindberg, *The Reformation Theologians: An Introduction to Theology in the Early Modern*

Abelard, Peter (1079–1142). French philosopher, theologian, and logician. He is known for his contributions to scholasticism, his controversial views on theology, and his love affair with Héloïse. His works, such as *Sic et Non*, and *Theologia 'Summi Boni'*, engaged in dialectical reasoning and explored theological and philosophical questions. Famously, Abelard applied Aristotelian logic to both philosophy and theology.

Albertus Magnus (*ca.* 1200–1280), also called Albert the Great, was a German Dominican friar, philosopher, and theologian, known for his vast knowledge and contributions to various fields of study. He played a significant role in the development of scholasticism and his works, such as *Summa Theologiae sive De mirabilis scientia Dei* (uncompleted) and *De Animalibus*, explored topics ranging from theology and philosophy to natural science.

Alcuin (730–804), an English scholar and theologian, was a leading figure in the Carolingian Renaissance. He served as an advisor to Charlemagne and played a crucial role in the revival of learning and the promotion of education in the Frankish Empire.

Period (Oxford: Blackwell, 2002); Donald W. Musser and Joseph L. Price, eds., *A New Handbook of Christian Theologians* (Nashville, TN: Abingdon, 1996); Gerald O'Collins and Edward G. Farrugia, *The Modern Theologians: An Introduction to Christian Theology in the Twentieth Century* (New York: Paulist, 2000); Dean G. Peerman and Martin E. Marty, eds., *A Handbook of Christian Theologians* (Nashville, TN: Abingdon, 1984); Michael Walsh, ed., *Dictionary of Christian Biography* (Collegeville, MN: Liturgical, 2001).

Alexander of Alexandria (d. 328) was a bishop and theologian in the early church. He played a significant role in the Council of Nicaea and his works engaged with topics like Christology, the nature of the Trinity, and the relationship between the Father and the Son.

Alexander of Hales (*ca.* 1186–1245), an English theologian and Franciscan friar, made significant contributions to scholastic theology. His work *Summa Theologiae* provided a comprehensive treatment of Christian doctrine and influenced later theologians, including Thomas Aquinas.

Allis, Oswald T. (1880–1973) was an American theologian and professor at Westminster Theological Seminary. He is known for his defense of biblical inerrancy and authored *The Five Books of Moses: A Reexamination of the Modern Theory that the Pentateuch is a Late Compilation from Diverse and Conflicting Sources*, and *The Unity of Isaiah.*

Ambrose of Milan (*ca.* 340–*ca.* 397) was a fourth-century bishop and theologian, and one of the most influential figures in the early Christian church. He served as the bishop of Milan and played a crucial role in the conversion of Augustine. He was known for his strong leadership and defense of the Church's independence. Among his many writings, of note here are his dogmatic works: *De fide ad Gratianum*, *De Spiritu Sancto*, *De incarnationis dominicae sacramento*, *Explanatio symboli ad initiandos*, *Expositio fidei*, *De mysteriis*, *De sacramentis*, *De paenitentia* and *De sacramento regenerationis sive de philosophia*.

Ames, William (1576–1633) was an English Puritan theologian and professor. He taught at various universities and his works—including *Technometria, Medulla Theologiae*, and *The Marrow of Sacred Divinity*—engage with topics like ethics, casuistry, and the nature of the Christian life.

Amyraut, Moses (1596–1664), a French Reformed theologian, is known for his contributions to the theological debate on predestination. His teachings, known as Amyraldianism or hypothetical universalism, proposed a modified view of Calvinism that emphasized God's universal love and the possibility of salvation for all.

Anselm of Canterbury (1033–1109), an Italian theologian and archbishop, is known for his contributions to scholasticism and his ontological argument for the existence of God. His works, such as *Monologion*, *Proslogion*, and *Cur Deus Homo*, explored topics like faith, reason, and the nature of God.

Apollinarius of Laodicea (*ca.* 310–390) was a bishop and theologian in early Christianity. He was involved in the Christological controversies of the 4th century, and his views on the nature of Christ (now termed Apollinarianism) were condemned as heretical. His works, such as *Apodeixis*, engage with topics like Christology, the incarnation, and the relationship between the divine and human natures of Christ.

Aquinas, Thomas (1224–1274), a Dominican friar and theologian from Italy, is considered one of the most influential figures in Western philosophy and theology. His synthesis of Aristotelian philosophy and Christian theology, as seen in his monumental work *Summa Theologicae*, shaped the development of Catholic thought. Among his other works are *Scripta Super Libros Sententiarum* and *Summa contra Gentiles.*

Arius of Alexandria (270–336), was a priest and theologian in early Christianity, and a central figure in the Arian controversy of the 4th century. His teachings, which denied the full divinity of Christ, led to the Council of Nicaea and the formulation of the Nicene Creed. The only extant works of Arius are two letters, a profession of faith, and a passage from a pamphlet in both verse and prose entitled *Thalia.*

Arminius, Jacob (1560–1609), a Dutch theologian and professor, is known for his views on predestination and free will. His teachings, which challenged the supralapsarianism of Theodore Beza, led to the development of Arminianism and the Remonstrant movement. He authored numerous writings, including *Declaration of Sentiments*, *Examination of Perkins' Pamphlet*, *Public Disputations*, and (posthumously) *Seventy-Nine Private Disputations*.

Athanasius (296–373), an Egyptian bishop and theologian, played a crucial role in defending orthodox Christianity against the Arian heresy. His writings, such as *On the Incarnation*, emphasized the divinity of Christ and his role in salvation.

Augustine of Hippo (*ca.* 354–*ca.* 430) was a theologian and philosopher from North Africa. His works, such as *Confessions*, *City of God*, and *The Trinity* had a profound impact on Western Christianity and philosophy, addressing topics like original sin, predestination, and the nature of God. He also wrote *On Christian Teaching* and *Reconsiderations* (or *Retractions*).

Aulén, Gustaf (1879–1977) was a Swedish theologian and bishop. He is known for his work on Christ's atonement, particularly his book *Christus Victor*, which presents a different understanding of the atonement as a victory over the powers of evil.

Bacon, Roger (1214–1294), an English philosopher and Franciscan friar, made significant contributions to the fields of natural science and philosophy. His works, such as *Opus Majus* and *Opus Tertium*, advocated for the use of empirical observation and experimentation in scientific inquiry.

Baillie, Donald (1887–1954) was a Scottish theologian and professor at the University of Edinburgh. He is known for his work on the theology of Karl Barth and authored *God Was in Christ*.

Baillie, John (1886–1960) was a Scottish theologian and professor at the University of Edinburgh. Espousing a form orthodox liberal Protestantism, Baillie is known for his work on the theology of the Reformation and authored *The Theology of John Calvin*, as well as *Our Knowledge of God* and his posthumously published Gifford Lectures, *The Sense of the Presence of God.*

Balthasar, Hans Urs von (1905–1988) was a Swiss Catholic theologian and cardinal. He is known for his work in systematic theology and his writings, such as the seven-volume *The Glory of the Lord: A Theological Aesthetics* and the five-volume *Theo-drama*, explored themes like beauty, theodicy, and the relationship between theology and the arts.

Bangs, Nathan (1778–1862), an American Methodist theologian and historian, played a significant role in the development of American

Methodism. His works, such as *A History of the Methodist Episcopal Church* and *The Life of Freeborn Garrettson*, documented the history and growth of the Methodist movement in the United States.

Bannerman, D. Douglas (1842–1903) was a Scottish theologian and professor at the University of Edinburgh. He is known for his work on the doctrine of the church and authored *The Church of Christ: A Treatise on the Nature, Powers, Ordinances, Discipline, and Government of the Christian Church.*

Bannerman, James (1807–1868) was a Scottish theologian and professor. He is known for his work on the doctrine of the church and his defense of Presbyterianism. Among his more important works are *Systematic Theology*, *Apologetic Theology*, *Inspiration: The Infallible Truth and Divine Authority of the Holy Scriptures*, and the two-volume *The Church.*

Barackman, Floyd H. (1923–2007), an American pastor, theologian, and professor at Practical Bible Training School (now, Davis College). One of his better-known works is *Practical Christian Theology: Examining the Great Doctrines of the Faith.*

Barrett, C. K. (1917–2011) was a British biblical scholar and theologian. He is known for his work in New Testament studies. His commentaries, such as *The Gospel According to St. John* and *The Epistle to the Romans*, contributed to the understanding of the biblical text.

Barrett, Matthew (b. 1982), an American theologian and professor, is known for his work in systematic theology and historical theology. He has authored books such as *God's Word Alone: The Authority of Scripture* and has taught at various seminaries and universities.

Barth, Karl (1886–1968), a Swiss theologian, is considered one of the most influential theologians of the 20th century. His work, particularly his monumental and massive *Church Dogmatics*, in twelve part-volumes, emphasized the primacy of God's revelation in Jesus Christ and challenged traditional theological frameworks.

Basil of Caesarea (Basil the Great) (330–379) was a fourth-century bishop and theologian, from Caesarea in Cappadocia. He was a prominent figure in the development of communal monasticism and early Christian theology, particularly the doctrine of the Trinity against Arianism and the Pneumatomachai. His works engage with topics like asceticism, the nature of the Holy Spirit, and the relationship between faith and works. Of note are *Moral Rules*, *De Spiritu Sancto*, and *Against Eunomium.*

Baur, Ferdinand Christian (1792–1860) was a German Protestant theologian and professor, and founder of the Tübingen School of New Testament criticism. He played a significant role in the development of historical–critical methods in biblical studies and his works engage with topics like New Testament theology, the development of early Christianity, and the relationship between history and faith.

Bavinck, Herman (1854–1921) was a Dutch Reformed theologian and professor at Kampen and then the Free University of Amsterdam. His four-volume *Reformed Dogmatics* (*Gereformeerde Dogmatiek*) is considered a classic in Reformed theology and his writings contributed to the development of neo-Calvinism.

Baxter, Richard (1615–1691), an English Puritan theologian and pastor, played a significant role in the development of practical theology. His works, such as *The Reformed Pastor*, *The Saints' Everlasting Rest*, and *A Call to the Unconverted*, emphasized the importance of pastoral care, personal holiness, and the pursuit of God. Of note, too, are Baxter's *Methodus Theologiae Christianae*.

Beale, Gregory K. (b. 1949) is an American New Testament scholar and theologian. He taught at Westminster Theological Seminary and his works, such as *The Temple and the Church's Mission: A Biblical Theology of the Dwelling Place of God*, contributed to the understanding of the biblical text and its theological themes.

Beasley–Murray, G. R. (1916–2000) was a British New Testament scholar, professor and Principal at Spurgeon's College, and later professor at Southern Baptist Theological Seminary. He is known for his work on the book of Revelation, and authored *Baptism in the New Testament, Jesus and the kingdom of God,* and *Jesus and the Last Days*.

Becket, Thomas (1118–1170) was an English archbishop and martyr. He served as the Archbishop of Canterbury and his conflict with King Henry II led to his assassination. His life and works engage with topics like ecclesiology, the relationship between church and state, and the defense of church authority.

Bede (*ca.* 673–735), also known as the Venerable Bede, was an English monk and scholar who made significant contributions to the fields of history, theology, and biblical studies. His most famous work, *Historia Ecclesiastica Gentis Anglorum*, is a valuable source of information on early medieval England, beginning with the conquest of Britain by Julius Caesar. Among those works deemed to be authentic are *Super Acta*

Apostolorum expositio, *Libellus retractationis in Actus Apostolorum*, *De nominibus locorum quae leguntur in libro Actus Apostolorum*, and *De locis sanctis*.

Beeke, Joel (b. 1952), a Dutch-American theologian and pastor, is known for his work in Reformed theology and Puritan studies. His numerous books, including *Reformed Preaching*, *Puritan Reformed Theology*, and the three-volume *Reformed Systematic Theology* (with Paul R. Smalley), have made significant contributions to the understanding and promotion of Reformed theology.

Benedict of Nursia (*ca.* 480–547) was an Italian monk and founder of the Benedictine Order, known as the patriarch of Western monasticism. He is known for his *Rule of Saint Benedict*, providing guidelines for monastic life and spirituality that served as the norm in the West from the eighth through the twelfth centuries.

Berengar of Tours (*ca.* 999–1088), a French theologian, was involved in the Eucharistic controversies of the 11th century. His teachings, for instance in *De corpore et sanguine Christi*, emphasized a symbolic understanding of the Eucharist and were met with harsh opposition from church authorities.

Berkhof, Hendrikus (1914–1995) was a Dutch Reformed theologian and professor. He is known for his work on systematic theology and his emphasis on the social implications of the Christian faith. His works include *Introduction to the Study of Dogmatics*, *Christian Faith: An Introduction to the Study of the Faith*, and *Christ the Meaning of History*.

Berkhof, Louis (1873–1957) was a Dutch-American Reformed theologian and professor. He taught at Calvin Theological Seminary and his works, such as *Systematic Theology*, engage with topics like Reformed theology, theological method, and the doctrines of God, Christ, and salvation.

Berkouwer, G. C. (1903–1996) was a Dutch Reformed theologian and professor. He taught at Free University of Amsterdam and his works, such as the multi-volume *Studies in Dogmatics*, engage with topics like theological method, the nature of faith, the relationship between theology and culture, and various theological loci.

Bernard of Clairvaux (1090–1153) was a French abbot and theologian. He played a significant role in the Cistercian monastic movement and was a key figure in the 12th-century reformation. His writings, such as *On Loving God* and *Sermons on the Song of Songs*, emphasized the importance of mystical experience and devotion to Christ.

Beza, Theodore (1519–1605) was a French Reformed theologian and pastor. He was a close associate of and successor to John Calvin, and he played a significant role in the development of Reformed theology. His works, such as the three-volume *Tractationes Theologicae* (*Theological Tractates,* 1570–82), defended Reformed doctrines and engaged in theological controversies, particularly predestination.

Biel, Gabriel (*ca.* 1415–1495) was a German scholastic theologian and professor. He taught at the University of Tübingen and his works, such as *Collectorium circa quattuor libros sententiarum*, engage with topics like sacramental theology, grace, and the nature of God.

Bird, Michael F. (b. 1974) is an Australian Anglican priest, theologian, New Testament scholar, and professor at Ridley College. His popular *Evangelical Theology: A Biblical and Systematic Introduction* evinces a Gospel-centered ethos, and has the strength of being a systematic theology written by a biblical scholar.

Blaising, Craig A. (b. 1949) is an American theologian and professor, and former Executive Vice President and Provost of Southwestern Baptist Theological Seminary. He is known for his work on eschatology and co-authored *Progressive Dispensationalism*.

Blaurock, Georg (Jörg vom Haus Jacob)(*ca.* 1491–1529) was a Swiss Anabaptist leader and theologian. A Roman Catholic priest prior to this conversion, Blaurock played a significant role in the early Anabaptist movement, and co-founded the Swiss Brethren in Zürich. While he engaged with topics like believer's baptism, nonviolence, and the relationship between church and state, the only extant writings (all penned during the last three weeks of this life) are a letter and two hymns.

Blocher, Henri A. G. (b. 1937) is a French Baptist evangelical theologian and professor. He taught at Faculté Libre de Théologie Évangélique and his works, such as *Original Sin: Illuminating the Riddle* and *Evil and the Cross: An Analytical Look at the Problem of Pain*, engage with topics like sin, salvation, and the nature of evil.

Bloesch, Donald (1928–2010). An American evangelical theologian and professor, Bloesch taught at the University of Dubuque Theological Seminary. His works, such as his two-volume *Essentials of Evangelical Theology* and the seven-volume *Christian Foundations*, contributed to the development of evangelical theology and engaged with topics like systematic theology, the nature of God, and the relationship between theology and spirituality.

Blomberg, Craig (b. 1955) is an American New Testament scholar and professor. He teaches at Denver Seminary and his works, such as *The Historical Reliability of the Gospels*, engage with topics like biblical interpretation, the historical Jesus, and the reliability of the New Testament.

Bock, Darrell L. (b. 1935) is an American New Testament scholar and professor at Dallas Theological Seminary. He is known for his work on the historical Jesus and authored, among other titles, *Jesus According to Scripture: Restoring the Portrait from the Gospels*.

Boethius (*ca.* 477–*ca.* 524), a philosopher and statesman, made significant contributions to medieval philosophy and theology. His work *The Consolation of Philosophy* explored topics such as the nature of God, free will, and the problem of evil.

Boettner, Loraine (1901–1990) was an American Reformed theologian and author. He is known for his work on systematic theology and his defense of Reformed theology. He authored many works, including *Studies in Theology*, *The Reformed Faith, Immortality,* and *Roman Catholicism.*

Boice, James Montgomery (1938–2000) was an American Reformed pastor and theologian. He served as the senior minister of Tenth Presbyterian Church in Philadelphia and his works, such as *Foundations of the Christian Faith*, provided a comprehensive treatment of Reformed theology.

Bonaventure (1221–1274). An Italian Franciscan friar and theologian, Bonaventure is known for his mystical writings and his leadership within the Franciscan Order. His works, such as *The Journey of the Mind to God* and *The Life of St. Francis*, emphasized the importance of spiritual contemplation and the imitation of Christ.

Bonhoeffer, Dietrich (1906–1945) was a German Lutheran pastor, theologian, and anti–Nazi dissident who was executed in the Nazi concentration camp, Flossenbürg. He is known for his works, such as *The Cost of Discipleship, Life Together,* and *Letters and Papers from Prison*, which explored themes of Christian ethics, the nature of discipleship, and resistance against injustice.

Boyce, James Petigru (1827–1888) was an American Baptist theologian and educator. He was one of the founders and the first president of the Southern Baptist Theological Seminary, and his *Abstract of Systematic Theology* contributed to the development of Baptist theology in the United States.

Boyd, Gregory A. (b. 1957) is an American theologian, pastor, and author. He is known for his work on open theism and his books, such as *God of the Possible*, engaging with topics like divine providence, free will, and the problem of evil.

Braaten, Carl E. (b. 1929) is an American Lutheran theologian and professor. He taught at Lutheran School of Theology at Chicago and his works, such as *The Future of God: A Practical Approach to Spirituality for Our Times*, engaged with topics like ecumenism, eschatology, and the relationship between theology and culture. With Robert W. Jensen, Braaten authored *Christian Dogmatics*.

Bray, Gerald L. (b. 1948), a British theologian and church historian, has made significant contributions to the study of Reformation theology and the history of Christianity. He has authored numerous books, including *The Doctrine of God*, *The Church: A Theological and Historical Account*, *God Has Spoken: A History of Christian Theology,* and *God Is Love: A Biblical and Systematic Theology.*

Bromiley, Geoffrey W. (1915–2009), a British-born historical theologian and church historian. Ordained in the Church of England, he taught at Fuller Theological Seminary for nearly three decades. Among his many writings, he authored *Historical Theology: An Introduction*, *Children of Promise: The Case for Baptizing Infants*, and *Introduction to the Theology of Karl Barth*.

Brown, Harold O. J. (1933–2007) was an American theologian and professor. He taught at Reformed Theological Seminary and his works, such as *Heresies: The Image of Christ in the Mirror of Heresy and Orthodoxy from the Apostles to the Present*, engaged with topics like heresy, orthodoxy, and the relationship between Christianity and culture.

Bruce, F. F. (1910–1990) was a Scottish-British biblical scholar and theologian, who associated with Plymouth Brethren Assemblies. A celebrated exegete, Bruce is known for his work in New Testament studies, particularly the historical reliability of the New Testament. His writings, such as *The New Testament Documents: Are They Reliable?* and

The Canon of Scripture, contributed to the field of biblical criticism and the study of early Christianity.

Brunner, Emil (1889–1966), a Swiss theologian, was a prominent figure in the neoorthodox movement. His works, such as *The Mediator: A Study of the Central Doctrine of the Christian Faith* (1927), sought to bridge the gap between liberal theology and traditional orthodoxy.

Bucer, Martin (1491–1551). A German Reformed theologian and reformer, Bucer played a significant role in the Protestant Reformation in Strasbourg. His works, such as *De Regno Christi* and *Concerning the True Care of Souls,* emphasized the importance of church reform and the role of the church in society. His *Summary of Christian Doctrine and Religion* affirmed the Lutheran emphasis on justification by faith alone, and emphasized the importance of the guidance of the Holy Spirit in reading Scripture.

Bulgakov, Sergei Nikolaevich (1870–1944). A Russian Orthodox theologian, priest, philosopher, and economist. Though never officially censured, his orthodoxy (particularly his teaching on sophiology) was challenged in some quarters. Among his many publications are *Unfading Light* (1917), *Jacob's Ladder* (1929), *The Orthodox Church* (1935), *The Comforter* (1936), and *The Wisdom of God: A Brief Summary of Sophiology* (1937).

Bullinger, E. W. (1837–1913). Anglican clergyman, biblical scholar, and ultradispensationalist theologian. A recognized scholar in biblical languages and an accomplished musician, among Bullinger's more important works are *A Critical Lexicon and Concordance to the English* *and Greek New Testamen*t; *Number in Scripture; Figures of Speech Used in the Bible; The Companion Bible* (he was the primary editor).

Bullinger, Johann Heinrich (1504–1575). A Swiss reformer, theologian, and pastor, Bullinger succeeded Huldrych Zwingli as the leader of the Reformed Church in Zürich. His works, such as *Decades* (1549–1551), provided a systematic exposition of Reformed theology and played a significant role in shaping the Reformed tradition, particularly with reference to ecclesiology, the Lord's Supper, and the relationship between church and state

Bunyan, John (1628–1688) was an English Puritan preacher and writer. He is best known for his allegorical work *The Pilgrim's Progress*, which engages with topics like the Christian journey, spiritual warfare, and the pursuit of holiness. He also authored a spiritual autobiography, *Grace Abounding to the Chief of Sinners*, as well as the weighty *Defense of Justification by Faith.*

Bushnell, Horace (1802–1876) was an American Congregationalist theologian and pastor. He played a significant role in the development of American theology in the 19th century. His works engage with topics like theology of childhood, the nature of conversion, and the relationship between faith and culture. Among his published works are *Christian Nurture* (1847), *God in Christ* (1849), *Nature and the Supernatural* (1858), and *The Vicarious Sacrifice* (1866).

Buswell, J. Oliver, Jr. (1895–1977) was an American Presbyterian theologian and educator. He served as the president of Wheaton College and Covenant College and his works, such as *A Systematic Theology of the Christian Religion*, contributed to the development of Reformed theology.

Butler, Joseph (1692–1752) was an English Anglican bishop and theologian, known for his moral philosophy. His magisterial *The Analogy of Religion, Natural and Revealed, to the Constitution and Course of Nature* (1736), is widely considered to be primarily responsible for the defeat of deism.

Caird, G. B. (1917–1984) was a British biblical scholar and theologian. He taught at Oxford University and his works, such as *The Language and Imagery of the Bible* and *The Revelation of St. John the Divine*, engaged with topics like biblical interpretation, hermeneutics, and the book of Revelation.

Cajetan, Thomas de Vio (1469–1534). Philosopher, theologian, Bible scholar, and Roman Catholic cardinal, remembered for his heated encounter with Martin Luther at Augsburg. A prolific author, Cajetan published some 115 works, including a classic commentary on Aquinas's *Summa Theologicae*.

Calvin, John (1509–1564), a French theologian and pastor, was a prominent figure in the Protestant Reformation. His theological system, known as Calvinism or Reformed theology, emphasized the sovereignty of God, predestination, and the authority of Scripture. Calvin commented extensively on Scripture, and authored the classic *Institutes of the Christian Religion*, as well as *Summa Pietatis*.

Campbell, John McLeod (1800–1872) was a Scottish minister and theologian. He is known for his views on Christ's atonement, which were controversial at the time. His works engage with topics like the nature of Christ's atonement, the love of God, and the relationship between sin and salvation.

Carlstadt, Andreas von (1486–1541) was a German theologian and reformer. He was an early associate of Martin Luther and his works engage with topics like ecclesiology, the nature of the sacraments, and the relationship between faith and works.

Carnell, Edward John (1919–1967) was an American evangelical theologian and apologist. He taught at Fuller Theological Seminary and his works, such as *The Case for Orthodox Theology*, engage with topics like theological method, and the defense of the Christian faith.

Carson, D. A. (b. 1946) is a Canadian–born American evangelical theologian and professor. He taught at Trinity Evangelical Divinity School and his works, such as *The Gospel According to John*, contributed to the understanding of the New Testament and its theological themes. He has also written works such as *Exegetical Fallacies*, *The Enduring Authority of the Christian Scriptures,* and *The Gagging of God: Christianity Confronts Pluralism.*

Cassian, John (*ca.* 360–*ca.* 435), a monk and theologian, played a significant role in the development of Western monasticism. His works, such as *Conferences* and *Institutes*, provided guidance on the spiritual life and influenced the Rule of St. Benedict.

Catherine of Siena (1347–1380), an Italian mystic and theologian, played a significant role in the 14th-century papal politics and the Avignon

Papacy. Her writings, such as *The Dialogue*, addressed spiritual and political matters and emphasized the importance of personal holiness.

Chafer, Lewis Sperry (1871–1952) was an American theologian and pastor. He founded Dallas Theological Seminary and his eight-volume *Systematic Theology* provided a dispensationalist perspective on Christian doctrine. Chafer wrote numerous other works, including *Major Bible Themes, He That Is Spiritual, Salvation: A Clear Doctrinal Analysis,* and *Satan: His Motives and Methods.*

Charnock, Stephen (1628–1680) was an English Puritan theologian and preacher. He is best known for his work *The Existence and Attributes of God*, which explores the nature and character of God.

Chemnitz, Martin (1522–1586) was a German Lutheran theologian and reformer. He played a significant role in the development of Lutheran theology. His works include the four-volume *Examen Concilii Tridentini* and *Loci Theologici*. Of note, too, is Chemnitz's *De Duabus Naturis in Christo* (*The Two Natures in Christ*, 1578) a significant work on the incarnation.

Clark, Gordon H. (1902–1985) was an American philosopher and theologian. He taught at Butler University and his works, such as *Religion, Reason, and Revelation*, engage with topics like epistemology, the relationship between faith and reason, and the nature of truth. He is known for his defense of presuppositional apologetics and his works, such as *The Philosophy of Science and Belief in God*, engaged with the intersection of philosophy and theology.

Clarke, Adam (1762–1832), an Irish Methodist theologian and biblical scholar, is known for his extensive commentary on the Bible. His work *Commentary on the Bible* provided detailed explanations of the Scriptures and engaged with critical scholarship.

Clement of Alexandria (*ca.* 150–*ca.* 215), a Christian theologian from Egypt, was known for his synthesis of Greek philosophy and Christian theology. His works, such as *Stromata*, explored the relationship between faith and reason and emphasized the importance of moral development in the Christian life.

Cocceius, Johannes (1603–1669) was a Dutch Reformed theologian and professor. He is known for his work on covenant theology and his emphasis on the continuity between the Old and New Testaments, particularly in his *Summa doctrinae de foedere et testament Dei* (*The Doctrine of the Covenant and Testament of God*).

Cone, James Hal (1938–2018) was an American theologian and advocate for black liberation theology. He is known for his influential works, such as *Black Theology and Black Power*, which engage with topics like racial justice, the relationship between Christianity and black liberation, and the intersection of theology and social activism.

Congar, Yves (1904–1995) was a French Dominican theologian and cardinal. He played a significant role in the development of Catholic ecumenism and his works, such as *The Meaning of Tradition*, contributed to the renewal of Catholic theology in the 20th century.

Conn, Harvie M. (1933–1999) was an American missiologist and theologian. He taught at Westminster Theological Seminary and his works, such as *Eternal Word and Changing Worlds: Theology, Anthropology, and Mission in Trialogue*, engaged with topics like missiology, cultural engagement, and the relationship between theology and mission.

Copan, Paul (b. 1962) is an American philosopher and theologian. He teaches at Palm Beach Atlantic University and his works engage with topics like ethics, biblical interpretation, and the problem of evil. Among his many titles are *Loving Wisdom: A Guide to Philosophy and Christian Faith*, *That's Just Your Interpretation*, and *Is God a Moral Monster? Making Sense of the Old Testament God.*

Craig, William Lane (b. 1949) is an American philosopher, theologian, and apologist. He is known for his work in philosophy of religion and apologetics, particularly in the areas of theistic arguments and the historical evidence for the resurrection of Jesus. Among his better-known works are *Reasonable Faith, The Kalām Cosmological Argument*, and *In Quest of the Historical Jesus.*

Cranmer, Thomas (1489–1556) was an English archbishop and theologian. He played a significant role in the English Reformation, in the development of the *Book of Common Prayer*, and in the establishment of the Church of England.

Cullmann, Oscar (1902–1999) was a French Protestant theologian and professor. He taught at the University of Basel and his works engage with topics like New Testament theology, eschatology, and the relationship between history and faith. His works include *Christ in Time, Early*

Christian Worship, *Salvation in History*, and *The Christology of the New Testament*.

Culver, Robert D. (1916–2015) was an American theologian and professor. He taught at Wheaton College and his works, such as *Systematic Theology: Biblical and Historical*, provide a comprehensive treatment of Christian doctrine from an evangelical perspective.

Cunningham, William (1805–1861) was a Scottish theologian and professor. He is known for his work on historical theology and his engagement with theological controversies of his time. His works include the classic two-volume *Historical Theology*.

Cyprian of Carthage (d. 258) was a bishop and theologian in early Christianity. He is known for his writings on the unity of the church and his defense of the authority of bishops. His works engage with topics like ecclesiology, the nature of the sacraments, and the relationship between church and state. Along with a large corpus of letters (the *Epistles*), Cyril also authored a dozen or so treatises, including an appeal *To Donatus*; the compendium of Scripture texts, *To Quirinus*; as well as *On the Unity of the Church*, *On the Lord's Prayer*, and *On the Lapsed*.

Cyril of Alexandria (*ca.* 376–*ca.* 444), a bishop and theologian from Alexandria, played a significant role in the Christological controversies of the 5th century. He defended the orthodox understanding of the Incarnation and the unity of Christ's divine and human natures. His writings include *Discourse Against the Arians* and *Dialogues on the Trinity*.

Cyril of Jerusalem (*ca.* 313–*ca.* 386), a bishop and theologian from Jerusalem, is known for his *Catechetical Lectures* that provided instruction to new converts to Christianity. His teachings on the sacraments and the nature of Christ had a lasting impact on the development of Christian doctrine.

Dabney, Robert Lewis (1820–1898) was an American Presbyterian theologian and professor. He taught at Union Theological Seminary and his works, such as *Systematic Theology*, engage with topics like theology proper, the doctrine of God, and the relationship between theology and culture.

Damian, Peter (1007–1072), an Italian cardinal and theologian, played a significant role in church reform during the 11th century. His voluminous writings (treatises, letters, sermons, hymns, etc.) addressed a wide variety of issues, including clerical celibacy, simony, the need for moral and spiritual renewal within the Church, and Mary. Notable works include *De Divina Omniptentia*, *Dominus vobiscum*, *Officium Beatae Virginis*, and *De Institutione moralis*.

Darby, John Nelson (1800–1882) was an Irish theologian and pastor. He is known for his role in the development of dispensationalism and his works (e.g., the popular five-volume *Synopsis of the Books of the Bible*) engage with topics like eschatology, the nature of the church, and the interpretation of biblical prophecy. His voluminous writings (fifty-two volumes in his *Collected Writings*) cover a myriad of topics, including apologetics, doctrine, biblical exposition, prophecy, and so forth.

Davis, John Jefferson (b. 1946), an American theologian, is known for his work in the fields of systematic theology and ethics. He has authored several books, including *Foundations of Evangelical Theology* and *Evangelical Ethics: Issues Facing the Church Today*, and has taught at various seminaries and universities.

de Molina, Luis (1535–1600), a Spanish Jesuit theologian, is known for his contributions to the theological debate on divine grace and human free will. His works, such as *Concordia* and *On Divine Foreknowledge,* proposed a middle ground between the views of Thomas Aquinas and John Calvin.

Demarest, Bruce A. (1935–2021) was an American theologian and professor. He taught at Denver Seminary and his works, such as *The Cross and Salvation: The Doctrine of Salvation*, provided a comprehensive treatment of soteriology from an evangelical perspective. With Gordon Lewis he coauthored the three-volume *Integrative Theology*.

Denney, James (1856–1917) was a Scottish theologian and professor at the United Free Church College in Glasgow. He is known for his work on Christ's atonement and authored *The Death of Christ*.

Dulles, Avery (1918–2008) was an American Jesuit priest, theologian, and cardinal. He played a significant role in the development of Catholic theology in the United States and his works, such as *Models of the Church* and *The Craft of Theology*, engaged with topics like ecclesiology and the nature of theology.

Dunn, James D. G. (1939–2020) was a British New Testament scholar and professor emeritus at University of Durham. He is known for his work on the New Perspective on Paul and authored *The Theology of Paul the Apostle*.

Duns Scotus, John (1266–1308), a Franciscan friar and philosopher from Scotland, was known for his intricate philosophical system and defense of the Immaculate Conception. His work on metaphysics and theology had a significant impact on later scholastic thought.

Dwight, Timothy (1752–1817) was an American Congregationalist theologian and educator. He served as the president of Yale University and his works, such as *Theology Explained and Defended*, engage with topics like systematic theology, the doctrines of God, Christ, and the Church, and the relationship between theology and education.

Eck, Johann (1486–1543) was a German Catholic theologian and opponent of Martin Luther. He engaged in theological debates with Luther and his works engage with topics like ecclesiology, justification by faith, and the authority of Scripture. His writings include *Enchiridion locorum communium adversus Lutherum et alios hostes ecclesiae*.

Eckhart, Johannes (1260–1328), a German theologian and mystic known popularly as Meister Eckhart, was a leading figure in the medieval mystical tradition. His sermons and writings, such as *The Talks of Instruction*, explored topics like the nature of God, the soul, and the union of the individual with the divine.

Edwards, Jonathan (1703–1758) was an American theologian and pastor, was a key figure in the First Great Awakening. Known for his powerful sermons and writings, such as *Sinners in the Hands of an Angry God* and *Religious Affections,* Edwards emphasized the sovereignty of God and the importance of personal religious experience.

Enns, Paul (b. 1937) was a professor at Dallas Theological Seminary and is an adjunct professor at Southeastern Baptist Theological Seminary, who has written extensively on systematic theology. His notable publications include *The Moody Handbook of Theology*.

Erasmus, Desiderius (1469–1536), a Dutch humanist and theologian, was a leading figure in the Northern Renaissance. His works, such as *The Praise of Folly* and *The Handbook of the Christian Soldier*, criticized the corruption and abuses within the Church and advocated for a return to the teachings of Christ.

Erickson, Millard J. (b. 1932), an American theologian and professor, is known for his work in systematic theology. His book *Christian Theology* is widely used as a textbook in evangelical seminaries and provides a comprehensive overview of Christian doctrine, and has been abridged as *Introducing Christian Doctrine*. Among Erickson's other writings are the handy *Concise Dictionary of Christian Theology.*

Eriugena, John Scotus (815–877), an Irish theologian, philosopher, and poet, was known for his synthesis of Neoplatonism and Christian theology. His work *De Divisione Naturae* explored the relationship between God, creation, and the human soul.

Eusebius of Caesarea (*ca.* 260–*ca.* 340), a historian and bishop, is known as the Father of Church History. His work *Ecclesiastical History* is a valuable source of information on the early Christian Church and its development.

Farel, Guillaume (1489–1565) was a French Reformed theologian and pastor. He played a significant role in the Reformation in Switzerland and his works engage with topics like evangelism, church discipline, and the authority of Scripture.

Fee, Gordon (b. 1934) is an American Pentecostal theologian and professor. He taught at Regent College and his works, such as *God's Empowering Presence: The Holy Spirit in the Letters of Paul*, contributed to the understanding of the Holy Spirit and the interpretation of the New Testament. He has also authored (with Douglas Stuart) the widely-used *How to Read the Bible for All Its Worth.*

Fenelon (1651–1715), a French archbishop and spiritual writer, is known for his devotional and mystical works. His writings, such as *The Maxims of the Saints* and *Spiritual Letters*, emphasized the importance of inner transformation, humility, and the pursuit of union with God.

Ferguson, Sinclair (b. 1948) is a Scottish Reformed theologian and pastor. He served as the senior minister of First Presbyterian Church in Columbia. He has written extensively on various theological topics, including *The Holy Spirit,* and *The Whole Christ: Legalism, Antinomianism, and Gospel Assurance—Why the Marrow Controversy Still Matters.*

Finney, Charles G. (1792–1875) was an American evangelist and theologian. He played a significant role in the Second Great Awakening and his works, such as *Lectures on Revivals of Religion*, engage with topics like revivalism, conversion, and the nature of faith.

Fisher, Edward (fl. 1627–1655) was an English Puritan theologian and pastor. He is known for his work *The Marrow of Modern Divinity*, which engages with topics like the nature of the gospel, the relationship between law and grace, and the doctrine of justification.

Flavel, John (1627–1691), an English Puritan preacher and writer, is known for his devotional and practical works. His writings, such as *The Mystery of Providence* and *The Fountain of Life*, emphasized the sovereignty of God, the importance of faith, and the pursuit of holiness.

Flowers, Leighton (b. 1974) is an American theologian and pastor, Professor of Theology at Trinity Seminary and Director of Evangelism and Apologetics for Texas Baptists. He is associated with the provisionist perspective within Southern Baptist theology and his works and podcasts (especially on Soteriology101) engage with topics like soteriology, divine sovereignty, and the nature of human free will. His published books include *The Potter's Promise: A Biblical Defense of Traditional Soteriology,* and *God's Provision for All: A Defense of God's Goodness*.

Fox, George (1624–1691) was an English founder of the Quaker movement. He emphasized the direct experience of God's presence and his works engage with topics like mysticism, pacifism, and the nature of the church.

Frame, John M. (b. 1939) is an American Reformed theologian and professor. He taught at Reformed Theological Seminary and his works, such as *The Doctrine of the Knowledge of God*, contributed to the development of presuppositional apologetics and engaged with topics like epistemology and the nature of God. He has also authored *Systematic Theology: An Introduction to Christian Belief* and the briefer *Salvation Belongs to the Lord: An Introduction to Systematic Theology.*

France, R. T. (1938–2012) was an English Anglican theologian and biblical scholar. He is known for his work on the New Testament, particularly his commentaries on the Gospels. He has also written *The Evidence for Jesus* and *Jesus and the Old Testament.*

Garrett, James Leo, Jr. (1925–2020), was an American Baptist theologian who taught at Southern Baptist Theological Seminary, Baylor University, and was Distinguished Professor Emeritus of Theology at Southwestern Baptist Theological Seminary. He was a leading figure in Baptist theology and church history. His works, such as the exhaustive *Baptist Theologians: A Four-Century Study* and the meticulously footnoted two-volume *Systematic Theology: Biblical, Historical, and Evangelical*, have been influential in shaping Baptist thought and practice.

Garrigou–Lagrange, Reginald (1877–1964) was a French philosopher, Dominican theologian, and professor at the Pontifical University of St. Thomas Aquinas in Rome. He is known for his work in Thomistic philosophy and theology, particularly on the topics of grace and predestination. Among his many works are *Reality: A Synthesis of Thomistic Thought, Predestination*, *Providence*, and *God, His Existence and Nature: A Thomistic Solution of Certain Agnostic Antinomies.*

Geisler, Norman L. (1932–2019), an American systematic theologian, apologist, and philosopher. Cofounder of two nondenominational evangelical seminaries (Veritas International University and Southern Evangelical Seminary), founder and first president of the International Society of Christian Apologetics, and one of the primary architects of the Chicago Statement on Biblical Inerrancy. Geisler made scholarly contributions (as author, coauthor, or editor of over ninety books and hundreds of articles) to the subjects of systematic theology, classical Christian apologetics, ethics, philosophy of religion, and more. Among his authored works are *Christian Apologetics, Christian Ethics,* and the four-volume *Systematic Theology*.

George, Timothy (b. 1950) is an American Baptist theologian and professor. He taught at Beeson Divinity School and his works, such as *Theology of the Reformers*, contributed to the understanding of the Protestant Reformation and its theological themes.

Gerhard, Johannes (1582–1637), a German Lutheran theologian, made significant contributions to Lutheran orthodoxy. His works, such as *Loci Theologici*, provided a systematic exposition of Lutheran theology and engaged with theological controversies of his time.

Gerson, Jean (1363–1429), a French theologian and chancellor of the University of Paris, played a significant role in the Western Schism and the Council of Constance. His works, such as *On the Unity of the Church*, addressed issues of church reform and the authority of the papacy.

Gerstner, John H. (1914–1996) was an American Reformed theologian and professor. He is known for his work on historical theology and his defense of Reformed theology. His works include *A Predestination*

Primer and *Repent or Perish: With Special Reference to the Conservative Attack on Hell.*

Gill, John (1697–1771), an English Baptist pastor and theologian, is known for his extensive biblical commentaries. His works, such as *Exposition of the Old and New Testaments*, provided detailed explanations of the Scriptures from a Calvinistic perspective.

Gottschalk (*ca.* 808–*ca.* 867), a theologian and monk, was known for his controversial views on predestination. His teachings on double predestination and the inability of humans to resist God's grace led to conflicts with church authorities and his eventual condemnation.

Greggs, Tom (b. 1980), is a British theologian, Professor of Divinity at the University of Aberdeen, Methodist preacher, and serves in the Faith and Order Commission of the World Council of Churches. Among his published works are *New Perspectives for Evangelical Theology* (2010) and Introduction *to Christian Theology: A Comprehensive, Systematically and Biblically Based Approach* (2024).

Gregory of Nazianzus (*ca.* 329–389), also known as Gregory the Theologian or Gregory Nazianzen, was a prominent theologian and bishop in the 4th century. His writings, such as his *Five Theological Orations*, played a significant role in shaping the doctrine of the Trinity and defending orthodox Christianity.

Gregory of Nyssa (*ca.* 335–395), a theologian and bishop, was one of the Cappadocian Fathers who shaped early Christian thought. His writings, such as *The Life of Moses* and *On the Soul and the Resurrection,* explored topics like the nature of God, the human soul, and the process of sanctification.

Gregory the Great (*ca.* 540–604), also known as Pope Gregory I, was a pope and theologian who had a profound impact on the development of medieval Christianity. His writings, such as *Pastoral Rule* and *Dialogues*, addressed topics like pastoral care, monasticism, and the authority of the papacy.

Grenz, Stanley J. (1950–2005) was an American evangelical theologian and professor. He taught at Carey Theological College and his writings engage with topics like theological method, ecclesiology, and the relationship between theology and postmodernity. Among his works are *Theology for the Community of God, Created for Community: Connecting Christian Belief with Christian Living, Renewing the Center: Evangelical Theology in a Post–Christian Era,* and *Revisioning Evangelical Theology: A Fresh Agenda for the 21st Century*

Grider, J. Kenneth (1913–2006) was an American theologian and professor. He taught at Nazarene Theological Seminary and his works, such as *A Wesleyan–Holiness Theology*, contributed to the development of Wesleyan–Holiness theology.

Groote, Gerhard (1340–1384) was a Dutch theologian and founder of the Brethren of the Common Life. He emphasized the importance of personal piety and his works engage with topics like spiritual formation, the imitation of Christ, and the pursuit of holiness.

Groothuis, Douglas (b. 1957) is a prominent American Christian philosopher and apologist. He taught at Denver Seminary for three decades and his many works, such as *Christian Apologetics: A Comprehensive Case for Biblical Faith*, engage with topics like apologetics and philosophy of religion.

Grotius, Hugo (1583–1645), a Dutch jurist and theologian, is known for his contributions to international law and natural law theory. His work *The Law of War and Peace* emphasized the importance of just war theory and influenced the development of international legal principles.

Grounds, Vernon (1914–2010) was an American evangelical theologian and educator. He served as the president of Denver Seminary and his works, such as *The Reason for Our Hope* and *The Challenge of Humanism,* engaged with topics like apologetics, ethics, and the relationship between Christianity and culture.

Grudem, Wayne (b. 1948), an American evangelical theologian and professor, is known for his work in systematic theology and biblical studies. He is a professor of theology and biblical studies at Phoenix Seminary and has also taught at several other institutions. His book *Systematic Theology: An Introduction to Biblical Doctrine* is widely used in evangelical seminaries and provides a comprehensive treatment of Christian doctrine. He has also written *Christian Ethics: An Introduction to Biblical Moral Reasoning* and *Politics—According to the Bible: A Comprehensive Resource for Understanding Modern Political Issues in Light of Scripture.*

Gulley, Norman R. (1932–2019) was an American Seventh–day Adventist theologian and professor. He taught at Southern Adventist

University and his works, such as his four-volume *Systematic Theology* provided a comprehensive treatment of Adventist theology.

Gunton, Colin (1941–2003) was an English Reformed systematic theologian. He made significant contributions to the doctrine of creation and the doctrine of the Trinity. He taught at King's College, London. With Christoph Schwoebel he co-founded the Research Institute for Systematic Theology. He also co-founded the *International Journal of Systematic Theology* with John B. Webster.

Harnack, Adolf von (1851–1930). German theologian and church historian. He played a significant role in the development of liberal theology and his works, such as *History of Dogma* and *What Is Christianity?*, influenced the study of early Christian history and theology.

Harwood, Adam (b. 1974), an American theologian and professor, is known for his work in theological anthropology and soteriology. He has written on topics such as the nature of human free will and the extent of Christ's atonement. He gained attention with his *The Spiritual Condition of Infants: A Biblical-Historical Survey and Systematic Proposal,* and recently published *Christian Theology: Biblical, Historical, Systematic.*

Helwys, Thomas (*ca.* 1575–*ca.* 1616), an English Baptist leader, is considered one of the founders of the Baptist tradition. He advocated for religious freedom and separation of church and state, and his work *A Short Declaration of the Mystery of Iniquity* defended the rights of conscience.

Henry, Carl F. H. (1913–2003), an American evangelical theologian, was a leading figure in the mid-20th-century evangelical movement. He co–founded *Christianity Today* and authored numerous books, including *God, Revelation, and Authority*, which addressed issues of biblical authority and the nature of God.

Heppe, Heinrich (1820–1879) was a German Reformed theologian and professor. He taught at the University of Marburg and his works, such as *Reformed Dogmatics*, engage with topics like Reformed theology, the doctrines of God, Christ, the church, and the sacraments.

Hilary of Poitiers (*ca.* 310–*ca.* 368), a bishop and theologian, played a significant role in the development of early Christian theology. His works, such as *On the Trinity* and *On the Councils*, defended orthodox Christian beliefs and engaged with theological controversies of his time.

Hodge, A. A. (1823–1886), the son of Charles Hodge, was an American Presbyterian theologian and educator. He followed in his father's footsteps and became a professor at Princeton Theological Seminary. His work focused on defending Reformed theology and addressing contemporary theological challenges. He authored the widely used *Outlines of Theology*.

Hodge, Charles (1797–1878), an American Presbyterian theologian, was a leading figure in 19th-century Reformed theology. He served as a professor at Princeton Theological Seminary and his three-volume *Systematic Theology* became a standard text in Reformed circles.

Hoekema, Anthony A. (1913–1988) was a Dutch-American Reformed theologian and professor. He taught at Calvin Theological Seminary and his works, such as *Created in God's Image* and *The Bible and the Future*, provided a systematic exposition of Reformed theology, particularly in the areas of anthropology and eschatology.

Hoeksema, Herman (1886–1965) was a Dutch-American Reformed theologian and pastor. He is known for his defense of the Reformed doctrine of predestination and his contributions to the field of systematic theology, particularly in his *Reformed Dogmatics*.

Hollaz, David (1648–1713), a German Lutheran theologian, made significant contributions to Lutheran orthodoxy. His work *Examen Theologicum Acroamaticum* provided a comprehensive treatment of Lutheran theology and engaged with theological controversies.

Holsteen, Nathan D. (b. 1961), is an American theologian and professor. He teaches at Dallas Theological Seminary and his works, such as *The Historical Reliability of the New Testament: Countering the Challenges to Evangelical Christian Beliefs,* engage with topics like biblical criticism, the reliability of the New Testament, and the historical Jesus. With Michael J. Svigel he has edited the three-volume *Exploring Christian Theology.*

Hooker, Richard (1554–1600), an English theologian and Anglican priest, is known for his work *Of the Laws of Ecclesiastical Polity*. His writings defended the authority of the Church of England and advocated for a moderate approach to theological controversies.

Horton, Michael (b. 1964) is an American Reformed theologian and professor. He teaches at Westminster Seminary California and his works, such as *The Christian Faith: A Systematic Theology for Pilgrims on the*

Way, engage with topics like systematic theology, the doctrine of God, and the nature of the church.

Hovey, Alvah (1820–1903) was an American Baptist theologian and educator. He served as the president of Newton Theological Institution (now Andover Newton Seminary) and his works, such as *Outlines of Theology*, contributed to the development of Baptist theology in the United States.

Hoyt, Herman A. (1914–1992), was an American theologian and educator. He served as the president of Grace Theological Seminary and his works, such as *The End Times* and *The Judgment Seat of Christ*, engaged with topics like eschatology and Christian ethics.

Hugh of St. Victor (1078–1151), a German theologian and mystic, was a leading figure in the 12th-century Renaissance. His works, such as *Didascalicon*, emphasized the importance of education and the integration of faith and reason.

Hus, Jan (1369–1415) was a Czech theologian and reformer. He played a significant role in the Bohemian Reformation and his works, particularly *De Ecclesia*, engage with topics like ecclesiology, the authority of Scripture, and the relationship between church and state. His teachings, which emphasized the authority of Scripture and criticized church corruption, led to his condemnation and execution.

Ignatius of Antioch (*ca.* 35–*ca.* 108), an early Christian bishop and martyr, was known for his strong defense of orthodox Christian beliefs. His seven letters, written during his journey to martyrdom, provide valuable insights into early Christian theology and the organization of the Church.

Irenaeus of Lyons (*ca.* 120–*ca.* 202), a bishop and theologian, played a crucial role in combating heresies and defending orthodox Christianity. His work *Against Heresies* provided a comprehensive refutation of Gnostic teachings and emphasized the importance of apostolic tradition.

Ironside, H. A. (1876–1951) was a prominent American Bible teacher and pastor. He served as the pastor of Moody Church in Chicago and is known for his expository preaching. Ironside authored numerous books, including *The Four Hundred Silent Years, Except Ye Repent*, and *Holiness: The False and the True*.

Isidore of Seville (*ca.* 560–*ca.* 626), a bishop and scholar, was a leading figure in early medieval education and scholarship. His work *Etymologiae* was an influential encyclopedia that covered a wide range of topics, including theology, philosophy, and natural sciences.

Jenson, Robert (1930–2017) was a leading American Lutheran and ecumenical theologian. He served as the director for the Center for Theological Inquiry at Princeton Theological Seminary, and was the co-founder of the Center for Catholic and Evangelical Theology. He is known for his two-volume *Systematic Theology*.

Jewett, Paul K. (1919–1991) was an American theologian and professor at Fuller Theological Seminary. He is known for his work on gender and theology, particularly his book *Man as Male and Female: A Study in Sexual Relationships from a Theological Point of View*.

John Chrysostom (347–407), an Archbishop of Constantinople, was a renowned preacher and theologian in the early Church. Known for his eloquence and moral teachings, his sermons and writings had a lasting impact on Christian spirituality and social ethics.

John of Damascus (*ca.* 675–749) was a Syrian monk, theologian, and hymnographer. He played a significant role in the development of Eastern Orthodox theology and his works, such as *Exact Exposition of the Orthodox Faith*, defended orthodox Christianity against various heresies and contributed to the development of Eastern Orthodox theology. He is also known for his defense of the use of icons in Christian worship.

Johnson, S. Lewis (1915–2004) was an American Presbyterian theologian and professor. He taught at Dallas Theological Seminary and his expository preaching and teaching ministry focused on biblical theology and the study of the Old Testament. Among his writings are *The Old Testament in the New: An Argument for Biblical Inspiration*.

Julian of Norwich (1342–1413), an English mystic and theologian, is known for her mystical experiences and her work *Revelations of Divine Love*. Her writings emphasized God's love and the importance of contemplative prayer.

Jüngel, Eberhard (1934–2021), was a German Lutheran theologian. He was Emeritus Professor of systematic Theology and the Philosophy of Religion at the Faculty of Protestant Theology at the University of Tübingen. He is known for his work on the theology of Martin Luther and Karl Barth, mand his contributions to the understanding of sacraments.

Among his works are *God's Being is in Becoming: The Trinitarian Being of God in the Theology of Karl Barth.*

Justin Martyr (*ca.* 110–*ca.* 165), an early Christian apologist and philosopher, sought to reconcile Christianity with Greek philosophy. His works, such as *First Apology* and *Dialogue with Trypho*, defended Christian beliefs and engaged in dialogue with non–Christians.

Kaiser, Walter, Jr. (b. 1933) is an American Old Testament scholar and theologian. He taught at Gordon–Conwell Theological Seminary and his works, such as *Toward an Old Testament Theology*, contributed to the understanding of the Old Testament and its theological themes.

Kapic, Kelly M. (b. 1972) is an American theologian and professor. He teaches at Covenant College and his works, such as *A Little Book for New Theologians: Why and How to Study Theology*, engage with topics like theological education, spiritual formation, and the importance of theology for the Christian life.

Kärkkäinen, Veli-Matti (b. 1958) is a Finnish theologian and a professor of Systematic Theology at Fuller Seminary. He is known for his work in global theology and has published books on the subject, including a five-volume series on *Constructive Christian Theology for the Pluralistic World.*

Keener, Craig S. (b. 1960) is an American New Testament scholar and professor. He teaches at Asbury Theological Seminary and his works, such as *The IVP Bible Background Commentary: New Testament*, engage with topics like biblical interpretation, historical context, and the social world of the New Testament. Among his many works are *The Jesus of the Gospels, Christobiography,* and *Miracles: The Credibility of the New Testament Gospels.*

Kelly, Douglas F. (b. 1943) is a Scottish-American Reformed theologian and professor. He teaches at Reformed Theological Seminary and his works include a three-volume *Systematic Theology.*

Kempis, Thomas à (*ca.* 1380–1471) was a German–Dutch monk and author. He is best known for his devotional work *The Imitation of Christ*, which has had a significant influence on Christian spirituality.

Kierkegaard, Søren (1813–1855) was a Danish philosopher, theologian, and writer. He is considered one of the founders of existentialism and his works, such as *Fear and Trembling* and *The Sickness Unto Death*, engage with topics like faith, despair, and the nature of the self.

Kline, Meredith G. (1922–2007) was an American Reformed theologian and professor. He is known for his work on biblical theology and his contributions to the field of covenant theology, particularly in *The Treaty of the Great King* and *The Structure of Biblical Authority*.

Knight, George A. F. (1909–2002) was a New Testament scholar and professor at the University of St. Andrews, and President of the Pacific Theological College. He is known for his work on the historical Jesus and authored *The Jesus of History*.

Knox, John (*ca.* 1513–1572), a Scottish reformer and theologian, was a key figure in the Scottish Reformation. His works, such as *The First Blast of the Trumpet Against the Monstrous Regiment of Women* and *The Book of Common Order,* advocated for the establishment of a reformed church in Scotland.

Küng, Hans (1928–2021), a Swiss Catholic theologian, is known for his work in ecumenism and interreligious dialogue. He has written extensively on topics such as the nature of God, the role of the Church, and the relationship between Christianity and other religions. His writings include *Justification: The Doctrine of Karl Barth and a Catholic Reflection, The Church, Infallible? An Inquiry,* and *On Being a Christian.*

Kuyper, Abraham (1837–1920) was a Dutch theologian, politician, and journalist. He played a significant role in the development of Reformed theology and was a key figure in the formation of the Anti–Revolutionary Party in the Netherlands. Among his better-known works is *Principles of Sacred Theology.*

CHAPTER SIX:
BIOGRAPHICAL SKETCHES OF KEY THEOLOGIANS, PART II

THE following continues from the previous chapter, and covers letters L through Z.

Lactantius (*ca*. 250–*ca*. 325), an early Christian author from North Africa, was known for his apologetic and theological writings. His work *Divine Institutes* defended Christianity against pagan criticisms and influenced the development of Christian thought.

Ladd, George E. (1911–1982) was an American New Testament scholar and professor at Fuller Theological Seminary. He is known for his work on the kingdom of God and authored *A Theology of the New Testament* and *The Presence of the Future: The Eschatology of Biblical Realism*.

Lane, A. N. S. (b. 1945) is a British Anglican theologian and professor. He taught at London School of Theology and his works, such as *The Gospel According to Mark*, contributed to the understanding of the New Testament and its theological themes. He has written *Exploring Christian Doctrine: A Guide to What Christians Believe.*

Lane, William L. (1931–1999) was an American biblical scholar and theologian. He taught at Western Kentucky University and his works, such as the commentary on the Gospel of Mark in the *New International Commentary on the New Testament* series, contributed to the understanding of the biblical text.

Lemke, Steve (b. 1951) is an American theologian and professor. He teaches at New Orleans Baptist Theological Seminary and his works, such as *Baptist Theology: A Four-Century Study*, engage with topics like Baptist history, theology, and the distinctive beliefs and practices of Baptists.

Leo the Great (*ca.* 400–*ca.* 461), also known as Pope Leo I, was a pope and theologian who played a crucial role in shaping the doctrine of the papacy and defending orthodox Christianity. His writings, such as his *Tome to Flavian* and his sermons on the incarnation, had a lasting impact on the development of Christian theology.

Letham, Robert (b. 1947) is a British Reformed theologian and Professor of Systematic and Historical Theology at Union School of Theology, and is an Adjunct Professor at Westminster Theological Seminary. His works, such as *The Holy Trinity: In Scripture, History, Theology, and Worship*, contributed to the understanding of the doctrine of the Trinity. He has also authored *Systematic Theology*.

Lewis, Gordon R. (1917–1991) was an American theologian and professor. He taught at Denver Seminary and his works, such as the three-volume *Integrative Theology* (co-authored with Bruce Demarest) provided a comprehensive treatment of Christian doctrine from an evangelical perspective.

Lightner, Robert P. (1931–2018), an American theologian and professor, specialized in systematic theology and eschatology. He taught at Dallas Theological Seminary and authored books such as *The Last Days Handbook, The Death Christ Died*, and *Handbook of Evangelical Theology*.

Lindsell, Harold (1913–1998) was a one of the founding members of and a professor at Fuller Theological Seminary and served as the editor of Christianity Today. He is best known for his 1976 book *The Battle for the Bible*, which addressed the issue of biblical inerrancy.

Litton, Edward Arthur (1813–1897) was an English Anglican theologian and bishop. He served as the Bishop of Salisbury and his works, such as *Introduction to Dogmatic Theology*, engage with topics like systematic theology, the nature of God, and the doctrines of the Christian faith.

Lombard, Peter (*ca.* 1096–1159), an Italian theologian and bishop, is best known for his work *Sentences*, which became a standard theological textbook in the Middle Ages. His compilation of theological opinions and arguments influenced later scholastic thinkers.

Lonergan, Bernard (1904–1984) was a Canadian Jesuit priest, philosopher, and theologian. He is known for his work in systematic theology and philosophy of religion, particularly in the areas of epistemology and method in theology. His works include *Method in Theology, Insight: A Study of Human Understanding,* and the two-volume *De Deo Trino.*

Lucian of Antioch (*ca.* 240–312) was a theologian and martyr in early Christianity. He played a significant role in the development of biblical textual criticism and his works engage with topics like the nature of the Trinity, the authority of Scripture, and the relationship between faith and reason.

Luther, Martin (1483–1546), a German monk and theologian, was a key figure in the Protestant Reformation. His Ninety–Five Theses, which criticized the Catholic Church's sale of indulgences, sparked a movement that led to the formation of Protestant Christianity.

MacArthur, John (b. 1939), an American pastor and author, is known for his conservative evangelical theology and his emphasis on expository preaching. He has written numerous books, including *The Gospel According to Jesus,* and is the founder of Grace to You, a Christian radio ministry. With Richard Mayhue, he has authored *Biblical Doctrine: A Systematic Summary of Bible Truth.*

Machen, J. Gresham (1881–1937) was an American Presbyterian theologian and professor. He played a significant role in the defense of orthodox Christianity against liberal theology and his work *Christianity and Liberalism* critiqued the theological liberalism of his time.

MacRae, Allan A. (1902–1997) was an American Presbyterian theologian and professor. He served as the president of Faith Theological Seminary and his works, such as *Christianity and the World Religions*, engaged with the study of comparative religion and apologetics.

Marshall, I. Howard (1934–2015) was a British New Testament scholar and theologian. He taught at the University of Aberdeen and his works, such as *New Testament Theology: Many Witnesses, One Gospel,* contributed to the understanding of the New Testament and its theological themes.

Martin, Walter R. (1928–1989). American Baptist minister and author who founded Christian Research Institute in 1960 as a parachurch ministry specializing in general Christian apologetics and counter-cult apologetics. His best-known work is the classic *The Kingdom of the Cults.*

Mayhue, Richard (b. 1944), an American theologian and professor, has made significant contributions to the field of biblical and systematic theology. He has served as the dean of The Master's Seminary and has written on topics such as the doctrine of the Holy Spirit and the role of women in ministry. With John MacArthur, he has authored *Biblical Doctrine: A Systematic Summary of Bible Truth.*

McClain, Alva J. (1888–1968) was an American theologian and educator. He founded Grace Theological Seminary, and his work *The Greatness of the Kingdom* provided a dispensationalist perspective on the biblical concept of the kingdom of God.

McClendon, James William, Jr. (1924–2000) was an American Baptist theologian and professor, He is known for his work in systematic theology and ethics, particularly in the areas of theological method and the role of the church in society. He authored a three-volume *Systematic Theology.*

McCune, Rolland (1934–2019), an American theologian and professor, was known for his work in systematic theology and dispensationalism. He served as a professor at Detroit Baptist Theological Seminary and authored the three-volume *A Systematic Theology of Biblical Christianity*.

McGrath, Alister E. (b. 1953) is a British theologian and professor. He taught at the University of Oxford and his works, such as *Christian Theology: An Introduction* and *Historical Theology: an Introduction to the History of Christian Thought*, contributed to the understanding of Christian theology and engaged with topics like the relationship between science and religion.

Melanchthon, Philip (1497–1560), a German theologian and humanist, was a close collaborator of Martin Luther and played a significant role in the development of Lutheran theology. He was known for his scholarly works and his efforts to promote education and reform within the Protestant movement.

Migliore, Daniel L. (b. 1935) is an American Reformed theologian and professor. He taught at Princeton Theological Seminary and his works, such as *Faith Seeking Understanding: An Introduction to Christian Theology*, engaged with topics like theological method, the nature of God, and the relationship between faith and reason.

Miley, John (1813–1895) was an American Methodist theologian and professor. He is known for his work *Systematic Theology*, which provided a comprehensive treatment of Wesleyan–Arminian theology and engaged with theological controversies of his time.

Mohler, R. Albert, Jr. (b. 1959) is an American Southern Baptist theologian and president of The Southern Baptist Theological Seminary. He is known for his conservative theological views and his writings and speeches engage with topics like biblical authority, cultural engagement, and the role of the church in society. Among his works are *We Cannot Be Silent, Culture Shift: Engaging Current Issues with Timeless Truth, He Is Not Silent*, and *Preaching in a Postmodern World.*

Moltmann, Jürgen (b. 1926) is a German Reformed theologian and professor. He is known for his work on theology of hope and his emphasis on the eschatological dimension of Christian faith. His works engage with topics like eschatology, the nature of God, and the relationship between theology and social justice. Among his better known writings are *Theology of Hope* and *The Crucified God.*

Montgomery, John Warwick (b. 1931) is an American lawyer, theologian, and philosopher. He is known for his work in Christian apologetics and his writings, such as *Evidence for Faith: Deciding the God Question,* engage with topics like the historical reliability of the Bible and the defense of the Christian faith.

Moody, D. L. (1837–1899) was an American evangelist and founder of the Moody Bible Institute. He played a significant role in the revivalist movement and his works engage with topics like evangelism, the Christian life, and the pursuit of holiness.

Moody, Dale (1915–1992) was a theologian and professor at the Southern Baptist theological Seminary until forced into retirement for expressing his views on the issue of apostasy (Moody believed that a believer who fails to abide in Christ may apostatize and forfeit their salvation)—as expressed in his *Apostasy: A Study in the Epistle to the Hebrews and in Baptist History* (1997). Moody authored the comprehensive systematic theology text, *The Word of Truth: A Summary of Christian Doctrine Based on Biblical Revelation* (1981).

Moreland, J. P. (b. 1948) is an American evangelical philosopher and theologian. He taught at Biola University and his works, such as *Love Your God with All Your Mind: The Role of Reason in the Life of the Soul*, engaged with topics like philosophy of mind, apologetics, and the integration of faith and reason.

Morgan, Christopher W. (b. 1971) is an American theologian and professor. He teaches at California Baptist University. With Robert A. Peterson he has written *Christian Theology: The Biblical Story and Our Faith* as well as *A Concise Dictionary of Theological Terms.*

Morris, Leon L. (1914–2006) was an Australian biblical scholar and theologian. He is known for his work in New Testament studies and his commentaries, such as *The Gospel According to John* and *The Epistle to the Romans*, contributed to the understanding of the biblical text.

Moule, H. G. C. (1841–1920) was an English Anglican bishop and theologian. He served as the Bishop of Durham and his works, such as *The Epistle to the Romans* and *The Second Epistle to the Corinthians*, provided insightful commentaries on the New Testament.

Muller, Richard A. (b. 1948) is an American Reformed historical theologian and professor. He taught at Calvin Theological Seminary and his works, such as the magisterial four-volume *A Post–Reformation Reformed Dogmatics: The Rise and Development of Reformed Orthodoxy, ca. 1510 to 1725*, engage with topics like Reformed theology, historical theology, and the development of Protestant thought.

Mullins, E. Y. (1860–1928) was an American Baptist theologian and educator. He served as the president of Southern Baptist Theological Seminary and his work *The Christian Religion in Its Doctrinal Expression* (1917) provided a comprehensive treatment of Baptist theology in nontechnical language.

Murray, John (1898–1975) was a Scottish–born Reformed theologian and professor. He taught at Westminster Theological Seminary and his works, such as *Redemption Accomplished and Applied*, provided a systematic exposition of Reformed theology, particularly in the areas of soteriology and the atonement.

Nestorius (*ca*. 386–451) was the bishop of Constantinople and theologian in early Christianity, who was involved in the Christological controversies of the fifth century. His teachings on the nature of Christ led to the Nestorian controversy and the Council of Ephesus, which condemned his views as heretical.

Nicholas of Cusa (1401–1464), a German philosopher, theologian, and cardinal, made significant contributions to the fields of mathematics, philosophy, and theology. His works, such as *On Learned Ignorance* and *The Vision of God*, explored topics like the limits of human knowledge and the nature of God.

Nicole, Roger R. (1915–2010) was a Swiss-American Reformed theologian and professor. He taught at Gordon–Conwell Theological Seminary and at Reformed Theological Seminary. His works, such as *Revelation and the Bible* and *Our Sovereign Savior: The Essence of the*

Reformed Faith, engaged with topics like biblical inspiration, hermeneutics, and the doctrine of God.

Niebuhr, H. Richard (1894–1962) was an American theologian and ethicist. He is known for his work *Christ and Culture*, which explored different approaches to the relationship between Christianity and culture.

Niebuhr, Reinhold (1892–1971) was an American theologian, ethicist, and political commentator. He played a significant role in the development of Christian realism and his works, such as *Moral Man and Immoral Society* and *The Nature and Destiny of Man*, engaged with the ethical and political challenges of his time.

Novatian (*ca.* 200–258) was a theologian and antipope in early Christianity. He is known for his strict views on church discipline and his works engage with topics like ecclesiology, the nature of the sacraments, and the relationship between sin and forgiveness.

Oberman, Heiko (1930–2001) was a German-American historian and theologian. He played a significant role in the study of Martin Luther and the Reformation and his works, such as *Luther: Man Between God and the Devil*, contributed to the understanding of the historical context and theological significance of the Reformation.

Oden, Thomas C. (1931–2016) was an American Methodist theologian and professor. He taught at Drew University and his works, such as *The Transforming Power of Grace*, contributed to the development of paleo–orthodoxy and engaged with topics like the authority of Scripture and the early church fathers.

Olevianus (Olevian), Caspar (1536–1587) was a German Reformed theologian and pastor. He played a significant role in the development of the Heidelberg Catechism and his works engage with topics like covenant theology, justification by faith, and the sacraments.

Olson, Roger E. (b. 1952) is an American theologian and professor. He taught at Baylor University and his works, such as *The Story of Christian Theology: Twenty Centuries of Tradition and Reform*, provide a comprehensive treatment of the history of Christian theology.

Origen (*ca.* 184–*ca.* 253), an influential early Christian biblical and systematic theologian from Alexandria, was known for his extensive biblical scholarship and his philosophical approach to theology. He played a significant role in shaping early Christian thought. Possibly the most prolific writer in antiquity, Origen produced by dictation some two thousand works: commentaries on almost every biblical book, hundreds of homilies, numerous scholia on particular passages, and the massive and long-unsurpassed *Hexapala.* Among his better-known extant writings are the apologetic *Against Celsus* and the speculative *On First Principles*.

Orr, James (1844–1913) was a Scottish Presbyterian theologian and professor. He is known for his work on apologetics and his engagement with contemporary intellectual challenges to the Christian faith. His works, including *The Progress of Dogma* and *The Christian View of God and the World,* engage with topics like the defense of Christianity, the relationship between faith and reason, and the nature of revelation.

Osborne, Grant (1942–2018) was an American New Testament scholar and theologian. He taught at Trinity Evangelical Divinity School and his works, such as the commentary on the Gospel of Matthew in the *Zondervan Exegetical Commentary on the New Testament* series, contributed to the understanding of the biblical text. He authored the widely-acclaimed *The Hermeneutical Spiral: A Comprehensive Introduction to Biblical Interpretation.*

Ott, Ludwig (1906–1985) was a German Catholic theologian and professor. He taught at the University of Bonn and his works, such as *Fundamentals of Catholic Dogma*, provide a masterful expression of pre-Vatican II Roman Catholic theology.

Owen, John (1616–1683), an English Puritan theologian and pastor, is known for his extensive writings on theology and spirituality. His works, such as *The Death of Death in the Death of Christ* and *Communion with God*, explored topics like Christ's atonement, the Holy Spirit, and the believer's union with Christ. His *Theologoumena Pantodapa* (1611, published as *Biblical Theology: A History of Theology from Adam to Christ*) traces the development of theology through the biblical covenants.

Pache, René (1904–1979) was a Swiss-French theologian and biblical scholar, and professor at the Faculté Libre de Théologie Évangélique in Vaux–sur–Seine, France. He is known for his work in biblical theology and authored several books, including *The Inspiration and Authority of Scripture* and *The Return of Jesus Christ.*

Packer, J. I. (1926–2020), an English–born Canadian theologian, was a prominent figure in Reformed theology and evangelicalism. His book *Knowing God* is considered a classic in Christian literature, and his writings on topics such as the sovereignty of God and the authority of Scripture have had a significant impact. Among his many titles are *Evangelism and the Sovereignty of God*, *"Fundamentalism" and the Word of God*, *God Has Spoken: Special Revelation and the Word of God*, and *A Quest for Godliness*.

Pannenberg, Wolfhart (1928–2014) was a German Lutheran theologian who taught at the Universities of Heidelberg, Mainz, and Munich. Known for his concept of history as a form of revelation centered on the resurrection of Christ, Pannenberg made significant contributions to modern theology. In *Revelation as History* (1961), he argues that God reveals Himself in universal history, the whole of which is summed up in the resurrection of Jesus. His *Jesus, God and Man* (1964; trans. 1968) develops a Christology "from below" from the data of Jesus' life, death, and resurrection. He also authored the three-volume *Basic Questions in Theology* (trans. 1970–73), and the two-volume *Systematic Theology* (1988–93; trans. 1991, 1994).

Pascal, Blaise (1623–1662) was a French mathematician, physicist, and theologian. He is known for his influential work *Pensées*, which engages with topics like the nature of faith, the problem of skepticism, and the relationship between reason and religious belief.

Patterson, Paige (b. 1942) is an American Southern Baptist theologian and pastor. He was a pivotal part of the Southern Baptist Convention conservative resurgence, and served as the president of Southwestern Baptist Theological Seminary. His works engaged with topics like biblical interpretation, ecclesiology, and the role of women in ministry.

Payne, J. Barton (1922–1979) was an American theologian and professor at Covenant Theological Seminary. He is known for his work on biblical prophecy and authored *The Encyclopedia of Biblical Prophecy.*

Peckham, John C. (b. 1981) is associate professor of theology and Christian philosophy at the Seventh-Day Adventist Theological Seminary of Andrews University. Among his many publications are *The Love of God: A Canonical Model, The Doctrine of God: Introducing the Big Questions*, and *Divine Attributes: Knowing the Covenantal God of Scripture.* He has recently released *God With Us: An Introduction to Adventist Theology.*

Pelagius (*ca.* 354–418) was a British monk and theologian. He is known for his views on free will and his emphasis on human moral responsibility. His works engaged with topics like original sin, the nature of grace, and the relationship between human effort and divine assistance. Among his extant writings are *De fide Trinitatis libri III*, *Eclogarum ex divinis Scripturis liber primus*, and *Commentarii in epistolas S. Pauli.*

Pelikan, Jaroslav (1923–2006) was an American historian and theologian. He taught at Yale University and his works, such as the five-volume *The Christian Tradition: A History of the Development of Doctrine*, contributed to the understanding of Christian history and theology.

Pentecost, J. Dwight (1915–2014) was an American theologian and professor. He taught at Dallas Theological Seminary and his work *Things to Come* provided a comprehensive treatment of biblical prophecy and eschatology. He also wrote *Things Which Become Sound Doctrine* and *The Words and Works of Jesus Christ.*

Perkins, William (1558–1602) was an English Puritan theologian and pastor. He played a significant role in the development of Reformed theology in England and is known for his influential works on practical theology, such as *The Art of Prophesying* and *A Golden Chain,* engaging with topics like preaching, pastoral ministry, and the pursuit of godliness.

Peterson, Robert A. (b. 1948) is an American theologian and professor. He teaches at Covenant Theological Seminary and his works, such as *Salvation Accomplished by the Son: The Work of Christ*, engage with topics like soteriology, Christology, and the atonement. With Christopher W. Morgan, he has written *Christian Theology: The Biblical Story and Our Faith* as well as *A Concise Dictionary of Theological Terms.*

Pieper, Franz August Otto (1852–1931) was a German-American Lutheran theologian and professor. He was a prominent figure in the Lutheran Church–Missouri Synod and his four-volume *Christian Dogmatics* provided a systematic exposition of Lutheran theology.

Pinnock, Clark (1937–2010) was a Canadian evangelical theologian and professor. He taught at McMaster Divinity College and his works, such as *The Openness of God: A Biblical Challenge to the Traditional Understanding of God*, engaged with topics like divine sovereignty, human freedom, and the nature of God.

Piper, John (b. 1946) is an American Reformed Baptist pastor and theologian. He served as the pastor of Bethlehem Baptist Church in Minneapolis and his works, such as *Desiring God: Meditations of a Christian Hedonist*, emphasized the pursuit of joy in God and the sovereignty of God in all things.

Plantinga, Alvin (b. 1932) is an American philosopher and theologian. He is known for his work in philosophy of religion and epistemology, particularly in the areas of theistic arguments and the problem of evil. His works include *God and Other Minds, The Nature of Necessity*, and *Warranted Christian Belief.*

Pohle, Joseph (1852–1922) was a German Catholic theologian and professor. He is known for his work on dogmatic theology and his engagement with contemporary theological issues. He wrote *The Sacraments, Mariology, Grace: Actual and Habitual,* and, with Arthur Preuss, the twelve-volume *Manual of Dogmatics*.

Polycarp of Smyrna (*ca.* 69–*ca.* 155) was a bishop and martyr in early Christianity. He is known for his defense of the faith and his works engage with topics like ecclesiology, the nature of the church, and the relationship between faith and martyrdom.

Pope, William Burt (1822–1903) was an English Methodist theologian and writer. His work *A Compendium of Christian Theology: Being Analytical Outlines of a Course of Theological Study, Biblical, Dogmatic, Historical* provided a comprehensive treatment of Methodist theology and engaged with theological controversies of his time.

Poythress, Vern S. (b. 1946) is an American Reformed theologian and professor. He taught at Westminster Theological Seminary and his works, such as *Redeeming Science: A God-Centered Approach*, engaged with topics like the relationship between science and Christianity and the integration of faith and learning.

Purkiser, W. T. (1910–1992) was an American theologian and writer. He served as the president of Nazarene Theological Seminary and his works, such as *Exploring Our Christian Faith* and *Called Unto Holiness,* contributed to the development of Wesleyan–Holiness theology.

Quenstedt, Johannes Andreas (1617–1688), a German Lutheran theologian, made significant contributions to Lutheran scholasticism. His work *Theologia Didactico-polemica sive Systema Theologicae* provided a comprehensive treatment of Lutheran theology and engaged with theological controversies of his time.

Radbertus, Paschasius (785–865), a Benedictine monk and theologian, is known for his work on the doctrine of the Eucharist. His book *On the Body and Blood of the Lord* presented a controversial view of the real presence of Christ in the Eucharist, which sparked theological debates in the Middle Ages.

Rahner, Karl (1904–1984) was a German Jesuit theologian and philosopher. He played a significant role in the development of Catholic theology in the 20th century and his works, such as *Foundations of Christian Faith*, engaged with topics like the nature of God, Christology, and the relationship between faith and culture.

Ramm, Bernard L. (1916–1992) was a professor at California Baptist Theological Seminary and authored numerous books on theology and apologetics. His notable works include *Protestant Biblical Interpretation* and *The Christian View of Science and Scripture.*

Ratramnus (d. *ca.* 868), a monk and theologian known to the Reformers as "Bertram," engaged in theological debates during the Carolingian period. His work *De Corpore et Sanguine Domini* (*On the Body and Blood of Christ*) presented a moderate view on the Eucharist (opposing the teaching of Paschasius Radbertus), opposing the idea of a physical presence of Christ.

Rauschenbusch, Walter (1861–1918) was an American theologian and Baptist pastor. He is known for his work on the social gospel and his emphasis on the Christian responsibility to address social and economic injustices. His works—such as *Christianity and the Social Crisis*, and *The Social Principles of Jesus*—engage with topics like social ethics, the kingdom of God, and the relationship between faith and social activism.

Raymond, Miner (1811–1897) was an American Methodist theologian and educator. He served as the president of Wesleyan University and played a significant role in the development of Methodist higher education in the United States. He authored a three-volume *Systematic Theology*.

Reuchlin, Johannes (1455–1522) was a German humanist and theologian. He played a significant role in the revival of Hebrew and the study of Jewish texts in Christian Europe. His works, including *De Verbo Mirifico* and *De Arte Cabbalistica*, engage with topics like biblical interpretation, Jewish–Christian relations, and the relationship between faith and reason.

Reymond, Robert L. (1932–2013), an American Reformed theologian and professor, was known for his work in systematic theology and apologetics. He taught at Knox Theological Seminary and his works, such as *A New Systematic Theology of the Christian Faith*, provided a comprehensive and coherent treatment of Reformed theology from a conservative perspective.

Ritschl, Albrecht (1822–1889) was a German Protestant theologian and professor. He played a significant role in the development of the Ritschlian school of theology, which emphasized the ethical teachings of Jesus and the social implications of Christianity. Among his writings are *The Emergence of the Old Catholic Church* and *The Doctrine of Justification and Reconciliation.*

Rogers, Adrian (1931–2005) was a prominent Southern Baptist pastor and served as the president of the Southern Baptist Convention. He is known for his powerful preaching and conservative theological stance. His popular-level books include *What Every Christian Ought to Know* and *Discover Jesus: The Author and Finisher of Our Faith*.

Ryle, J. C. (1816–1900) was a 19th-century Anglican bishop and author. He is known for his practical and pastoral writings, including *Holiness* and *Expository Thoughts on the Gospels*.

Ryrie, Charles C. (1925–2016) was an American theologian and writer, best known for his work on systematic theology (especially his *Basic Theology* and *Dispensationalism*) and his *The Ryrie Study Bible*. He was a Professor of Theology at Dallas Theological Seminary, and served as the president of the Philadelphia College of Bible.

Sanders, Fred (b. 1968) is an American theologian and professor. He teaches at Biola University and his works, such as *The Deep Things of God: How the Trinity Changes Everything*, engage with topics like

Trinitarian theology, the nature of God, and the relationship between theology and spirituality.

Sauer, Erich (1898–1959) was a German theologian and writer. He is known for his works on biblical prophecy and eschatology, such as *The Dawn of World Redemption* and *The Triumph of the Crucified.*

Savonarola, Girolamo (1452–1498) was an Italian Dominican friar and preacher. He played a significant role in the religious and political life of Florence and his works engage with topics like moral reform, the pursuit of holiness, and the relationship between church and state.

Sawyer, M. James (b. 1951) was an American theologian and professor. He is a professor of A. W. Tozer Seminary and director of Sacred Saga Ministries. He is known for his work on systematic theology and his engagement with contemporary theological issues. Among his works are *Survivor's Guide to Theology.*

Schaeffer, Francis A. (1912–1984) was an American evangelical theologian and philosopher. He is known for his work on Christian apologetics and his engagement with contemporary cultural issues. He authored many works, including *How Then Should We Live?, A Christian Manifesto,* and *He Is There and He Is Not Silent.* His works engage with topics like the defense of Christianity, the relationship between faith and culture, and the nature of truth.

Schaff, Philip (1819–1893) was a Swiss-American theologian and church historian. He played a significant role in promoting ecumenism and interdenominational dialogue and his works, such as his magisterial eight-volume *History of the Christian Church*, have been widely influential in the field of church history.

Schleiermacher, Friedrich D. E. (1768–1834), a German theologian and philosopher, is considered the father of modern liberal theology. His work, particularly *On Religion: Speeches to Its Cultured Despisers,* sought to reconcile Christianity with Enlightenment thought and emphasized the role of religious feeling and experience.

Schweitzer, Albert (1875–1965) was a French–German theologian, philosopher, and physician. He is known for his work on the historical Jesus and his emphasis on the ethical teachings of Jesus. His works engage with topics like the quest for the historical Jesus, the nature of discipleship, and the pursuit of ethical living. His books include *The Quest for the Historical Jesus: A Critical Study of its Progress from Reimarus to Wrede*, and *The Mystery of the Kingdom of God.*

Scofield, C. I. (1843–1921) was an American theologian and writer, best known for his annotated Bible, *The Scofield Reference Bible.* His study notes and commentary had a significant impact on the development of dispensationalism, a theological framework that interprets biblical history in distinct dispensations or periods.

Scroggie, W. Graham (1877–1958), was a Baptist pastor and Bible teacher in the United Kingdom. He is known for his expository preaching and authored several commentaries and biblical works, including *A Guide to the Gospels* and *The Unfolding Drama of Redemption.*

Semler, Johann Salomo (1725–1791) was a German theologian and biblical scholar who gained notoriety for his critical approach to biblical interpretation and his role in the development of historical–critical methods in biblical studies. His writings (nearly two hundred) include *Commentatio de demoniacs*, *Selecta capita historiae ecclesiasticae*, and *Apparatus ad liberalem N. T. interpretationem*.

Shedd, William G. T. (1820–1894) was an American Presbyterian theologian and professor. Among his many works are included *Homiletics and Practical Theology,* the two-volume *History of Christian Doctrine,* and the classic *The Doctrine of Endless Punishment.* His multi-volume *Dogmatic Theology* provided a systematic exposition of Reformed theology and engaged with theological controversies of his time.

Simeon the New Theologian (949–1022) was a Byzantine Christian monk and theologian. He is known for his mystical writings and his works, such as *The Discourses*, engaging with topics like the experience of God, the nature of prayer, and the pursuit of holiness.

Simons, Menno (1496–1561), a Dutch Anabaptist leader and theologian, played a significant role in the development of the Mennonite movement. His writings, such as *The Foundation of Christian Doctrine*, emphasized the importance of nonviolence, discipleship, and separation from the world.

Smeaton, George (1814–1889) was a Scottish theologian and professor at New College, Edinburgh. He is known for his work on the doctrine of the atonement and authored *The Doctrine of the Atonement as Taught by Christ Himself.*

Smith, James K. A. (b. 1970) is a Canadian-American philosopher and theologian. He teaches at Calvin University and his works, such as *Desiring the Kingdom: Worship, Worldview, and Cultural Formation*, engage with topics like philosophy of education, liturgy, and the role of the imagination in Christian formation.

Smith, Morton H. (1923–2017), was an American Presbyterian scholar who taught at Belhaven College and Reformed Theological Seminary, and was Professor of Systematic and Biblical Theology at Greenville Presbyterian Theological Seminary. He wrote a two-volume *Systematic Theology*.

Socinus, Laelius (1525–1562) was an Italian theologian and one of the founders of the Socinian movement. He is known for his rejection of the Trinity and his emphasis on the unity of God.

Spener, Philipp Jakob (1635–1705) was a German Lutheran theologian and pastor. He is known as the father of Pietism, a movement that emphasized personal piety, Bible study, and practical Christian living. He authored the influential *Pia Desideria.*

Sproul, R. C. (1939–2017), an American theologian and pastor, was a leading figure in Reformed theology. He founded Ligonier Ministries and authored books such as *The Holiness of God* and *Chosen by God*, emphasizing the sovereignty of God and the importance of sound doctrine.

Spurgeon, Charles (1834–1892) was an English Baptist preacher and writer. Known as the "Prince of Preachers," Spurgeon's sermons and writings, such as *Morning and Evening* and *Lectures to My Students*, continue to be influential in evangelical Christianity.

Spykman, Gordon R. (1931–1993) was an American Reformed theologian and professor. He taught at Fuller Theological Seminary and his works, such as *Reformational Theology: A New Paradigm for Doing Dogmatics*, engaged with topics like worldview, cultural engagement, and the integration of faith and learning.

Stanley, Charles (1932–2023) was the pastor of First Baptist Atlanta and the founder of In Touch Ministries. He is known for his teaching on practical Christian living and has authored numerous books, including *The Charles F. Stanley Life Principles Bible*.

Stonehouse, Ned B. (1902–1962) was a professor at Westminster Theological Seminary and a biblical scholar. He is recognized for his work on the New Testament and co–authored *The Infallible Word: A Symposium by the Members of the Faculty of Westminster Theological Seminary*.

Stott, John (1921–2011) was an English Anglican cleric and theologian. He is known for his work in evangelical theology and his writings, such as *Basic Christianity* and *The Cross of Christ*, emphasized the importance of biblical exposition, social justice, and the centrality of the cross in Christian faith.

Strong, A. H. (1836–1921), an American Baptist theologian, was a prominent figure in the late 19th and early 20th centuries. His work, *Systematic Theology: A Compendium Designed for the Use of Theological Students*, became a standard text in Baptist seminaries and emphasized the authority of Scripture and the importance of Christian ethics.

Stuart, Moses (1780–1852), was a professor at Andover Theological Seminary and a biblical scholar. He is known for his work in biblical interpretation and authored several commentaries, including *A Commentary on the Book of Proverbs.*

Suarez, Francisco (1548–1617), a Spanish Jesuit philosopher and theologian, made significant contributions to the fields of metaphysics, ethics, and theology. His works, such as *Disputationes Metaphysicae* and *De Legibus*, explored topics like the nature of being, moral philosophy, and the relationship between faith and reason.

Summers, Thomas O. (1812–1882) was an American Methodist theologian and bishop. He was a prominent figure in the Methodist Episcopal Church, South, and his works, such as *Systematic Theology* and *Commentary on the Gospels*, contributed to the theological development of the denomination.

Svigel, Michael J. (b. 1973) is an American theologian and professor. He teaches at Dallas Theological Seminary and his works, such as *Theological Foundations for Ministry: An Introduction for Lay Leaders*, engage with topics like theological education, ministry, and the role of the laity in the church. With Nathan D. Holsteen, he edited the three-volume *Exploring Christian Theology*; with Glenn R. Kreider, he authored *A Practical Primer on Theological Method.*

Swete, Henry Barclay (1835–1918) was an Anglican theologian and professor at the University of Cambridge. He is known for his work on the New Testament, particularly his commentary on the Gospel of Mark.

Tauler, Johann (*ca.* 1300–1361) was a German mystic and preacher. He is known for his intensely practical sermons and writings on Christian spirituality, which emphasize the importance of inner transformation and union with God.

Taylor, Jeremy (1613–1667), an English bishop and theologian, is known for his devotional and pastoral writings. His works, such as *Holy Living* and *Holy Dying*, emphasized the importance of personal piety, moral virtue, and the practice of Christian spirituality.

Tenney, Merrill C. (1904–1985) was a professor at Wheaton College and served as the general editor of the *Zondervan Pictorial Encyclopedia of the Bible*. He is known for his expertise in New Testament studies and authored several books, including *New Testament Survey* and *John: The Gospel of Belief.*

Tertullian (*ca.* 160–*ca.* 220) was a prominent early Christian theologian from Carthage, known for his defense of orthodox Christian beliefs and his contributions to the development of Latin Christian literature. Among his writings are the well-known apologetic works, *Ad nationes* and the *Apologeticum.* Of note also are *Adversus Marcionem*, *De anima*, *De carne Christi*, and *De resurrectione mortuorum*.

Theodore of Mopsuestia (*ca.* 350–428) was an early Christian theologian and bishop. He is known for his exegetical works and his emphasis on the humanity of Christ, particularly in his most important and controversial doctrinal work, *Incarnation*. Among Theodore's other works are three ascetic treatises, *The Priesthood, To the Monks*, and *Perfect Direction*. However, some of his teachings were later deemed heretical.

Thielicke, Helmut (1908–1986) was a German Protestant theologian and pastor. He taught at the University of Hamburg and his works, such as the three-volume *The Evangelical Faith* and *Theological Ethics*, engaging with topics like ethics, preaching, and the relationship between theology and culture.

Thiessen, Henry C. (1883–1947), a Canadian–born American theologian, was known for his work in evangelical theology. His book *Lectures in Systematic Theology* provides a concise and accessible overview of Christian doctrine from an evangelical perspective.

Thiselton, Anthony C. (b. 1937) is a British theologian and professor. He taught at the University of Nottingham and his works, such as *The Hermeneutics of Doctrine*, contributed to the understanding of hermeneutics and the interpretation of Christian doctrine. He recently published his *Systematic Theology*.

Thomas, W. H. Griffith (1861–1924) was an Anglican theologian and professor at Wycliffe Hall, Oxford. He is known for his work on systematic theology and authored several books, including *The Principles of Theology* and *The Apostles' Creed: Its Relation to Primitive Christianity*.

Thorsen, Donald A. D. (b. 1955) is an American theologian and professor. He taught at Azusa Pacific University and his works, such as *An Exploration of Christian Theology*, provide a comprehensive treatment of

Christian theology from an evangelical perspective. He also wrote the important *The Wesleyan Quadrilateral: Scripture, Tradition. Reason, and Experience as a Model of Evangelical Theology.*

Tillich, Paul (1886–1965) was a German-American theologian and philosopher. He is known for his work in existentialist theology and his writings, such as *Systematic Theology* and *The Courage to Be*, explored the relationship between faith and culture.

Toon, Peter (1939–2009) was an Anglican priest, theologian, historian, and professor at the University of Birmingham. He is known for his work on Anglican theology and authored *The Anglican Way: Evangelical and Catholic.* He also authored numerous important theological works, including *Our Triune God: A Biblical Portrayal of the Trinity, Justification and Sanctification, Heaven and Hell: A Biblical and Theological Overview, The Art of Meditating on Scripture*, and the controversial *The Emergence of Hyper-Calvinism in English Nonconformity, 1689–1765.*

Torrance, Thomas F. (1913–2007), the Scottish Presbyterian dogmatician and minister, was an important modern thinker widely regarded as one of the most important theologians of the twentieth century. Torrance served as a professor of Christian dogmatics at the University of Edinburgh for nearly three decades. Torrance sought to unify the worlds of theology and science. *Theology in Reconstruction* (1965) represents his most unified theological work. Other important titles include *Theological Science* (1969); *Space, Time and Incarnation* (1969); *Space, Time and Resurrection* (1976); *Christian Theology and Scientific Culture* (1980); *The Ground and Grammar of Theology* (1980); *Reality and Evangelical*

Theology (1982); *Transformation and Convergence in the Frame of Knowledge* (1984) and *Reality and Scientific Theology* (1985).

Torrey, R. A. (1856–1928) was an American evangelist, pastor, and writer. He served as the superintendent of Moody Bible Institute and his works, such as *The Person and Work of the Holy Spirit* and the four-volume series he edited, *The Fundamentals: A Testimony to the Truth*, contributed to the development of fundamentalist/conservative theology and served to combat modernism and destructive higher criticism.

Tozer, A. W. (1897–1963) was an American pastor, writer, and speaker. He is known for his devotional writings, such as *The Pursuit of God* and *The Knowledge of the Holy*, which emphasized the importance of personal intimacy with God and the pursuit of a deeper spiritual life.

Trueman, Carl R. (b. 1967) is a British Reformed theologian and professor. He teaches at Grove City College and his works, such as *The Creedal Imperative*, engage with topics like church history, confessionalism, and the importance of creeds and confessions.

Turretin, Francis (1623–1687), a Swiss–Italian Reformed theologian, is known for his three-volume *Institutes of Elenctic Theology*. His writings, organized in a question–and–answer format, provided a systematic exposition of Reformed theology and engaged with theological controversies.

Tyndale, William (*ca.* 1494–1536) was an English scholar and translator. He is known for his translation of the Bible into English and his role in the Protestant Reformation. He also authored a number of important polemical works, including *The Parable of the Wicked Mammon*, *The Obedience of a Christian Man*, and *The Practice of Prelates*.

Ursinus, Zacharias (1534–1583) was a German Reformed theologian and professor. He was one of the primary authors of the Heidelberg Catechism and his works engage with topics like covenant theology, the doctrine of God, and the nature of the church.

Van Til, Cornelius (1895–1987) was a Dutch-American Reformed theologian and apologist. He played a significant role in the development of presuppositional apologetics and his works, such as *The Defense of the Faith*, emphasized the importance of the Christian worldview and the primacy of Christian presuppositions in defending the faith.

Vermigli, Peter Martyr (1499–1562) was an Italian Reformed theologian and professor. He taught at various universities and his works, such as *Loci Communes,* engaging with topics like biblical interpretation, the doctrine of God, and the nature of the sacraments.

Vincent of Lérins (d. 450), a monk and theologian, is known for his work *Commonitorium*, which provided guidelines for determining orthodox Christian doctrine. He emphasized the importance of holding to the faith that has been believed *quod ubique, quod semper, quod ab omnibus creditum est* ("everywhere, always, and by all").

Volf, Miroslav (b. 1956) is a Croatian-American theologian and professor. He teaches at Yale Divinity School and his works, such as *Exclusion and Embrace,* engage with topics like reconciliation, forgiveness, and the relationship between Christianity and culture.

Vos, Geerhardus (1862–1949) was a Dutch-American Reformed theologian and professor. He taught at Princeton Theological Seminary and his works, such as *Biblical Theology*, engage with topics like biblical interpretation, redemptive history, and the relationship between the Old and New Testaments.

Wakefield, Samuel (1799–1895) was a preacher in the Methodist Episcopal Church, and a composer and compiler of hymnbooks. He authored *A Complete System of Christian Theology; or, a Concise, Comprehensive, and Systematic View of the Evidences, Doctrines, Morals, and Institutions of Christianity*.

Waldo, Peter (*ca.* 1140–1218) was a French merchant and religious reformer. He is known for his role in the Waldensians (also called Waldenses or Vaudois) movement, which emphasized the importance of preaching and the translation of the Bible into the vernacular.

Walvoord, John F. (1910–2002) was an American theologian and writer, known for his work on biblical prophecy and eschatology. He served as the president of Dallas Theological Seminary and authored numerous books on theology, including *The Rapture Question*, *The Millennial Kingdom*, and *Jesus Christ Our Lord.*

Ware, Bruce (b. 1953) is an American evangelical theologian and professor. He taught at The Southern Baptist Theological Seminary and his works, such as *God's Lesser Glory: The Diminished God of Open Theism*, engaged with topics like the nature of God, divine sovereignty, and the relationship between God and creation.

Warfield, Benjamin B. (1851–1921) was an American Presbyterian theologian and professor. He is known for his defense of biblical inerrancy and his contributions to the field of systematic theology. Among his any works are *Counterfeit Miracles, Biblical Doctrines, and Studies in Theology.*

Watson, Richard (1781–1833), an English Methodist theologian, is known for his three-volume *Theological Institutes*. His writings provided a systematic exposition of Methodist theology and engaged with theological controversies of his time.

Watson, Thomas (1620–1686) was an English Puritan theologian and pastor. He is known for his works on practical theology, which engage with topics like the Christian life, spiritual growth, and the pursuit of godliness. Notable works include his *The Art of Divine Contentment* and *A Body of Divinity* (consisting of one hundred seventy-six sermons upon the Westminster Assembly's Catechism in question and answer format).

Webster, John B. (1955–2016) was an Anglican priest and Reformed theologian and professor. He taught at the University of Aberdeen and the University of St. Andrew's. He co-founded the *International Journal of Systematic Theology.* His works, such as *Holiness*, engaged with topics like the nature of God, theological anthropology, and the doctrine of the Trinity.

Wells, David F. (b. 1939) is an American theologian and professor at Gordon–Conwell Theological Seminary. He is known for his critique of modernity and the impact of secularism on the church. Wells authored several influential books, including *No Place for Truth* and *God in the Wasteland.*

Wenham, John (1913–1996) was a British theologian and author. He is known for his work on biblical criticism and apologetics, including *The Goodness of God* and *Redating Matthew, Mark, and Luke.*

Wesley, Charles (1707–1788), an English hymn-writer and theologian, played a crucial role in the development of Methodism. His hymns, such as "Hark! The Herald Angels Sing" and "And Can It Be," expressed theological truths and played a significant role in Methodist worship.

Wesley, John (1703–1791), an English Anglican cleric and theologian, is known as the founder of Methodism. His teachings, which emphasized personal holiness, social justice, and the pursuit of Christian perfection, had a significant impact on the development of the Methodist movement.

White, James R. (b. 1962) is an American Reformed theologian and apologist. He is known for his work in Christian apologetics and his writings and debates engage with topics like the defense of the Christian faith, the reliability of the Bible, and the relationship between Christianity and other religions. Among his writings are *The King James Only Controversy: Can You Trust the Modern Translations?, The Forgotten Trinity: Recovering the Heart of Christian Belief,* and *The God Who Justifies: A Comprehensive Study of the Doctrine of Justification.*

Whitefield, George (1714–1770) was an English Anglican preacher and evangelist. He played a significant role in the Great Awakening and his powerful sermons drew large crowds.

Whitehead, Alfred North (1861–1947) was a British mathematician and philosopher. He is known for his process philosophy and his work on the relationship between science, metaphysics, and theology. His works include *Process and Reality* and *Religion in the Making*. With Bertrand Russell, Whitehead authored the three-volume *Prinicipia Mathematica*.

Wiley, H. Orton (1877–1961) was an American Methodist theologian and educator. He served as the president of Asbury Theological Seminary and his three-volume *Christian Theology* provided a systematic exposition of Methodist theology.

William of Ockham (*ca.* 1285–1349), an English Franciscan friar and philosopher, is known for his philosophical principle known as "Ockham's Razor." His works, such as *Summa Logicae* and *Ordinatio*, challenged prevailing scholastic views and emphasized the importance of simplicity and logical reasoning.

Williams, J. Rodman (1918–2008) was an American Pentecostal theologian and professor. He taught at Regent University and his works, such as his three-volume *Renewal Theology*, engage with topics like pneumatology, the gifts of the Holy Spirit, and the nature of the church.

Williams, Roger (*ca.* 1604–1683) was an English theologian and founder of the colony of Rhode Island in North America. He is known for his advocacy of religious freedom and his writings on the separation of church and state.

Witsius, Herman (1636–1708), a Dutch Reformed theologian, is known for his work *The Economy of the Covenants Between God and Man*. His writings emphasized the covenantal framework of salvation and the relationship between law and grace.

Wycliffe, John (*ca.* 1320–1384) was an English theologian and reformer. He is known for his translation of the Bible into English and his criticism of the Catholic Church.

Wynkoop, Mildred Bangs (1905–1997) was an American theologian and writer. She is known for her work *A Theology of Love,* which explored the Wesleyan–Arminian understanding of sanctification and emphasized the role of love in the Christian life.

Yarnell, Malcolm B., III (b. 1962) is an American Baptist theologian and professor. He teaches at Southwestern Baptist Theological Seminary and his works engage with topics like Baptist theology, ecclesiology, and the relationship between church and state. He has written *The Formation of Christian Doctrine*, *God the Trinity: Biblical Portraits,* and *Who Is the Holy Spirit?*

Zanchi, Jerome (1516–1590) was an Italian Reformed theologian and professor. He taught at various universities (most notably at Strasbourg) and his works engage with topics like predestination, the doctrine of God, and the nature of the church.

Zinzendorf, Nikolaus Ludwig von (1700–1760) was a German theologian and founder of the Moravian Church. He is known for his emphasis on "heart religion," Christian unity, and his missionary work.

Zwingli, Huldrych (1484–1531), a Swiss reformer and theologian, played a crucial role in the Protestant Reformation. His teachings, which emphasized the authority of Scripture and rejected certain Catholic practices, influenced the development of Reformed theology.

THE long and honorable history of the discipline now generally denominated systematic theology is a fascinating and dynamic journey that spans two millennia of Christian thought and reflection. From the early catechesis of the ancient church, to the massive *Summae* of Scholastic theology, to the resurgence of systematic theology in recent times, the development of this discipline reflects the ongoing effort of Christians to understand and articulate the truths of the faith in a manner that is biblically faithful, rationally coherent, doxologically oriented, and existentially relevant.

Throughout, this small book has surveyed the key thinkers and their writings that have shaped the development of systematic theology. From the early church fathers, to the medieval Scholastics, to the Reformers, and the modern theologians, each era has contributed to the richness and diversity of the Christian tradition. We have also seen how the development of systematic theology has been shaped by historical, cultural, and broader intellectual contexts.

Far from being a mere academic discipline, systematic theology has played a vital role in shaping the Christian faith, providing a framework for understanding the nature of God and our relationship to Him. It has also been instrumental in shaping the way we think about the world and our place in it. Recent developments in systematic theology—such as the current resurgence of interest in the field, the establishment of professional groups, and the growth of analytical theology—have brought fresh perspectives and insights to the discipline. This has led to an explosion of excellent texts that are accessible to a wide range of readers in various mediums, providing a richer understanding of the Christian faith and facilitating a deeper understanding of and a more meaningful engagement with the living and redeeming God.

Considering the past, observing the present, and looking towards the future of systematic theology nurtures a sense of hope and anticipation. The discipline has continually developed and matured, adapting to the changing needs and contexts of the church it serves, while maintaining the purity of "the faith once delivered to the saints" (Jude 3). The ongoing dialogue between theologians, pastors, and laypeople ensures that systematic theology remains a relevant, accessible, and meaningful discipline for all. This book is written on the firm belief that the future of systematic theology is brimming with promise and possibility, eagerly awaiting the contributions and insights that will emerge in the years to come.

APPENDIX 1: IMPORTANT EVENTS IN CHRISTIAN HISTORY

THE study of systematic theology is a journey that navigates the intricate labyrinth of thought, belief, and interpretation that has shaped the Christian faith for over two millennia.[1] This appendix serves as a chronological guide, providing a succinct and comprehensive timeline of significant individuals and events that have indelibly marked the landscape and trajectory of Christian history in general, and systematic theology in particular.

The dates and events listed herein are not merely historical markers; they represent pivotal moments of theological development, periods of doctrinal consolidation, and instances of profound intellectual and spiritual insight. From the early church fathers who laid the foundational stones of Christian doctrine, to the mediaeval scholastics who sought to

---

[1] Good histories of Christianity can be had in the following: Kurt Aland, *A History of Christianity*, 2 vols., trans. James L. Schaff (Philadelphia, PA: Fortress, 1985); Earle E. Cairns, *Christianity Through the Centuries* (Grand Rapids, MI: Zondervan, 1996); Justo L. González, *The Story of Christianity,* 2 vols., rev. ed. (San Francisco, CA: HarperOne, 2010); Kenneth Scott Latourette, *A History of Christianity,* 2 vols. (1954; reprint, Peabody, MA: Hendrickson, 1997–99); Nick Needham, *2,000 Years of Christ's Power,* 4 vols. (Fearn, Ross-Shire, Scotland: Christian Focus, 2016); Jaroslav Pelikan, *The Christian Tradition: A History of the Development of Doctrine*, 5 vols. (Chicago, IL: University of Chicago, 1971–89).

reconcile faith with reason, to the Reformers who challenged the status quo and reshaped the contours of Christian belief, the entries in this appendix carry theological significance.

This appendix is therefore more than a mere reference aid; rather, it is an invitation to delve deeper into the historical context of systematic theology, to understand the significant personalities and temporal progression of ideas, and to appreciate the dynamic interplay between theology and the social–cultural milieu in which it is embedded. It is hoped that this appendix will serve, not only as an aid to this book, but as a valuable companion in exploring the rich and fascinating world of systematic theology.

30–325 Beginnings: from the Resurrection of Christ to Nicaea

30–100 Apostolic Age

***ca.* 85–150** Writings of the Apostolic Fathers

***ca.* 93–94** Josephus writes *Antiquities of the Jews*

***ca.* 95–98** Severe persecution of Christians under Emperor Domitian

***ca.* 95–99** The *Didache* written

96 Clement of Rome writes his letter to the church in Corinth

101–284 Early Church Era

***ca.* 108** Ignatius writes seven epistles

132–135 Bar Kokhba Revolt/Second Jewish Rebellion

150 Justin Martyr dedicates his *First Apology*

***ca.* 150** Polycarp writes his epistle to the Philippians

161–180 Widespread persecution of Christians under Marcus Aurelius

180 Irenaeus writes *Against Heresies*

***ca.* 195–203** Clement of Alexandria writes three major theological works

***ca.* 196–220** Tertullian begins writing dozens of influential works; coins the term "Trinity"

***ca.* 215–290** Rise of the Christian schools at Alexandria and Antioch

215 Origen begins writing

249–251 Severe persecution of Christians under Decius

250 Origen publishes *Contra Celsum*

284–305 Severe persecution of Christians under Diocletian

312 Donatist schism begins

313 "Edict of Milan" (Constantine I granted Christians freedom of worship)

325 Eusebius competes *Ecclesiastical History,* the first major church history

325 Council of Nicaea; Arianism condemned

***ca.* 328** Athanasius writes *On the Incarnation*

329–395 Cappadocian Fathers (Basil the Great, Gregory of Nyssa, and Gregory Nazianzus) produce brilliant theological works, making significant contributions to Trinitarian theology

330 Constantine moves capital from Rome to Byzantium (Constantinople)

341 Fourth Creed of Antioch

343 Council of Serdica

344 Antiochene Council

351 Council at Sirmium

358 Hilary of Poitiers writes his epistles to the Arians

367 Athanasius' *Easter Letter* confirms the books of the Bible

376 Goths invade Roman Empire

358 Basil the Great founds monastic community

367 Athanasius' letter defines New Testament canon

378 Constantinian dynasty ends

***ca.* 375–425** Pelagian Controversy

380 Theodosius declares Christianity official religion of Roman Empire

381 First Council of Constantinople; Nicene Creed revised

386 Augustine converts to Christianity; becomes the most influential theologian in Christian history

391 Edict of Theodosius

397 Synod of Carthage, confirms the 27 books of the New Testament

***ca.* 397–400** Augustine writes *Confessions*

***ca.* 400–428** Augustine writes *On the Trinity*

405 Jerome publishes the *Latin Vulgate*, which would become the standard version of the Bible in the west for the next 1,100+ years

409 Goths establish semi–independent kingdom in Spain

410 Fall of Rome

411 Council of Carthage

***ca.* 413–426** Augustine writes *City of God*

430 Goths establish semi-independent kingdom in North Africa

431 Council of Ephesus; Nestorianism and Pelagianism condemned

449 Leo the Great claims papal authority; lays foundation for the Bishop of Rome (later, the Pope) to lay claim to papal supremacy

***ca.* 450–500** Athanasian Creed

451 Council of Chalcedon; condemns several heresies related to the nature of Christ, issues the Chalcedonian Definition

476 Goths establish semi–independent kingdom in Italy

476 Fall of the Western Roman Empire; last Western emperor deposed, imperial regalia sent to Constantinople

500 Dionysius the Pseudo-Aeropagite writes

513 Great Synod in Antioch

524 Boethius completes *Consolation of Philosophy*

540 Benedict writes his monastic *Rule*

553 Second Council of Constantinople

555–559 Council of Toledo

589 Visigoths in Spain converted to Catholicism

590–628 Persia invades Eastern Empire, takes most of Syria, Palestine, Egypt

626 Constantinople besieged by Avars

632–642 Muslim Arabs invade Syria, Palestine, Egypt

663 Synod of Whitby

680–681 Third Council of Constantinople

692 Council in Trullo in Constantinople

698 Muslim conquest of North Africa

706 Arabic becomes dominant language in eastern Roman Empire

711–778 Spread of Islam

725–842 Iconoclastic Controversy

726 Controversy over icons begins in Eastern Church

730 Bede's *Ecclesiastical History* published

732 Franks repulse Arabs at Poitiers

750 Donation of Constantine written about this time

751 Ravenna falls to Lombards

***ca.* 754–787** John of Damascus writes *Exact Exposition of the Orthodox Faith*

787 Second Council of Nicaea

794 Anti–Byzantine synods at Frankfurt

797 Anti–Byzantine synods at Friuli

800 Charlemagne crowned as Holy Roman Emperor by Pope Leo III; the Holy Roman Empire existed as a political entity in Central Europe until 1806

809 Anti–Byzantine synods at Aachen (Aix–la–Chapelle)

843 Treaty of Verdun divides Carolingian Empire

861 East–West conflict over Photius begins

1054 The Great Schism/East–West Split

1093 Anslem becomes Archbishop of Canterbury; writes numerous influential works; formulates the famous Ontological Argument for God's existence

1095–1204 Crusades

1095 First Crusade launched by Council of Clermont by Pope Urban II

1096 Oxford University founded

1122 Concordat at Worms ends investiture controversy

1141 Hildegard of Bingen begins writing

1150 Universities of Paris and Oxford founded

1150 Peter Lombard publishes *The Four Books of Sentences,* which became the standard theology textbook in the west for the next 400+ years

1175 Waldensian movement launched by proto–Reformer Peter Waldo

1200–1500 Scholasticism emerges and dominates

1204 Constantinople sacked

1215 Fourth Lateran Council

1229 Frederick II leads crusade to Holy Land, retakes Jerusalem

1250–1252 Bonaventure writes *Commentary on the Sentences*

1259–1272 William of Moerbeke translates classical Greek texts, fostering a resurgence in the study of the classics

1261 Rulers of Nicaea recapture Constantinople

***ca.* 1266–1272** Thomas Aquinas pens his massive *Summa Theologicae*

1274 Second Council of Lyon

***ca.* 1300–1399** Hesychasm controversy

1302 *Unam Sanctum* proclaims papal supremacy

1305–1377 Papacy in Avignon ("Babylonian captivity")

1321 Dante completes *Divine Comedy*

1370 Catherine of Sienna begins her *Letters*

1376 John Wycliffe writes *Civil Dominion*, arguing for church reform

1378–1471 Great Papal Schism, during which there were rival popes

1380 John Wycliffe supervises English Bible translation

1414–1417 Council of Constance

1415 John Hus is martyred

1418 Thomas á Kempis writes *The Imitation of Christ*

1438 Council of Basel

1438–1516 Pragmatic sanction of Bourges

1439 Council of Florence

***ca.* 1450** Emergence of the Renaissance

1453 Constantinople falls to the Turks; end of Eastern Roman Empire

1456 Johannes Gutenberg produces first printed Bible; his press becomes a means for disseminating new ideas, catalyzing changes in politics and theology

1479 Spanish Inquisition established

1488 First complete printed single-volume Hebrew Old Testament

1494 Treaty of Tordesillas

1497 Girolamo Savonarola excommunicated

1516 Erasmus publishes Greek New Testament

1517 Martin Luther posts *Ninety–five Theses* in Wittenburg; sparks the Protestant Reformation

1520 Martin Luther publishes *The Babylonian Captivity of the Church*

1521 Diet of Worms; Luther is put on trial by the Roman Catholic Church

1522 Martin Luther publishes his German New Testament

1523 Zwingli leads Swiss Reformation

1525 William Tyndale's New Testament published

1525 Anabaptist movement begins

1527 Schleitheim Confession of Faith

1529 Treaty of Zaragoza

1529 Colloquy of Marburg

1530 Augsburg Confession

1534 Act of Supremacy; Church of England breaks with Rome

1522 Martin Luther publishes his famous commentary on Galatians

1535–1536 Wittenberg Articles

1536 English Ten Articles

1536 John Calvin publishes the first edition of his *Institutes of the Christian Religion*

1537 Smalcald Articles

1545–1563 Council of Trent—Roman Catholic Counter–Reformation

1549 Thomas Cranmer publishes the *Book of Common Prayer* in England (revised 1662)

1553 Forty–two Articles of Church of England

1555 Peace of Augsburg signed

1559–1622 Period of Protestant Orthodoxy

1559 Elizabethan Settlement establishing Anglicanism as official Church of England

1559 Final edition of John Calvin's *Institutes of the Christian Religion*

1559 French Confession of La Rochelle

1561 Belgic Confession

1563 John Foxe's *Book of Martyrs* published

1563 *Heidelberg Catechism* published

1565 Teresa of Avila writes *The Way of Perfection*

1566 Second Helvetic Confession

1570 Elizabeth I excommunicated

1571 Thirty–nine Articles of Church of England

1572 Thomas Wilcox and supporters called "Puritans"

1577 Formula of Concord

1580 *Book of Concord* published

1580/81 Second Mennonite (Waterland) Confession

1595 Lambeth Articles

1598 Edict of Nantes

1603 James VI of Scotland to English throne as James I

1609 Smyth baptizes self and first Baptists

1611 King James Version of the Bible published

1615 Irish Articles

1618–1648 Thirty Years War

1618–1619 Synod of Dort

1620 Mayflower Compact drafted

1636 Harvard College founded to train New England's pastors

1644 First London Baptist Confession published

1646–1647 Westminster Confession and Catechisms published

1648 Peace of Westphalia ends Thirty Years' War

1649 Cambridge Platform

***ca.* 1650** Emergence of Quakers

1662 Book of Common Prayer

1667 John Milton publishes *Paradise Lost*

1670 Blaise Pascal's *Pensées* published posthumously

1675 Emergence of Pietism with Jacob Spencer's *Pia Desideria*

1679–1685 Francis Turretin writes *Institutes of Elenctic Theology*

1678 John Bunyan writes *Pilgrim's Progress*

1685 Edict of Nantes revoked

1688–1689 "Glorious Revolution" (English parliament ejects Catholic King James II)

1689 Second London Baptist Confession

1694–1784 Writers of the French Revolution

1707–1748 Isaac Watts writes nearly 800 hymns and spiritual songs, publishes several books

1720–1780 The Enlightenment begins

***ca.* 1730–1770** The First Great Awakening

1746 Jonathan Edwards publishes *Religious Affections*

1750–present Modern Christianity

1750–1800 Emergence of Puritanism

1773 Isaac Backus publishes *An Appeal to the Public for Religious Liberty*

1785 Andrew Fuller publishes *The Gospel Worthy of All Acceptation*

1789 French Revolution begins

***ca.* 1790–1840** The Second Great Awakening

1792 William Carey publishes *An Enquiry*

1799 Friedrich Schleiermacher publishes *On Religion*

1811 The Campbells begin the "Disciples of Christ"; the Stone–Campbell Restoration Movement begins

***ca.* 1830** John Nelson Darby helps found the Plymouth Brethren

1844 Søren Kierkegaard publishes *Philosophical Fragments*

1845 Phoebe Palmer publishes *The Way of Holiness*

1854 Søren Kierkegaard publishes *Attacks on Christianity*

1864 John Henry Newman publishes *Apologia Pro Vita Sua*

1869–1870 First Vatican Council; dogma of papal infallibility proclaimed

1875 First Keswick Convention

1875–1897 Niagara Bible Conference

1878 William and Catherine Booth found the Salvation Army

1880 Abraham Kuyper founds the Free University at Amsterdam

1886 Beginning of the Student Volunteer Movement

***ca.* 1890–1900** Emergence of Modernism

***ca.* 1900** Emergence of Evangelicalism

1906–1908 Emergence of Pentecostal/ Charismatic Movement with the Azusa Street Revival

1908 G. K. Chesterton publishes *Orthodoxy*

1909 C. I. Scofield's *Scofield Reference Bible* published

1910–1915 *The Fundamentals* are published, critiquing modernistic theology

1919 Karl Barth publishes *Commentary on Romans*

***ca.* 1920s** Fundamentalist–Modernist controversy

1923 J. Gresham Machen publishes *Christianity and Liberalism*

1929–1930 Westminster Seminary founded by J. Gresham Machen *et al.*, in the wake of the Fundamentalist–Modernist controversy

1932 Karl Barth begins publishing *Church Dogmatics*

1937 Dietrich Bonhoeffer publishes *The Cost of Discipleship*

1941 Reinhold Niebuhr publishes *The Nature and Destiny of Man*

1942 National Association of Evangelicals founded

1942 Wycliffe Bible Translators founded by William Cameron

1947 Fuller Theological Seminary founded

1947 Carl F. H. Henry publishes *The Uneasy Conscience of Modern Fundamentalism*

1947 Evangelical Theological Society founded

1947 Dead Sea scrolls discovered at Qumran

1948 World Council of Churches founded

1950–1956 C. S. Lewis publishes *The Chronicles of Narnia*

1951 Richard Niebuhr publishes *Christ and Culture*

1956 *Christianity Today* founded

1960s Jesus People movement

1960s Charismatic renewal movement

1962–1965 Second Vatican Council

1965 Chuck Smith founds Calvary Chapel

1965 Joint Catholic–Orthodox Declaration issued, lifting the mutual excommunication stemming from the Great East–West of 1054

1968 Medellin Conference ushers in liberation theology

***ca.* 1970** Emergence of Postmodernism

1970s The Jesus Movement begins in the U.S.

1971 New American Standard Bible published

1971 R. C. Sproul launches Ligonier Ministries

1973 Emergence of feminism

1973 New International Version of the Bible first published

1974 International Congress on World Evangelization in Lausanne, Switzerland

***ca.* 1974** Postliberalism

1976 Francis Schaeffer publishes *How Then Should We Live?*

1977 New Perspective on Paul movement begun by E. P. Sanders

1978 Chicago Statement on Biblical Inerrancy issued

1980s–1990s Conservative Resurgence in the Southern Baptist Convention

1982 Chicago Statement on Biblical Hermeneutics issued

1986 Chicago Statement on Biblical Application issued

1987 Danvers Statement published by the Council of Biblical Manhood and Womanhood

1990 The Alpha Course developed by Nicky Gumbel at Holy Trinity Brompton in London.

1992 Publication of the *Catechism of the Catholic Church*

1994 Evangelicals and Catholics Together document signed

1994 Wayne Grudem publishes *Systematic Theology: An Introduction to Biblical Doctrine*

1999 Signing of the *Joint Declaration on Justification* by Lutheran and Roman Catholic Churches

1999 Charles Colson publishes *How Now Shall We Live?*

2000 The Baptist Faith and Message is revised to address contemporary issues, including family, gender roles, and the sanctity of life

2009 The ecumenical Manhattan Declaration: A Call of Christian Conscience is issued by Orthodox, Catholic, and Evangelical Christians

2009 Formation of the Anglican Church in North America

2001 English Standard Version of the Bible published

2011 Lexham English Bible published

2013 Strange Fire Conference, organized by Grace to You, addressed theological errors and dangers of the Charismatic/Pentecostal movements.

2017 The Protestant Reformation marks its 500th anniversary

2017 Nashville Statement published by the Council of Biblical Manhood and Womanhood

2022 Legacy Standard Bible published

2023 The Southern Baptist Convention voted to affirm the decision made earlier to remove Rick Warren and his megachurch (Saddleback Church) due to its having women pastors.

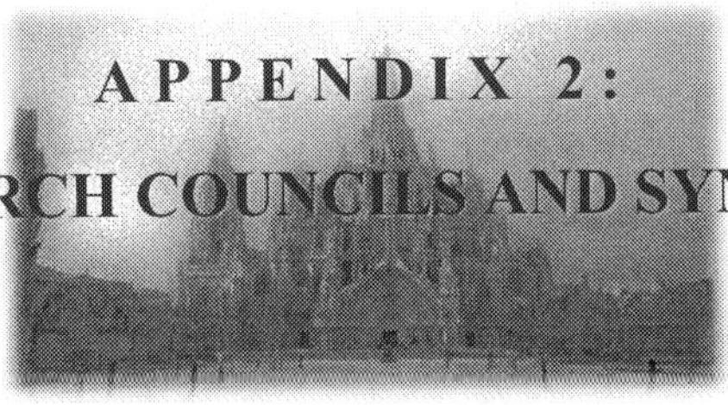

APPENDIX 2: CHURCH COUNCILS AND SYNODS

AS Gerald Bray (b. 1948) has defined it, "A church council is a gathering of all those members of the church who are responsible for guarding the deposit of the apostolic faith."[1] To be precise, there are three types of official assemblies often termed a "council." Ecumenical or general councils, local councils, and synods are different types of gatherings within the Christian church that serve various purposes. They differ in terms of their scope, authority, and the extent of their representation within the church.[2] This Appendix offers an explanation of the differences, and then lists, in chronological order, key examples with summary descriptions.

---

[1] G. L. Bray, "Councils," in *NDT*^{2}, 221.

[2] See Bray, "Councils," 221–25; J. H. Hall, "Councils, Church," in *EDT*^{3} 213–14; Wolfgang Beinert, "Council," in *ECT*, 366–68; idem, "Synod," in *ECT*, 1638–40; Charles Munier, "Council," in *EAC*, 1:625–26; D. A. Rausch, "Ecumenical Councils," in *EDT*^{3} 261. More fully, see Charles Joseph Hefele, *A History of the Councils of the Church*, 5 vols. (Edinburgh: T&T Clark, 1883–96); Philip Hughes, *The Church in Crisis: A History of the General Councils, 325–1870* (1961; reprint, Providence, RI: Cluny Media, 2020); Hubert Jedin, *Ecumenical Councils of the Catholic Church* (New York: Herder, 1960); Hans J. Margull, ed., *The Councils of the Church: History and Analysis* (Philadelphia, PA: Fortress, 1966).

Ecumenical (Gr. *oikoumene*, "the inhabited world") *councils*, also known as general councils, are the highest authoritative gatherings within the church. They bring together bishops or representatives from various regions and branches of the church to discuss and make decisions on matters of universal significance, such as doctrinal, theological, and disciplinary issues affecting the entire church. Ecumenical councils are typically rare and have occurred at specific historical junctures, and are usually convened to address significant challenges or controversies that have widespread implications. The decisions made in ecumenical councils are considered binding on the entire church and have a profound impact on its theology, governance, and practices.

There are seven ecumenical councils that every branch of Christianity recognizes today, whether Orthodox, Catholic, or Protestant: Nicaea I (325), Constantinople I (381), Ephesus (431), Chalcedon (451), Constantinople II (553), Constantinople III (681), and Nicaea II (787). In addition, Roman Catholicism recognizes fourteen more: Constantinople IV (870), Lateran I (1123), Lateran II (1139), Lateran III (1179), Lateran IV (1215), Lyon I (1245), Lyon II (1274), Vienne (1312), Constance (1414–18), Basel, Ferrara and Florence (1431–45), Lateran V (1512–17), Trent (1545–63), Vatican I (1870), and Vatican II (1962–65).

Local councils, also known as regional or provincial councils, are similar to synods (see below), but they specifically involve the bishops or representatives from a province (a specific geographic area or region, a territorial division) within the church. Local councils address matters that concern the particular province, including regional disputes, local practices, and organizational issues. The decisions made in provincial councils primarily affect the province they represent and are not necessarily binding on the entire church. In other words, local councils have authority within their respective regions and their decisions may be binding for the local churches. However, their decisions do not have the same universal authority as ecumenical councils. Local councils may also serve as a means of communication and coordination between the local churches within a province.

Synods (Gk. *synodos*, "a group of people traveling together") are gatherings of bishops, clergy, and sometimes laity, from a particular region or branch of the church, convened to discuss and make decisions on matters of doctrine, disciplinary concerns, or pastoral challenges within a particular church or jurisdiction. Synods can be local, regional, or national in scope. They serve as a means of governance and decision-making within a specific church or ecclesiastical structure. Synods are often convened periodically and are considered a regular part of the governance structure of a particular church. While synods can have significant influence and authority within their respective regions, their decisions generally pertain to the specific area or church they represent (as in, e.g., a denomination) and may not have universal or binding implications for the entire church.

The following are summary explanations of some of the key councils and synods of the church, listed in chronological order:

Synod of Antioch (264): Convened to address the heresy of Paul of Samosata, who denied the divinity of Christ.

Synod of Elvira (*ca.* 306): This synod, held in Spain, addressed various disciplinary matters and established canons on topics such as marriage, penance, and the treatment of heretics.

Synod of Arles (314): This synod, held in Gaul (modern-day France), addressed various theological and disciplinary matters, including the Donatist controversy, and affirmed the primacy of the See of Rome.

First Council of Nicaea (325): This council addressed the Arian controversy and formulated the Nicene Creed, affirming the divinity of Jesus Christ and establishing key doctrines of the Christian faith.

Synod of Antioch (341): Held in Antioch, this synod addressed the teachings of the Arian heresy and reaffirmed the Nicene Creed, while also regulating the metropolitan constitution of the church.

Council of Serdica (343): Held in Serdica (modern-day Sofia, Bulgaria), it addressed the Arian controversy and attempted to reconcile Eastern and Western bishops.

Synod of Milan (355): This synod, held in Milan, addressed the Arian controversy and condemned the teachings of Arius.

First Council of Constantinople (381): Building upon the Nicene Creed, this council affirmed the divinity of the Holy Spirit and expanded the creed to clarify the nature of the Trinity.

Synod of Carthage (393): Defines the canon of Scripture.

Synod of Carthage (397): Reaffirmed the canon of Scripture, previously defined by the Synod of Hippo (393).

Council of Toledo (Various Councils): A series of councils held in Toledo, Spain, from the 4th to the 7th centuries, which played a significant role in shaping the development of the church in the Iberian Peninsula.

Council of Ephesus (431): Condemning Nestorianism, this council affirmed the title of Mary as Theotokos (Mother of God) and emphasized the unity of Christ's divine and human natures.

Council of Ephesus (431): While there were actually three councils held in Ephesus (two in 431 and one in 449), all addressing christological debates of the fifth century, it is the larger council held in 431 that is considered an ecumenical council. This council also functioned as a provincial council for the Eastern Church, as it primarily addressed the Nestorian controversy. The smaller council of 431 is typically termed the Conciliabulum ("little council"). The other council in Ephesus, in 449, is known as the Latrocinium (robber synod) and is rejected.

Council of Chalcedon (451): Similar to the ecumenical council of Ephesus (431), Chalcedon is considered an ecumenical council, but it also had a provincial character as it addressed theological disputes within the Eastern Church, particularly the Monophysite controversy. Chalcedon defined the nature of Christ, affirming that Jesus has two distinct natures, human and divine, united in one person, rejecting both Nestorianism and Monophysitism.

Council of Orange (529): Held in Gaul (modern-day France), this council addressed the teachings of Pelagius and affirmed the doctrines of original sin and predestination.

Second Council of Constantinople (553): Condemning certain Nestorian and Origenist teachings, this council reaffirmed the orthodox understanding of Christ's nature and clarified theological controversies.

Council of Toledo (589): This council, held in Spain, played a crucial role in the conversion of the Visigothic Kingdom to Catholicism and addressed issues of church discipline and governance.

Synod of Whitby (664): This synod, held in England, resolved the conflict between the Celtic and Roman Christian traditions and established Roman ecclesiastical practices as the norm in the English church.

Third Council of Constantinople (680–681): Addressing the Monothelitism controversy, this council affirmed the orthodox belief in the two wills of Christ, human and divine.

Council of Hieria (754): Convened by the Byzantine Emperor Constantine V, this council condemned the veneration of icons, declaring that images of Jesus misrepresented Him and that images of Mary and the saints were idols.

Second Council of Nicaea (787): Restoring the veneration of icons, previously condemned at the Council of Hieria (754), this council affirmed the use of religious images in worship, resolving the iconoclastic controversy.

Council of Frankfurt (794): This council, held in Germany, condemned the heresy of Adoptionism, which denied the full divinity of Christ.

Synod of Frankfurt (794): Convened by Charlemagne to address the iconoclast controversy and affirmed the veneration of images.

Synod of Worms (868): Convened to address the issues raised by the theologian Gottschalk of Orbais, including the doctrine of predestination.

Fourth Council of Constantinople (869–870): Deposing Patriarch Photius, this council addressed the Photian Schism and attempted to reconcile and restore unity between the Eastern and Western churches.

Synod of Constantinople (879–880): Addressed the Photian Schism and reinstated Photius as the Patriarch of Constantinople.

First Lateran Council (1123): Addressing church reforms and the Investiture Controversy and clerical celibacy, this council sought to regulate the appointment of bishops and reaffirm the authority of the church over secular rulers.

Second Lateran Council (1139): Addressed issues related to the Investiture Controversy and enacted reforms within the church.

Third Lateran Council (1179): Addressed issues related to papal elections, simony, and clerical discipline.

Fourth Lateran Council (1215): Addressing various doctrinal and disciplinary matters, this council affirmed the doctrine of transubstantiation and addressed various issues related to the sacraments, heresy, church governance, and the Crusades.

Council of Toulouse (1229): Held in France, this council addressed the issue of heresy, particularly the Cathar heresy, and established measures for the suppression of heretics.

Councils of Lyons (Various Councils): Held in Lyon, France, in the 13th and 14th centuries, these councils addressed matters related to the Crusades, the relationship between the Latin and Greek churches, and other issues.

Council of Constance (1414–1418): This council, held in Germany, was convened to resolve the Western Schism and elect a single pope. It also addressed various reform issues within the church.

Council of Florence (1438–1445): Held in Florence, Italy, it aimed to reunite the Eastern and Western churches, addressing theological, doctrinal, and jurisdictional matters.

Council of Trent (1545–1563): In response to the Protestant Reformation, this council clarified and reaffirmed Catholic doctrine, and initiated significant reforms within the Roman Catholic Church.

Synod of Dort (1618–1619): This synod, held in the Netherlands, was a significant gathering of Reformed theologians that addressed the teachings of Arminius and affirmed the doctrines of predestination and divine grace.

Synod of Jerusalem (1672): This synod, also known as the Council of Jerusalem, was held in the Eastern Orthodox Church and addressed various theological and liturgical issues, including the relationship between the Eastern Orthodox and Oriental Orthodox Churches.

Council of Westminster (Various Councils): A series of councils held in Westminster, England, in the 19th and 20th centuries, addressing matters related to the Anglican Church, including doctrine, liturgy, and governance.

First Vatican Council (1869–1870): Defining papal infallibility, this council addressed the relationship between the Pope and the Roman Catholic Church, as well as the role of faith and reason in Catholic theology.

Synod of Jerusalem (1872): Convened by the Russian Orthodox Church to address various internal matters and reaffirm traditional Orthodox teachings.

All-African Synod (1958): Convened in Ghana, it brought together African bishops to discuss issues related to the African Catholic Church and its role in the post-colonial era.

Second Vatican Council (1962–1965): Marking a significant renewal in the Roman Catholic Church, this council addressed various aspects of church life, including liturgy, ecumenism, interfaith dialogue, and the role of the laity.

In summary, ecumenical councils are the highest authority in the Church, involve representatives from various regions and branches of the Church, and address matters of universal importance. Their decisions are binding on the entire Church and have far-reaching implications. On the other hand, local councils and synods address regional or local matters within specific jurisdictions. Their decisions are limited in scope and applicability to their respective regions.

APPENDIX 3: NOTABLE THEOLOGIANS

THIS appendix—dedicated to those individuals who have left an indelible imprint on theology throughout two millennia of Christian history—provides a list of notable Christian theologians listed chronologically by century of birth.[1] Several explanatory comments bear making.

First, the figures listed herein represent a broad spectrum of theological thought, encompassing both orthodox and heterodox perspectives. As such, inclusion in this list does not imply agreement with the individual's positions. Some, such as Arius and Mary Eddy Baker, are rank heretics; others, like Hans Küng and James Hal Cone, at best espouse a theological position quite different from my own. Those listed herein are included because they have, for better or worse, exercised a significant impact on Christian theology. Even where we might disagree with a person's theology there is still the potential to learn from them—see in this regard

---

[1] This appendix is an edited and greatly expanded version of Wikipedia's "List of Christian Theologians," retrieved from https://en.m.wikipedia.org/wiki/List_of_theologians, accessed January 11, 2022. I use the term "Christian" to distinguish individuals who identify with or have a nominal affiliation with Christianity, regardless of their level of adherence to or potential deviations from orthodox beliefs. Please note that this usage does not imply endorsement or validation with their beliefs or practices.

Uche Anieor's excellent volume, *How to Read Theology: Engaging Doctrine Critically and Charitably.*[2]

Second, in compiling this list, I have tried to avoid several common errors. Most lists tend to slant towards being patriarchal. I have sought to take note of significant woman theologians, including such historical luminaries as Kassia, Julian of Norwich, and Catherine of Siena; more recently, notable women theologians include Nancy Wilson, Mary McClintock Fulkerson, Sarah Coakley, Daniela Müller, Elizabeth Stuart, and Seung–Moo Ha.[3]

Another typical shortcoming in these sort of lists is predominant focus on Anglophones, particularly from Britain and America. To remedy this and to more accurately represent the body of Christ—which includes people "from every nation, from all tribes and peoples and languages" (Rev. 7:9)—an attempt has been made to include theologians representing a wide cultural diversity.

---

[2] Uche Anieor, *How to Read Theology: Engaging Doctrine Critically and Charitably* (Grand Rapids, MI: Baker Academic, 2018).

[3] Again, inclusion does not mean that I am thereby affirming egalitarianism (the position that men and women are equal to one another in nature, relationships, and roles, and that their participation in all capacities should not be limited by gender). To the contrary, I affirm complementarianism (the position that men and women are complementary to one another, equal in nature yet distinct in relationships and roles). That said, I readily recognize the reality that there *are* women theologians who in fact have made significant contributions to theology in general, and systematic theology in particular. For a definition of terms and further discussion, see Wayne Grudem, *Systematic Theology: An Introduction to Biblical Doctrine,* 2nd ed. (Grand Rapids, MI: Zondervan, 2020), 1150–70.

A desire to accurately depict the actual state of affairs rather than some ideal is the reason I have also resisted the urge to "clean up" the list by removing the names of those whose moral failures have come to light and created scandal. Christian thinkers such as Karl Barth, Paul Tillich, and more recently John Howard Yoder and Ravi Zacharias, have left a lasting impact on Christianity, even when their own sinful shortcomings have unfortunately done the same.[4]

The astute reader will undoubtedly notice the presence of a significant number of the theological movers and shakers of the evangelical world. As my own convictions fall within the pale of evangelicalism, my sympathies naturally gravitate to those of kindred convictions. Still, it is hoped that the reader will note the broad swath of *–ists*, *–isms*, and *–ologies* represented, including those with which I profoundly disagree.

Finally, in addition to vocational theologians, I have also sought to include both pastors (e.g. Adrian Rogers) and theologians actively involved in missions (e.g. Orlando Costas).

Accordingly, this appendix serves as a testament to the diversity and dynamism inherent in the field of systematic theology. It is a tribute to the complex tapestry of thought that constitutes the history of systematic theology, and to those who have made lasting contributions to the development and articulation of sound doctrine.

[4] Here, speaking of Tillich's infidelity, Eugene Peterson offers a relevant and helpful personal anecdote in his *The Wisdom of Each Other: A Conversation Between Spiritual Friends* (Grand Rapids, MI: Zondervan, 1998) 47-8.

1ST CENTURY

Clement of Rome (ca. 35–ca. 101)

Ignatius of Antioch (ca. 35–ca. 108)

Papias of Hierapolis (ca. 60–ca. 130)

Polycarp of Smyrna (ca. 69–ca. 155)

Aristides the Athenian (d. 140)

2ND CENTURY

Valentinus (ca. 100–ca. 160)

Quadratus of Athens (fl. 124/125)

Basilides (d. ca. 132)

Aristo of Pella (fl. ca. 140)

Marcion (ca. 110–ca. 160)

Justin Martyr (ca. 110–ca. 165)

Hegesippus (ca. 110–180)

Tatian the Assyrian (ca. 120–ca. 180)

Irenaeus of Lyons (ca. 120–ca. 202)

Melito of Sardis (d. ca. 180)

Athenagoras of Athens (ca. 133–ca. 190)

Dionysius of Corinth (fl. ca. 171)

Heracleon (fl. ca. 175)

Apollinaris Claudius (fl. ca. 177)

Ptolemy (fl. ca. 180)

Pantaenus (d. ca. 200)

Serapion of Antioch (d. 211)

Bardaisan (154–222/3)

Tertullian (ca. 160–ca. 220)

Apollonius of Ephesus (fl. ca. 180–ca. 210)

Origen (ca. 184–ca. 253)

Theophilus of Antioch (d. 184)

Clement of Alexandria (ca. 150–ca. 215)

Hippolytus of Rome (ca. 170–ca. 235)

Julius Africanus (ca. 160–ca. 240)

Marcus Minucius Felix (d. 250)

Cyprian of Carthage (d. 258)

Pontius of Carthage (d. 259)

Dionysius of Rome (ca. 200–ca. 268)

Dionysius of Alexandria (d. 264

3RD CENTURY

Caius, Presbyter of Rome (early 3rd cent.)

Sabellius (fl. ca. 215)

Cyprian (ca. 200–ca. 258)

Novatian (ca. 200–258)

Paul of Samosata (ca. 200–ca. 275)

Dionysius of Alexandria (d. 265)

Lucian of Antioch (ca. 240–312)

Arius of Alexandria (270–336)

Athanasius of Alexandria (296–373)

Dionysius of Rome (ca. 200–ca. 268)

Gregory Thaumaturgus (ca. 213–ca. 270)

Anatolius of Laodicea (d. 283)

Victorinus of Pettau (d. 304)

Pamphilus of Caesarea (d. 309)

Methodius of Olympus (d. ca. 311)

Lactantius (ca. 250–ca. 325)

Alexander of Alexandria (d. 328)

Arnobius of Sicca (d. 330)

Eusebius of Caesarea (ca. 260–ca. 340)

Eusebius of Nicomedia (d. 342)

Aphrahat (ca. 280–ca. 345)

Pachomius the Great (ca. 292–ca. 348)

Anthony the Great (ca. 251–ca. 356)

Hosius of Corduba (ca. 256–ca. 357)

4TH CENTURY

Ephrem the Syrian (ca. 306–373)

Apollinarius of Laodicea (ca. 310–390)

Basil of Caesarea (ca. 330–379)

Gregory of Nyssa (ca. 330–ca. 395)

Gregory Nazianzus (329–389)

Evagrius Ponticus (345–399)

John Chrysostom (347–407)

Jerome (347–420)

Nestorius (ca. 386–ca. 451)

Eusebius of Emesa (ca. 300–ca. 360)

Eustathius of Antioch (d. 360)

Potamius (d. 360)

Hilary of Poitiers (ca. 310–ca. 368)

Eusebius of Vercelli (ca. 283–ca. 371)

Lucifer of Cagliari (d. 371)

Marcellus of Ancyra (d. 374)

Eutyches (375–454)

Zeno of Verona (ca. 300–ca. 380)

Apollinaris of Laodicea (d. 382)

Ambrosiaster (d. 384)

Cyril of Jerusalem (ca. 313–ca. 386)

Ticonius (d. 390)

Nemesius (d. 390)

Diodorus of Tarsus (d. 390)

Pacian (ca. 310–ca. 391)

Gregory of Elvira (d. 392)

Phoebadius of Agen (d. 392)

Martin of Tours (ca. 313–ca. 397)

Ambrose of Milan (ca. 340–ca. 397)

Didymus the Blind (ca. 313–ca. 398)

Siricius (ca. 334–ca. 399)

Evagrius Ponticus (ca. 345–ca. 399)

Gaius Marius Victorinus (d. 400)

Optatus (d. 400)

Publilius (d. 400)

Rufinus the Syrian (d. 401)

Anastasius I (d. 401)

Epiphanius of Salamis (ca. 310–ca. 403)

Amphilochius of Iconium (d. 403)

Chromatius (d. 407)

Gaudentius of Brescia (d. 410)

Therasia of Nola (d. 410)

Macarius Magnes (d. ca. 410)

Tyrannius Rufinus (ca. 345–ca. 411)

Theophilus of Alexandria (d. 412)

Prudentius (ca. 348–ca. 413)

Nicetas of Remesiana (ca. 335–ca. 414)

Synesius (ca. 373–ca. 414)

John II of Jerusalem (d. 417)

Pelagius (ca. 354–418

Sulpicius Severus (ca. 360–ca. 420)

Maruthas (d. 420)

Martianus Capella (d. 420)

Paulinus the Deacon (d. 422)

Severian of Gabala (ca. 380–ca. 425)

Atticus of Constantinople (d. 425)

Augustine of Hippo (ca. 354–ca. 430)

Palladius of Galatia (ca. 363–ca. 430)

Nilus of Sinai (d. 430)

Philip of Side (ca. 380–ca. 431)

John Cassian (ca. 360–ca. 435)

Rabbula (d. 435)

Possidius (d. 437)

Isaac of Armenia (ca. 354–ca. 439)

Philostorgius (ca. 368–ca. 439)

Socrates Scholasticus (ca. 380–ca. 439)

Honoratus Antoninus (d. 440)

Flavius Lucius Dexter (ca. 368–ca. 444)

Cyril of Alexandria (ca. 376–ca. 444)

Eucherius of Lyon (ca. 380–ca. 449)

Poemen (ca. 340–ca. 450)

Peter Chrysologus (ca. 380–ca. 450)

Eznik of Kolb (ca. 380–ca. 450)

Agathangelos (d. 450)

Quodvultdeus (d. 450)

Vincent of Lérins (d. 450)

Isidore of Pelusium (d. 450)

Marius Mercator (*ca*. 390–*ca*. 451)

Salvian (*ca*. 405–*ca*. 451)

Prosper of Aquitaine (*ca*. 390–*ca*. 455)

Simeon Stylites (*ca*. 390–*ca*. 459)

Isaac of Antioch (d. 460)

Arnobius the Younger (d. 460)

Patrick (*ca*. 385–*ca*. 461)

Shenoute (*ca*. 348–*ca*. 466)

Theodoret (*ca*. 393–*ca*. 466)

Gennadius of Constantinople (d. 471)

Timothy Ælurus (d. 477)

Iakob Tsurtaveli (d. 483)

Narsai (*ca*. 399–*ca*. 502)

Isaiah the Solitary (d. 491)

Gelasius I (d. 496)

Gennadius of Massilia (d. 496)

Leo the Great (ca. 400–ca. 461)

Victor Vitensis (ca. 430–ca. 484)

Vigilius of Thapsus (d. 484)

Nonnus (d. 500)

Antipater of Bostra (d. 500)

Avitus of Vienne (ca. 450–ca. 519)

Benedict of Nursia (ca. 480–ca. 547)

Fulgentius Ferrandus (d. 547)

Isaiah the Solitary (d. 491)

Gelasius I (d. 496)

Gennadius of Massilia (d. 496)

Leo the Great (ca. 400–ca. 461)

Victor Vitensis (ca. 430–ca. 484)

Vigilius of Thapsus (d. 484)

Nonnus (d. 500)

Antipater of Bostra (d. 500)

Avitus of Vienne (ca. 450–ca. 519)

Benedict of Nursia (ca. 480–ca. 547)

Fulgentius Ferrandus (d. 547)

Cosmas Indicopleustes (d. 550)

Julianus Pomerius (d. 505)

Aeneas of Gaza (d. 518)

John Philoponus (ca. 490–ca. 570)

John Malalas (ca. 491–ca. 578)

Cassiodorus (ca. 480–ca. 585)

6TH CENTURY

Gregory the Great (ca. 540–604)

Martin of Braga (ca. 520–ca. 580)

Peter III of Callinicum (ca. 550–ca. 591)

Gregory of Antioch (d. 593)

Evagrius Scholasticus (ca. 536–ca. 594)

Gregory of Tours (ca. 538–ca. 594)

John IV of Constantinople (d. 595)

David the Invincible (d. 600)

Basil of Oxyrhynchus (d. 600)

Leander of Seville (ca. 534–ca. 601)

Eulogius of Alexandria (d. 608)

Venantius Fortunatus (ca. 530–ca. 609)

Isidore of Seville (ca. 560–ca. 626)

Gregory of Agrigento (ca. 559–ca. 630)

Theophylact Simocatta (ca. 580–ca. 630)

Andrew of Caesarea (ca. 563–ca. 637)

Sophronius of Jerusalem (ca. 560–ca. 638)

John Climacus (ca. 579–ca. 649)

Maximus the Confessor (580–662)

Gildas (ca. 500–ca. 570)

Victor of Tunnuna (d. 570)

Dorotheus of Gaza (ca. 505–ca. 565)

7TH CENTURY

Isaac of Nineveh (d. ca. 700)

Bede (ca. 673–735)

John of Damascus (ca. 675–749)

Anania Shirakatsi (ca. 610–ca. 685)

Jacob of Edessa (ca. 640–ca. 708)

8TH CENTURY

Alcuin (730–804)

Paschasius Radbertus (785–865)

Rabanus Maurus (ca. 780–856)

9TH CENTURY

Kassia (ca. 805–867/890)

Hincmar (806–882)

Gottschalk (ca. 808–ca. 867)

Claudius of Turin (d. 839)

Johannes Scotus Eriugena (810–877)

Ratramnus (d. ca. 868)

Heiric of Auxerre (ca. 835–887)

Remigius of Auxerre (ca. 841–908)

10TH CENTURY

Gerbert of Aurillac (ca. 950–1003)

Fulbert of Chartres (d. 1028)

Berengar of Tours (ca. 999–1088)

Lanfranc (d. 1089)

11TH CENTURY

Peter Damian (1007–1072)

Anselm of Canterbury (1033–1109)

Anselm of Laon (d. 1117)

William of St–Thierry (ca. 1075–1148)

Roscelin (d. 1125)

Hugh of St Victor (1078–1151)

Peter Abelard (1079–1142)

Bernard of Clairvaux (1090–1153)

12TH CENTURY

Peter Lombard (ca. 1100–1160)

Joachim of Fiore (ca. 1135–1202)

Peter Waldo (ca. 1140–1218)

Dominic (1170–1221)

Alexander of Hales (ca. 1186–1245)

Robert Grosseteste (ca. 1175–1253)

Francis of Assisi (ca. 1181–1286)

13TH CENTURY

Albertus Magnus (ca. 1200–1280)

Mechthild of Magdeburg (1210–1285)

Roger Bacon (1214–1294)

Bonaventure (1221–1274)

Thomas Aquinas (1224–1274)

Angela of Foligno (1248–1309)

Peter Quesnel (d. 1299)

Joannes Eckhart (1260–1328)

Johannes Duns Scotus (1266–1308)

Marsilius of Padua (1270–1342)

William of Ockham (ca. 1285–1349)

Thomas Bradwardine (ca. 1290–1349)

14TH CENTURY

Geert Groote (1340–1384)

Julian of Norwich (1342–1413)

Catherine of Siena (1347–1380)

Jean Gerson (1363–1429)

Jan Hus (ca. 1369–1415)

Thomas à Kempis (1380–1471)

15TH CENTURY

Nicholas of Cusa (1401–1464)

Cajetan, Thomas de Vio (1469–1534)

Desiderius Erasmus (1469–1536)

Martin Luther (1483–1546)

Huldrych Zwingli (1484–1531)

Andreas von Carlstadt (1486–1541)

Johann Eck (1486–1543

Bernardino Ochino (ca. 1487–1564)

Thomas Cranmer (1489–1556)

Blaurock, Georg (Jörg vom Haus Jacob)(ca. 1491–1529

Martin Bucer (1491–1551)

Ignatius of Loyola (ca. 1491–1556)

Menno Simons (1496–1561)

Philip Melanchthon (1497–1560)

Peter Martyr Vermigli (1499–1562)

16TH CENTURY

Alexander Alesius (1500–1565)

John of Avila (1500–1569)

Johann Heinrich Bullinger (1504–1575)

Juan de Valdés (1509–41)

John Calvin (1509–1564)

Michael Servetus (1511–1553)

John Knox (ca. 1513–1572)

Teresa of Avila (1515–1582)

Theodore Beza (1519–1605)

Jakob Andraea (1528–1590)

Peter Baro (1534–1599)

Luis de Molina (1535–1600)

Caspar Coolhaes (1536–1615)

Caspar Olevianus (1536–1587)

Francisco Suárez (1548–1617)

Charles Borromeo (1538–1584)

John of the Cross (1542–1591)

Johannes Piscator (1546–1625)

Francisco Saurez (1548–1617)

Richard Hooker (1554–1600)

Lancelot Andrewes (1555–1626)

Johannes Wtenbogaert (1557–1644)

William Perkins (1558–1602)

Jacob Arminius (1560–1609)

Anton Praetorius (1560–1613)

Daniel Tilenus (1563–1633)

Francis de Sales (1567–1622)

Johannes Polyander (1568–1646)

William Laud (1573–1645)

Willem van der Codde (1574–ca. 1630)

Thomas Helwys (ca. 1575–ca. 1616)

Jakob Boehme (1575–1624)

Samuel Brooke (1575–1631)

Eduard Poppius (ca. 1576–1624)

Jacobus Taurinus (1576–1618)

Gerardus Vossius (1577–1649)

Thomas Jackson (1579–1640)

Johannes Arnoldi Corvinus (ca. 1582–1650)

Johann Gerhard (1582–1637)

Simon Episcopius (1583–1643)

Hugo Grotius (1583–1645)

Caspar Barlaeus (1584–1648)

Zachary Boyd (1585–1653)

Dirk Rafelsz Camphuysen (1586–1627)

Étienne de Courcelles (1586–1659)

Johannes Wollebius (1586–1629)

John Goodwin (1593–1665)

Moses Amyraut (1596–1664)

17TH CENTURY

Petrus Serrarius (1600–1669)

Owen Feltham (ca. 1602–1668)

Henry Hammond (1605–1660)

John Milton (1608–1674)

Laurence Womock (1612–1686)

John Pearson (1613–1686)

Jeremy Taylor (1613–1667)

Richard Baxter (1615–1691)

John Owen (1616–1683)

Johannes Andreas Quenstedt (1617–1688)

Francis Turretin (1623–1687)

George Fox (1624–1691)

Simon Patrick (1626–1707)

John Flavel (1627–1691)

Stephen Charnock (1628–1680)

Philipp van Limborch (1633–1712)

George Bull (1634–1710)

Thomas Grantham (1634–1692)

Thomas Burnet (ca. 1635–1715)

Philipp Jakob Spener (1635–1705)

Edward Stillingfleet (1635–1699)

Herman Witsius (1636–1708)

Gilbert Burnet (1643–1715)

Isaac Jacquelot (1647–1708)

David Hollaz (1648–1713)

Fenelon (1651–1715)

Jean Leclerc (1657–1736)

Emanuel Swedenborg (1688–1772)

Johann Jakob Wettstein (1693–1754)

John Gill (1697–1771)

18TH CENTURY

Nicolas Ludwig Count von Zinzendorf (1700–1760)

Jonathan Edwards (1703–1758)

John Wesley (1703–1791)

Charles Wesley (1707–1788)

George Whitefield (1714–1770)

Samuel Hopkins (1721-1803)

John Brown (1722–1787)

John Fletcher (1729–1785)

Thomas Hartwell Horne (1780–1862)

Gotthold Ephraim Lessing (1729–1781)

John Hey (1734–1815)

Thomas Coke (1747–1814)

Aaron Bancroft (1755–1839)

Heinrich Paulus (1761–1851)

Adam Clarke (1762–1832)

Friedrich Schleiermacher (1768–1834)

Archibald Alexander (1772–1851)

Lyman Beecher (1775–1863)

Nathan Bangs (1778–1862)

Moses Stuart (1780–1852)

Richard Watson (1781–1833)

Nathaniel William Taylor (1786–1858)

Charles Grandison Finney (1792–1875)

Wilbur Fisk (1792–1839)

Charles Hodge (1797–1878)

Samuel Wakefield (1799–1895)

19TH CENTURY

John Henry Newman (1801–1890)

Christian Hermann Weisse (1801–1866)

Leonard Bacon (1802–1881)

Horace Bushnell (1802–1876)

Frederick Denison Maurice (1805–1872)

C. F. W. Walther (1811–1887)

Miner Raymond (1811–1897)

Thomas Osmond Summers (1812–1882)

Franz Delitzsch (1813–1890)

Søren Kierkegaard (1813–1855)

John Miley (1813–1895)

John McClintock (1814–1870)

George Smeaton (1814–1889)

James Stuart Russell (1816–1895)

J. C. Ryle (1816–1900)

Ransom Dunn (1818–1900)

Philip Schaff (1819–1893)

Robert Lewis Dabney (1820–1898)

Randolph Sinks Foster (1820–1903)

Alvah Hovey (1820–1903)

Henry C. Sheldon (1820–1877)

William G. T. Shedd (1820–94)

Mary Baker Eddy (1821–1910)

William Burt Pope (1822–1903)

Albrecht Ritschl (1822–1889)

James Strong (1822–1894)

Willibald Beyschlag (1823–1900)

A. A. Hodge (1823–1886)

William Alexander (1824–1911)

James Petigru Boyce (1827–88)

William Booth (1829–1912)

Frederic William Farrar (1831–1903)

Heinrich Julius Holtzmann (1832–1910)

James Strong (1833–1913)

William J. Erdman (1833–1923)

William Fairfield Warren (1833–1929)

Charles Spurgeon (1834–1892)

Henry Barclay Swete (1835–1917)

A. J. Gordon (1836–1895)

Augustin Gretillat (1837–1894)

Abraham Kuyper (1837–1920)

Louis Auguste Sabatier (1839–1901)

H. G. C. Moule (1841–1920)

D. Douglas Bannerman (1842–1903)

Peter Taylor Forsyth (1842–1921)

C. I. Scofield (1843–1921)

Albert Benjamin Simpson (1843–1919)

Borden Parker Bowne (1847–1910)

Hugh Price Hughes (1847–1902)

Bernhard Stade (1848–1906)

Solomon J. Gamertsfelder (1851–1925)

Adolf von Harnack (1851–1930)

B. B. Warfield (1851–1921)

James M. Gray (1851–1925)

Franz August Otto Pieper (1852–1931)

Herman Bavinck (1854–1921)

A. C. Dixon (1854–1925)

James Denney (1856–1917)

Reuben Archer Torrey (1856–1928)

Max Reischle (1858–1905)

Edgar Young Mullins (1860–1928)

W. H. Griffith Thomas (1861–1924)

Walter Rauschenbusch (1861–1918)

Billy Sunday (1862–1935)

Geerhardus Vos (1862–1949)

Richard C. H. Lenski (1864–1936)

George W. Truett (1867–1944)

Rudolf Otto (1869–1937)

William Henry Chamberlin (1870–1921)

Sergei Bulgakov (1871–1944)

Lewis Sperry Chafer (1871–1952)

Louis Berkhof (1873–1957)

Albert C. Knudson (1873–1953)

Nikolai Berdyaev (1874–1948)

Karl Heim (1874–1958)

Albert Schweitzer (1875–1965)

H. A. Ironside (1876–1951)

Reginald Garrigou–Lagrange (1877–1964)

W. Graham Scroggie (1877–1958)

H. Orton Wiley (1877–1961)

Oswald T. Allis (1880–1973

John Baillie (1886–1960)

Mary Ely Lyman (1887–1975)

Nikolaj Velimirović (1880–1956)

Edwin Lewis (1881–1959)

John Gresham Machen (1881–1937)

William Temple (1881–1944)

Henry Clarence Thiessen (1883–1947)

Johannes Pedersen (1883–1977)

Edgar S. Brightman (1884–1953)

Rudolf Karl Bultmann (1884–1976)

Étienne Gilson (1884–1978)

E. Stanley Jones (1884–1973)

Oliver Chase Quick (1885–1944)

Ernest S. Williams (1885–1981)

Karl Barth (1886–1968)

Paul Tillich (1886–1965)

Donald Baillie (1887–1954)

Friedrich Gogarten (1887–1967)

Vincent Taylor (1887–1968)

Alva J. McClain (1888–1968)

Emil Brunner (1889–1966)

Dietrich von Hildebrand (1889–1977)

Leonard Hodgson (1889–1969)

Anders Nygren (1890–1978)

Georgia Harkness (1891–1974)

Otto A. W. Piper (1891–1982)

Reinhold Niebuhr (1892–1971)

Dorothy Sayers (1893–1957)

H. Richard Niebuhr (1894–1962)

J. Oliver Buswell, Jr. (1895–1977)

Fulton Sheen (1895–1979)

Cornelius Van Til (1895–1987)

Henri de Lubac (1896–1991)

Mildred Barker (1897–1990)

Dorothy Day (1897–1980)

A. W. Tozer (1897–1963)
C. S. Lewis (1898–1963)
John Murray (1898–1975)
Erich Sauer (1898–1959)

20TH CENTURY

Gerhard von Rad (1901–1971)
Gordon Clark (1902–1985)
Oscar Cullmann (1902–1999)
Allan A. MacRae (1902–1997)
Watchman Nee (1903–1972)
Dumitru Stăniloae (1903–1993)
Yves Congar (1904–1995)
Bernard Lonergan (1904–1984)
René Pache (1904–1979)
Karl Rahner (1904–1984)
Merrill C. Tenney (1904–1985)
Hans Urs von Balthasar (1905–1988)
Eric Lionel Mascall (1905–1993)
Harold Ockenga (1905–1985)
Mildred Bangs Wynkoop (1905–1997)
Dietrich Bonhoeffer (1906–1945)
Joseph Clifford Fenton (1906–1969)
Albert C. Outler (1908–1989)
Addison H. Leitch (1908–1973)
Herman A. Hoyt (1909–2000)
F. F. Bruce (1910–1990)
W. T. Purkiser (1910–1992)
John F. Walvoord (1910–2002)
George Eldon Ladd (1911–1982)
Frank Stagg (1911–2001)
Alan Walker (1911–2003)
Francis Schaeffer (1912–1984)
Carl F. H. Henry (1913–2003)
Anthony A. Hoekema (1913–1988)
Bolaji Idowu (1913–1993)
Harold Lindsell (1913–1998)
Thomas F. Torrance (1913–2007)
Thomas Berry (1914–2009)
Anthony of Sourozh (Andrei Borisovich Bloom, 1914–2003)
Vernon Grounds (1914–2010)
Leon L. Morris (1914–2005)
Edward Schillebeeckx (1914–2009)
James Daane (1914–1983)
Markus Barth (1915–1994)
S. Lewis Johnson (1915–2004)
Thomas Merton (1915–1968)
J. Dwight Pentecost (1915–2014)
Derek Prince (1915–2003)

Roger R. Nicole (1915–2010)

Marie–Émile Boismard (1916–2004)

William Ragsdale Cannon (1916–1997)

Robert D. Culver (1916–2015)

Stanley Monroe Horton (1916–2014)

Bernard L. Ramm (1916–1992)

Victor Paul Wierwille (1916–1985)

C. K. Barrett (1917–2011)

G. B. Caird (1917–1984)

Edmund Clowney (1917–2005)

Avery Dulles (1918–2008)

Billy Graham (1918–2018)

J. Rodman Williams (1918–2008)

Edward J. Carnell (1919–1967)

Langdon Gilkey (1919–2004)

Paul K. Jewett (1919–1991)

John Macquarrie (1919–2007)

Catharina Halkes (1920–2011)

Karol Wojtyła (Pope John Paul II) (1920–2005)

J. Kenneth Grider (1921–2006)

George Wesley Buchanan (1921–2019)

Alexander Schmemann (1921–1983)

John Stott (1921–2011)

Hans Wilhelm Frei (1922–1988)

John Hick (1922–2012)

Meredith G. Kline (1922–2007)

J. Barton Payne (1922–1979)

Floyd H. Barackman (1923–2007)

Morton Howison Smith (1923–2017)

José Míguez Bonino (1924–2012)

James William McClendon, Jr. (1924–2000)

Jaroslav J. Pelikan (1924–2006)

John B. Cobb (b. 1925)

Daniel Fuller (1925–2003)

James Leo Garrett, Jr. (1925–2020)

John J McNeill (1925–2015)

Charles C. Ryrie (1925–2016)

Frederick Buechner (1926–2022)

H. Ray Dunning (b. 1926)

F. Leroy Forlines (1926–2020)

Gordon R. Lewis (1926–2016)

John Meyendorf (1926–92)

Jürgen Moltmann (b. 1926)

J. I. Packer (1926–2020)

Gordon Spykman (1926–1993)

Thomas J. J. Altizer (1927–2018)

Gerhard Forde (1927–2005)

Chuck Smith (1927–2013)

Joseph Ratzinger (Pope Benedict XVI) (b. 1927)

John Howard Yoder (1927–1997)

Shirley C. Guthrie, Jr. (1927–2004)

Mary Daly (1928–2010)

Gustavo Gutiérrez (b. 1928)

Hans Küng (1928–2021)

Martin E. Marty (b. 1928)

Johann Baptist Metz (1928–2019)

Wolfhart Pannenberg (1928–2014)

William Stringfellow (1928–1985)

Donald G. Bloesch (1928–2010)

Carl E. Braaten (b. 1929)

Kwesi Dickson (1929–2005)

Kosuke Koyama (1929–2009)

Dorothee Steffensky–Sölle (1929–2003)

James D. Strauss (1929–2014)

Joseph A. Bracken (b. 1930)

Ignacio Ellacuría (1930–1989)

Michael Green (1930–2019)

Robert William Jenson (1930–2017)

Heiko Oberman (1930–2001)

John Polkinghorne (1930–2021)

David Pawson (1930–2020)

Patricia Reif (1930–2002)

French L. Arrington (b. 1931)

Klaus Bockmühl (1931–1989)

William L. Lane (1931–1999)

John S. Mbiti (1931–2019)

William W. Menzies (1931–2011)

John Warwick Montgomery (b. 1931)

Thomas C. Oden (1931–2016)

Earl D. Radmacher (b. 1931)

Adrian Rogers (1931–2005)

John Shelby Spong (1931–2021)

John Zizioulas (b. 1931)

Millard J. Erickson (b. 1932)

Colin Brown (b. 1932)

Norman L. Geisler (1932–2019)

Douglas John Hall (b. 1932)

Rene Padilla (1932–2021)

Eugene H. Peterson (1932–2018)

Robert Picirilli (b. 1932)

Alvin Plantinga (b. 1932)

Robert L. Reymond (1932–2013)

Charles Stanley (1932–2023)

Roy B. Zuck (1932–2013)

Rubem Azevedo Alves (1933–2014)

Harold O. J. Brown (1933–2007)

Walter Brueggemann (b. 1933)

Everett Ferguson (b. 1933)

Roger T. Forster (b. 1933)

Norman R. Gulley (b. 1933)

Walter Kaiser, Jr. (b. 1933)

Michael Novak (1933–2017)

Marjorie Hewitt Suchocki (b. 1933)

Harvie M. Conn (1933–1999)

Charles E. Curran (b. 1934)

Gordon D. Fee (1934–2022)

Charles R. Swindoll (b. 1934)

I. Howard Marshall (1934–2015)

Mercy Oduyoye (b. 1934)

Henry Wansbrough (b. 1934)

Rolland McCune (1934–2019)

Bock, Darrell L. (b. 1935)

Bruce A. Demarest (1935–2021)

Daniel L. Migliore (b. 1935)

Dallas Willard (1935–2013)

Rosemary Radford Ruether (b. 1936)

Ronald H. Nash (1936–2006)

Henri A. G. Blocher (b. 1937)

Paul P. Enns (b. 1937)

Justo Gonzalez (b. 1937)

Clark Pinnock (1937–2010)

E. P. Sanders (1937–2022)

Anthony C. Thiselton (1937–2023)

David F. Wright (1937–2008)

Leonardo Boff (b. 1938)

James Montgomery Boice (1938–2000)

David J. A. Clines (b. 1938)

James Hal Cone (1938–2018)

Jack Cottrell (1938–2022)

Ronald M. Enroth (b. 1938)

Elisabeth Schüssler Fiorenza (b. 1938)

Keith Ward (b. 1938)

James Dunn (1939–2020)

John M. Frame (b. 1939)

George Marsden (b. 1939)

John F. MacArthur (b. 1939)

Ron J. Sider (b. 1939)

R. C. Sproul (1939–2017)

Peter Toon (1939–2009)

David F. Wells (b. 1939)

Alan Cairns (1940–2020)

Matthew V. Fox (b. 1940)

Stanley Hauerwas (b. 1940)

Walter Klaiber (b. 1940)

Donald Macleod (1940–2023)

Richard Mouw (b. 1940)

John N. Oswalt (b. 1940)

Stephen Tong (b. 1940)

Colin Gunton (1941–2003)

Elizabeth Johnson (b. 1941)

Erwin Lutzer (b. 1941)

David Hocking (b. 1941)

George Newlands (b. 1941)
Marcus Borg (1942–2015)
John P. Meier (1942–2022)
Grant R. Osborne (1942–2018)
Paige Patterson (b. 1942)
Lamin Sanneh (1942–2019)
Marilyn McCord Adams (1943–2017)
John Lennox (b. 1943)
Arnold G. Fruchtenbaum (b. 1943)
Douglas F. Kelly (b. 1943)
Douglas Stuart (b. 1943)
Gareth Lee Cockerill (b. 1944)
Andrew Louth (b. 1944)
Richard Mayhue (b. 1944)
Klyne Snodgrass (b. 1944)
John Ankerberg (b. 1945)
Kwame Bediako (1945–2008)
Keith Drury (b. 1945)
A. N. S. Lane (b. 1945)
D. A. Carson (b. 1946)
Mark Allan Noll (b. 1946)
John Piper (b. 1946)
Vern Poythress (b. 1946)
Andrew Puves (b. 1946)
William Willimon (b. 1946)
John Jefferson Davis (b. 1946)
Ravi Zacharias (1946–2020)
William J. Abraham (1947–2021)
P. D. L. Davis (b. 1947)
Paul S. Fiddes (b. 1947)
Larry D. Hart (b. 1947)
Robert Letham (b. 1947)
Jesse Mugambi (b. 1947)
Christopher Peppler (b. 1947)
Greg Bahnsen (1948–1995)
Gerald L. Bray (b. 1948)
David Brown (b. 1948)
Marva Dawn (1948–2021)
Sinclair Ferguson (b. 1948)
Bob Goss (b. 1948)
Wayne Grudem (b. 1948)
Scotty McLennan (b. 1948)
J. P. Moreland (b. 1948)
Richard A. Muller (b. 1948)
Robert A. Peterson (b. 1948)
William Placher (1948–2008)
Michael Plekon (b. 1948)
Charles Van Engen (1948)
N. T. Wright (b. 1948)
Gregory K. Beale (b. 1949)
Craig A. Blaising (b. 1949)
Graham A. Cole (b. 1949)
Ray Comfort (b. 1949)
William Lane Craig (b. 1949)
Tony Evans (b. 1949)
Graham McFarlane (b. 1949)
Michael J. Wilkins (b. 1949)
Chris Glaser (b. 1950)

Timothy George (b. 1950)

Stanley Grenz (1950–2005)

Gary Habermas (b. 1950)

Timothy J. Keller (1950–2023)

Douglas J. Moo (b. 1950)

Rowan Williams (b. 1950)

Nancy Wilson (b. 1950)

Donald K. McKim (b. 1950)

Mary McClintock Fulkerson (b. 1950)

Sarah Coakley (b. 1951)

Ken Ham (b. 1951)

Thomas Ice (b. 1951)

Steve Lemke (b. 1951)

Nancey Murphy (b. 1951)

Andrée Seu Peterson (b. 1951)

M. James Sawyer (b. 1951)

Ben Witherington III (b. 1951)

Marcella Althaus–Reid (1952–2009)

Alistair Begg (b. 1952)

Joel R. Beeke (b. 1952)

David K. Clark (b. 1952)

Kenneth J. Collins (b. 1952)

Franklin Graham (b. 1952)

Greg Laurie (b. 1952)

Bruce Lindley McCormack (b. 1952)

John Milbank (b. 1952)

Roger E. Olson (b. 1952)

Carsten Peter Thiede (1952–2004)

Daniel B. Wallace (b. 1952)

Rodney J. Decker (1953–2014)

Kent Hovind (b. 1953)

Michael Jenkins (b. 1953)

Musimbi Kanyoro (b. 1953)

Catherine Keller (b. 1953)

Randy L. Maddox (b. 1953)

Alister E. McGrath (b. 1953)

Scot McKnight (b. 1953)

Adele Reinhartz (b. 1953)

Bruce Ware (b. 1953)

Doug Wilson (b. 1953)

Kevin D. Zuber (b. 1953)

Gregg R. Allison (b. 1954)

Chad Brand (1954–2023)

Edith M. Humphrey (b. 1954)

Scott J. Jones (b. 1954)

Thomas R. Schreiner (b. 1954)

Tina Beattie (b. 1955)

Craig Blomberg (b. 1955)

Michael L. Brown (b. 1955)

Skip Heitzig (b. 1955)

Werner Günter Adolf Jeanrond (b. 1955)

Robert Jeffress (b. 1955)

Donald A. D. Thorsen (b. 1955)

Graham Ward (b. 1955)

John B. Webster (1955–2016)

Joel B. Green (b. 1956)
John E. Sanders (b. 1956)
Miroslav Volf (b. 1956)
Jeremy Sutherford Begbie (b. 1957)
Gregory A. Boyd (b. 1957)
Douglas Groothuis (b. 1957)
Daniela Müller (b. 1957)
Kevin J. Vanhoozer (b. 1957)
Gavin D'Costa (b. 1958)
Robert A. J. Gagnon (b. 1958)
Veli–Matti Kärkkäinen (b. 1958)
James Alison (b. 1959)
Peter Leithart (b. 1959)
Scott M. Manetsch (b. 1959)
R. Albert Mohler, Jr. (b. 1959)
Timothy Tennent (b. 1959)
Yves–Marie Adeline (b. 1960)
Mark Dever (b. 1960)
Craig S. Keener (b. 1960)
Peter Enns (b. 1961)
Nathan D. Holsteen (b. 1961)
Frank Turek (b. 1961)
Paul Washer (b. 1961)
Steven J. Wellum (b. 1961)
Paul Copan (b. 1962)
James R. White (b. 1962)
Elizabeth Stuart (b. 1963)
Malcolm B. Yarnell III (b. 1962)
Seung–Moo Ha (b. 1964)
Michael Horton (b. 1964)
K. Eric Thoennes (b. 1964)
David Bentley Hart (b. 1965)
Thomas Jay Oord (b. 1965)
R. C. Sproul, Jr. (b. 1965)
Philip Graham Ryken (b. 1966)
Ken Schenck (b. 1966)
Michael J. Vlach (b. 1966)
Marc Goodacre (b. 1967)
Carl R. Trueman (b. 1967)
Fred Sanders (b. 1968)
Robert Arp (b. 1970)
Mark Driscoll (b. 1970)
James K. A. Smith (b. 1970)
Kevin Gary Smith (b. 1970)
Christopher W. Morgan (b. 1971)
Kelly M. Kapic (b. 1972)
Scott R. Swain (b. 1972)
Daniel J. Treier (b. 1972)
Michael J. Svigel (1973)
Bruce Riley Ashford (b. 1974)
Michael F. Bird (b. 1974)
Leighton Flowers (b. 1974)
Adam Harwood (b. 1974)
Keith S. Whitfield (b. 1974)
Corneliu C. Simuţ (b. 1975)
Ulrich L. Lehner (b. 1976)
Tom Greggs (b. 1980)

Adam Kotsko (b. 1980)

R. Michael Allen (b. 1981)

Peckham, John C. (b. 1981)

Matthew Barrett (b. 1982)

Rhyne R. Putman (b. 1983)

APPENDIX 4: THE MAJOR LOCI OF SYSTEMATIC THEOLOGY

As noted previously in the discussion on the history of systematic theology in the Reformation and post-Reformation era, it was Philip Melanchthon (1497–1560)—Luther's lieutenant and the chief architect of Lutheranism—who worked out the elementary categorization schema for systematic theology by utilizing basic concepts—*topoi*, or *loci communes* ("common places"). Over time, these categories have been refined and expanded, and essentially standardized. This appendix lists and briefly explains eleven categories: Prolegomena, Bibliology, Theology Proper, Christology, Pneumatology, Angelology, Anthropology, Hamartiology, Soteriology, Ecclesiology, and Eschatology.

Prolegomena

Prolegomena (Gk. *pro*, "before"; *legō*, "to say") serves as an introduction to a subject—a propaedeutic. Here, prolegomena deals with foundational issues for constructing a systematic theology, including one's epistemology, the nature, task, source, scope, method of theology, and so forth.

Bibliology

Bibliology (Gk. *biblion*, "book" + *logos*, "word" or "discourse") is the doctrine of Scripture. It treats Scripture's inspiration (its God-breathed nature), authority (its supreme right to command faith and obedience), truthfulness (all its affirmations are wholly true), sufficiency (it provides wisdom leading to salvation and all the instruction Christians need to fully please God), necessity (it is the ultimate way in which God communicates), clarity (ability to be understood), power (it effects salvation and transformation of life), and canonicity (the collection of inspired writings that properly belong in Scripture). Bibliology also defends, and addresses challenges to, these matters.[1]

Theology Proper

Theology Proper (Gk. *theos*, "God" + *logos*, "word" or "discourse") is the doctrine of God Himself. It treats His existence (as evidenced through both special revelation and general revelation), and the traditional argumentation or "proofs" for such (typically falling into one of the following four categories: cosmological, teleological, ontological, and moral). Further, God's incomprehensibility and knowability is considered. God's attributes are also treated, typically organized into communicable (e.g., spirituality, wisdom, goodness, love, mercy) and incommunicable (e.g., independence, immutability, eternality, omnipresence, and unity) attributes. This loci further treats God's triune nature, as well as His decrees and works.

[1] Expanded from the definition in *BCDTT*, s.v. "bibliology," 33.

Christology

Christology (Gk. *christos*, "Christ" + *logos*, "word" or "discourse") treats the person and work of Jesus Christ. The doctrine affirms the preexistence of the Son of God; His eternal generation from the Father; and His work in creation, providence, redemption, and consummation. It treats His state of humiliation: the taking of human nature in the incarnation, His holy life, suffering, crucifixion, burial, and death. It covers His state of exaltation: His resurrection, ascension, session to the right hand of the Father, and future return. It further discusses Christ's work as a prophet, priest, and king, with emphasis on His atoning sacrifice.[2]

Pneumatology

Pneumatology (Gk. *pneuma*, "Spirit" + *logos*, "word" or "discourse") is the doctrine of the person and work of the Holy Spirit. It affirms the personality and deity of the Holy Spirit; His eternal procession from the Father and the Son; His work—together with those two—of creation, providence, redemption, and consummation; and the continuities and discontinuities between His work prior to Christ and His new covenant mission beginning at Pentecost. It further rehearses His many ministries, including conviction of sin, regeneration, sealing, assurance of salvation, prayer, illumination of Scripture, filling, empowerment for evangelism, guidance, distribution of spiritual gifts, and others.[3]

Angelology

Angelology (Gk. *angelos*, "angel" + *logos*, "word" or "discourse") is the doctrine of angels, treating the origin, nature, organization, works, and

---

[2] Expanded from ibid., s.v. "Christology," 40.

[3] Expanded from ibid., s.v. "Pneumatology," 164.

destiny of holy angels, Satan, and fallen angels. Sometimes this locus is subdivided into holy angels (angelology proper), Satan (Satanology), and fallen angels or demons (demonology); usually, all three topics are subsumed under a single locus.

Anthropology

Anthropology—in this case theological anthropology—is the doctrine of humanity (Gk. *anthropos*, "man" + *logos*, "word" or "discourse"). It treats humanity's origin (creation in the image of God), human nature (traditionally, either dichotomy—human nature is twofold: body and soul/spirit; or trichotomy—it is threefold: body, soul, and spirit), and the origin of the soul (traditionally, either creationism—God creates the soul; or traducianism—it is passed down from parents to their offspring). Contemporary discussion focuses on dualism (human nature is complex, being both material and immaterial) versus monism (it is simple, usually material only), and treats gender, embodiment, sexuality, and more.[4]

Hamartiology

Hamartiology (Gk. *hamartia*, "sin" + *logos*, "word" or "discourse") is the doctrine of sin. It treats the definition of sin (e.g., a lack of conformity to God's law and God's moral image), its elements (e.g., pride, unfaithfulness, disobedience), its origin (the rebellion of Adam and Eve), and its consequences (e.g., alienation from God, enslavement to sin, broken relationships). Further discussion focuses on controversial matters such as original sin (i.e., the state of guilt and/or corruption into which all people are born) and its transmission (creationism, traducianism), its

---

[4] Expanded from ibid., s.v. "anthropology, theological," 20.

elements (e.g., depravity, inability), and the imputation of Adam's sin (with the positions of Pelagianism, Arminianism, and Calvinism).[5]

Soteriology

Soteriology (Gk. *sotēria*, "salvation" + *logos*, "word" or "discourse") is the doctrine of salvation (God's gracious work of rescuing people from the power and curse of sin and restoring them to a right relationship with Himself), and all the mighty acts of God which fall under that blanket term, including the antecedent to, beginning, continuation, and completion of salvation. *Objective* soteriology (often addressed under Christology) speaks of the life, death, resurrection and exaltation of Christ in relation to salvation. *Subjective* soteriology (the work of the Spirit in the application of Christ's salvation) deals with the process whereby individuals are brought to God's saving goals. Topics generally covered include election, calling, regeneration, faith, repentance, conversion, justification, adoption, union, sanctification, and glorification.[6]

Ecclesiology

Ecclesiology (Gk. *ekklēsia*, "church, assembly" + *logos*, "word" or "discourse") is the doctrine of the church, including the origin, nature (universal and local), attributes or marks (one, holy, catholic or universal, and apostolic), offices (elders and deacons), governance (episcopal, presbyterian, congregational, nongovernmental), ministries (worship, proclamation, evangelism and missions, discipleship, and care),

---

[5] Expanded from ibid., s.v. "hamartiology," 97.

[6] Adapted from Stanley Grenz, David Guretzki, and Cherith Fee Nordling, *Pocket Dictionary of Theological Terms* (Downers Grove: InterVarsity, 1999) s.v. "soteriology," 108.

ordinances (baptism and the Lord's Supper), and relationships among the churches (complete independence, free church, network, multisite).

Eschatology

Eschatology (Gk. *eschatos*, "last" + *logos*, "word" or "discourse") is the doctrine of last things, both individual or personal (the future of the individual) and cosmic (the future of the human race and the entire creation). Personal eschatology addresses the subjects of death and the intermediate state (human existence between death and the resurrection of the body). Cosmic eschatology covers the return of Christ and its relation to the millennium (amillennialism, postmillennialism, premillennialism) and the tribulation, the resurrection, the last judgment, the eternal blessing of the righteous and the eternal judgment of the wicked, and the eternal state of the new heaven and new earth. Individual or personal eschatology occurs at death; cosmic eschatology occurs at the Second Coming.[7]

[7] Adapted slightly from the definition in *BCDTT*, s.v. "eschatology," 72.

BIBLIOGRAPHY

Nota bene: Nearly three millennia ago, King Solomon of Israel observed, "Of making many books there is no end, and much study is weariness of the flesh" (Ecc. 12:12 KJV).[1] Centuries later, the Roman philosopher Seneca (*d.* AD 65) would complain, "We suffer from an excess of literature as from an excess of anything" (*Epistles*, cvi). Significantly, both comments came long before the invention of the printing press (*ca.* 1450) and the World Wide Web (1989). Today, there is an overwhelming deluge of literature on every

---

[1] There is a translation issue with regards to Eccl. 12:12, as explained by *The NET Bible*:

> The verb עָשָׂה (*'asah*, "to do") may mean "to make" (*HALOT* 890 s.v. עשׂה 3) or "to acquire" (*HALOT* 891 s.v. עשׂה 6). The LXX rendered it as ποιησαι (*poiēsai*, "making"), as do most English versions: "making" (KJV, YLT, RSV, NRSV, NAB, ASV, MLB, NIV, NJPS). However, several English versions reflect a different nuance: "there is no end to the buying of books" (Moffatt); "the use of books is endless" (NEB); and "the writing of many books is endless" (NASB).

See *The NET Bible* (Dallas, Texas: Biblical Studies Press, 1996–2006) n. at Eccl. 12:12. Darby, Douay–Rheims, WEB, and BEB also read "making." Cf. NCV: "People are always writing books"; CJB: "one can write many books—there's no end to it"; *The Message*: "There's no end to the publishing of books"; *The Voice*: "There is no end to writing books"; *Tree of Life*: "There is no end to the making of many books"; LEB: "The writing of books is endless." The Latin Vulgate reads "Faciendi plures libros nullus est finis"; in Spanish, the Reina–Valera 1960 translates as "No hay fin de hacer muchos libros," while the Reina–Valera 1995 has "No tiene objeto escribir muchos libros."

conceivable subject. Just as the craftsman needs the right tools for the task, so too does every student of Scripture and theology. The following, therefore, is a collection of some of the more important works that every student ought to be familiar with, both specifically concerning the history of systematic theology and issues deemed otherwise germane. While this bibliography does not seek to be exhaustive (itself an impossible endeavor), it does offer the reader a reasonable collection of sources deemed helpful in exploring further the rich field of the history of systematic theology. These works are divided into standard reference works, church history, history of doctrine, primary systematic theologies, articles and chapters of importance, and monographs of note.

Standard Reference Works

Allen, R. Michael, ed. *The New Cambridge Companion to Christian Thought.* New York, NY: Cambridge University, 2023.

Burne, Peter, and Leslie Houlden, eds. *The Routledge Companion Encyclopedia of Theology.* London: Routledge, 2003.

Cross, F. L., and E. A. Livingstone, eds. *Oxford Dictionary of the Christian Church.* 3rd ed. Oxford: Oxford University, 1997.

Davie, Martin, *et al.*, eds. *New Dictionary of Theology: Historical and Systematic.* 2nd ed. Downers Grove, IL: InterVarsity Academic, 2016.

Di Berardino, Angelo, *et al.*, eds. *Encyclopedia of Ancient Christianity.* 3 vols. Trans. Joseph T. Papa, Erik A. Koenke, Eric E. Hewett, *et al.* Downers Grove, IL: IVP, 2014.

Elwell Walter A., ed. *Evangelical Dictionary of Theology.* Grand Rapids, MI: Baker, 1984.

Ferguson, Sinclair B., David F. Wright, and J. I. Packer, eds. *New Dictionary of Theology*. Downers Grove, IL: IVP, 1988.

Gunton, Colin E., ed. *The Cambridge Companion to Christian Doctrine*. Cambridge: Cambridge University, 1997.

Hart, Trevor, ed. *Dictionary of Historical Theology*. Grand Rapids, MI: Eerdmans, 2000.

Harrison, Everett F., Geoffrey W. Bromiley, and Carl F. H. Henry, eds. *Wycliffe Dictionary of Theology*. reprint; Peabody, MA: Hendrickson, 2004.

House, H. Wayne, ed. *Evangelical Dictionary of World Religions*. Grand Rapids, MI: Baker, 2018.

Kurian, Thomas George, ed. *Encyclopedia of Christian Civilization*. 4 Vols. Malden, MA: Wiley–Blackwell, 2011.

Lacoste, Jean–Yves, ed. *Encyclopedia of Christian Theology*. 3 vols. New York: Routledge, 2005.

Larsen, Timothy, and Daniel J. Treier, eds. *The Cambridge Companion to Evangelical Theology*. Cambridge: Cambridge University, 2007.

McFarland, Ian A., David S. Ferguson, Karen Kilby, and Iain R. Torrance, eds. *The Cambridge Dictionary of Christian Theology*. New York: Cambridge University, 2011.

McGrath, Alister, ed. *The Blackwell Encyclopedia of Modern Christian Thought*. Oxford: Blackwell, 1993.

Musser, Donald W., and Joseph L. Price, eds. *A New Handbook of Christian Theology*. Nashville, TN: Abingdon, 1992.

Richardson, Alan, and Jacob Bowden, eds. *The Westminster Dictionary of Christian Theology*. Philadelphia, PA: Westminster John Knox, 1983.

Treier, Daniel J., and Walter A. Elwell, eds. *Evangelical Dictionary of Theology*. 3rd ed. Grand Rapids, MI: Baker, 2017.

Webster, John, Kathryn Tanner and Iain Torrance, eds. *The Oxford Handbook of Systematic Theology*. Oxford: Oxford University, 2007.

Church History

Aland, Kurt. *A History of Christianity*. 2 vols. James L. Schaff, trans. Philadelphia, PA: Fortress, 1985.

Duesing, Jason G., and Nathan A, Finn, eds. *Historical Theology for the Church*. Wheaton, IL: Crossway, 2021.

Ferguson, Everett. *Church History,* vol. 1: *From Christ to the Pre-Reformation.* 2nd ed. Grand Rapids, MI: Zondervan, 2013.

González, Justo L. *The Story of Christianity.* 2 vols. Rev. ed. San Francisco, CA: HarperOne, 2010.

Hill, Jonathan. *Zondervan Handbook to the History of Christianity*. Grand Rapids, MI: Zondervan, 2006.

Latourette, Kenneth Scott. *A History of Christianity.* 2 vols. 1954. Reprint. Peabody, MA: Hendrickson, 1997–99.

Needham, Nick. *2,000 Years of Christ's Power*. 4 vols. Fearn, Ross-Shire, Scotland: Christian Focus, 2016.

Noll, Mark A. *Turning Points: Decisive Moments in the History of Christianity.* 3rd ed. Grand Rapids, MI: Baker, 2012.

Pelikan, Jaroslav. *The Christian Tradition: A History of the Development of Doctrine*. 5 vols. Chicago: University of Chicago, 1971–89.

Schaff, Philip. *History of the Christian Church.* 8 vols. 1910. Reprint. Grand Rapids, MI: Eerdmans, 1962.

Woodbridge, John D., and Frank A. James III. *Church History,* vol. 2: *From Pre-Reformation to the Present Day*. Grand Rapids, MI: Zondervan, 2013.

History of Doctrine

Allison, Gregg R. *Historical Theology: An Introduction to Christian Doctrine*. Grand Rapids, MI: Zondervan, 2011.

Berkhof, Louis. *The History of Christian Doctrines*. 1937. Reprint. Carlisle, PA: Banner of Truth, 1985.

Bromiley, Geoffrey W. *Historical Theology: An Introduction*. Grand Rapids, MI: Eerdmans, 1978.

Cunliffe-Jones, Hubert. *A History of Christian Doctrine*. Philadelphia. PA: Fortress, 1978.

Ford, David F., ed. *The Modern Theologians*. 2 vols. Oxford: Blackwell, 1997.

González, Justo L. *A History of Christian Thought*. 3 vols. Rev. ed. Nashville, TN: Abingdon, 1988.

Grillmeier, Aloys. *Christ in Christian Tradition*. 4 vols. Louisville, KY: Westminster John Knox, 1975–96.

Hägglund, Bengt. *History of Theology*. 4th rev. ed. Gene J. Lund, trans. St. Louis, MO: Concordia, 2007.

Hannah, John D. *Our Legacy: The History of Christian Doctrine*. Colorado Springs, CO: NavPress, 2001.

Pelikan, Jaroslav. *The Christian Tradition: A History of the Development of Doctrine*. 5 vols. Chicago: University of Chicago, 1971.

Quasten, Johannes. *Patrology*. 4 vols. Westminster: Christian Classics, 1983–86.

Schaff, Philip. *The Creeds of Christendom.* 3 vols. Grand Rapids, MI: Baker, 1983.

Shedd, William G. T. *A History of Christian Doctrine.* 2 vols. Reprint. Eugene, OR: Wipf & Stock, 1998.

PRIMARY SYSTEMATIC THEOLOGIES

Akin, Daniel L., ed. *A Theology for the Church.* Rev. ed. Nashville, TN: Broadman & Holman Academic, 2014.

Allen, Michael, and Scott R. Swain. *Christian Dogmatics: Reformed Theology for the Church Catholic.* Grand Rapids, MI: Baker, 2016.

Arrington, French L. *Christian Doctrine: A Pentecostal Perspective.* 3 vols. Cleveland, TN: Pathway Press, 1992–94.

Bancroft, Emery H. *Christian Theology: Systematic and Biblical.* 2nd ed. Rev. ed. Ronald B. Mayers, ed. Grand Rapids, MI: Zondervan, 1976.

Barackman, Floyd H. *Practical Christian Theology: Examining the Great Doctrines of the Faith.* 4th ed. Grand Rapids, MI: Kregel Academic, 2001.

Barrett, Matthew. *Reformation Theology: A Systematic Summary.* Wheaton, IL: Crossway, 2017.

Bavinck, Herman. *Reformed Dogmatics.* 4 vols. John Vriend, trans. John Bolt, ed. Grand Rapids, MI: Baker, 2003–06.

_____. *Reformed Dogmatics: Abridged in One Volume.* John Bolt, ed. Grand Rapids, MI: Baker Academic, 2011.

Beeke, Joel, and Paul M. Smalley, *Reformed Systematic Theology.* 3 vols. Wheaton, IL: Crossway, 2019–21.

Berkhof, Louis. *Systematic Theology*. 1958. Reprint. Carlisle, PA: Banner of Truth, 2003.

Bird, Michael. *Evangelical Theology: A Biblical and Systematic Introduction*. Grand Rapids, MI: Zondervan, 2013.

Bloesch, Donald G. *Christian Foundations*. 7 vols. Downers Grove, IL: IVP, 1992–2004.

_____. *Essentials of Evangelical Theology*. 2 vols. New York: Harper & Row, 1978–79.

Boice, James Montgomery. *Foundations of the Christian Faith*. Rev. one-vol. ed. Downers Grove, IL: InterVarsity, 1986.

Boyce, James Petigru. *Abstracts of Systematic Theology*. 1887. Reprint. Cape Coral, FL: Founders Press, 2006.

Braaten, Carl E. and Robert W. Jensen, eds. *Christian Dogmatics*. Minneapolis, MN: Fortress, 1984.

Bray, Gerald. *God Is Love: A Biblical and Systematic Theology*. Wheaton, IL: Crossway, 2012.

Buswell, James Oliver. *A Systematic Theology of the Christian Religion*. 2 vols. Grand Rapids, MI: Zondervan, 1962–63.

Calvin, John. *Institutes of the Christian Religion*. 2 vols. John T. McNeill, ed. Trans. and indexed by Ford Lewis Battles. In *The Library of Christian Classics*, Vols. 20–21. Philadelphia: Westminster, 1960.

Carter, Charles W., ed. *A Contemporary Wesleyan Theology: Biblical, Systematic, and Practical*. 2 vols. Grand Rapids, MI: Francis Asbury/Zondervan, 1983.

Chafer, Lewis Sperry. *Systematic Theology*. 8 vols. Dallas, TX: Dallas Seminary, 1947–48.

_____. *Systematic Theology.* 4 vols. John F. Walvoord, ed. Grand Rapids, MI: Kregel, 1993.

Culver, Robert Duncan. *Systematic Theology: Biblical and Historical.* Fearn, Ross–shire, Scotland: Mentor, 2005.

Dabney, Robert Lewis. *Systematic Theology.* 1878. Reprint. Edinburgh: Banner of Truth, 1985.

Dagg, John L. *Manual of Theology.* 1857. Reprint. Harrisonburg, VA: Gano, 1990.

Dunning, H. Ray. *Grace, Faith, and Holiness: A Wesleyan Systematic Theology.* Kansas City, MO: Beacon Hill, 1988.

Enns, Paul. *The Moody Handbook of Theology*, rev. and exp. Chicago, IL: Moody, 2008.

Erickson, Millard J. *Christian Theology.* 3rd ed. Grand Rapids, MI: Baker Academic, 2013.

_____. *Introducing Christian Doctrine.* 3rd ed. L. Arnold Hustad, ed. Grand Rapids, MI: Baker Academic, 2015.

Frame, John M. *Systematic Theology: An Introduction to Christian Belief.* Phillipsburg, NJ: Presbyterian and Reformed, 2013.

Gamertsfelder, Solomon J. *Systematic Theology.* Harrisburg, PA: Evangelical Publishing House, 1952.

Garrett, James Leo, Jr. *Systematic Theology: Biblical, Systematic, and Historical.* 2 vols. 1990, 1995. Reprint. Eugene, OR: Wipf & Stock, 2014.

Geisler, Norman L. *Systematic Theology in One Volume.* Minneapolis, MN: Bethany House, 2011.

_____. *Systematic Theology.* 4 vols. Minneapolis, MN: Bethany House, 2002–05.

Gill, John. *Complete Body of Doctrinal and Practical Divinity*. 2 vols. Grand Rapids, MI: Baker, 1978.

Grenz, Stanley J. *Theology for the Community of God*. Grand Rapids, MI: Eerdmans, 2000.

Grider, J. Kenneth. *A Wesleyan–Holiness Theology*. Kansas City, MO: Beacon Hill, 1994.

Grudem, Wayne. *Systematic Theology: An Introduction to Biblical Doctrine,* 2nd ed. Grand Rapids, MI: Zondervan, 2020.

Gulley, Norman R. *Systematic Theology*. 4 vols. Berrien Springs, MI: Andrews University, 2003–16.

Guthrie, Shirley C. *Christian Doctrine*. Rev. ed. Louisville, KY: Westminster John Knox, 1994.

Harwood, Adam. *Christian Theology: Biblical, Historical, Systematic*. Bellingham, WA: Lexham Academic, 2022.

Henry, Carl F. H. *God, Revelation, and Authority*. 6 vols. Waco, TX: Word, 1976–83.

Heppe, Heinrich. *Reformed Dogmatics: Set Out and Illustrated From the Sources*. Rev. ed. Ernst Bizer, ed. G. T. Thompson, trans. 1861. Reprint. Grand Rapids, MI: Baker, 1978.

Hodge, A. A. *Outlines of Theology*. 1878. Reprint. Grand Rapids, MI: Zondervan, 1949.

Hodge, Charles. *Systematic Theology*. 3 vols. 1871–1873. Reprint. Grand Rapids, MI: Eerdmans, 1975.

Holsteen, Nathan D., and Michael J. Svigel, eds. *Exploring Christian Theology*. 3 vols. Minneapolis, MN: Bethany House, 2014–15.

Horton, Michael. *The Christian Faith: A Systematic Theology for Pilgrims on the Way*. Grand Rapids, MI: Zondervan, 2011.

Horton, Stanley M. *Systematic Theology*. Rev. ed. Springfield, MO: Gospel, 1994.

Jones, Gareth. *Christian Theology*. Oxford: Polity, 1999.

Kelly, Douglas F. *Systematic Theology*. 3 vols. Fearn, Ross–shire, Scotland: Mentor, 2008, 2014, 2021.

Kuyper, Abraham. *Principles of Sacred Theology*. J. H. DeVries, trans. 1898. Reprint. Grand Rapids, MI: Eerdmans, 1968.

Lane, Tony. *Exploring Christian Doctrine: A Guide to What Christians Believe*. Downers Grove, IL: IVP Academic, 2014.

Letham, Robert. *Systematic Theology*. Wheaton, IL: Crossway, 2019.

Lewis, Gordon R. and Bruce A. Demarest. *Integrative Theology*. 3 vols. Grand Rapids, MI: Zondervan, 1987, 1990, 1994.

Litton, Edward Arthur. *Introduction to Dogmatic Theology*. Rev. ed. Philip E. Hughes, ed. 1882–92. Reprint. London: James Clarke, 1960.

MacArthur, John and Richard Mayhue, eds. *Biblical Doctrine: A Systematic Summary of Bible Truth*. Wheaton, IL: Crossway, 2017.

McBrien, Richard P. *Catholicism*. 2 vols. Minneapolis, MN: Winston, 1980.

McClendon, James William, Jr. *Systematic Theology*. 3 vols. Nashville, TN: Abingdon, 1986–2000.

McCune, Rolland. *A Systematic Theology of Biblical Christianity*. 3 vols. Allen Park, MI: Detroit Baptist Theological Press, 2009–10.

McGrath, Alister E. *Christian Theology: An Introduction*. 3rd ed. Oxford: Blackwell, 2001.

Menzies, William W., and Stanley M. Horton. *Bible Doctrines: A Pentecostal Perspective*. Springfield, MO: Gospel 1993.

Migliore, Daniel L. *Faith Seeking Understanding: An Introduction to Christian Theology*. 3rd ed. Grand Rapids, MI: Eerdmans, 2014.

Miley, John. *Systematic Theology*. 2 vols. Library of Biblical and Theological Literature, vols. 5–6. 1892, 1894. Reprint. Peabody, MA: Hendrickson, 1989.

Morgan, Christopher W., and Robert A Peterson. *Christian Theology: The Biblical Story and Our Faith*. Nashville, TN: B&H Academic, 2020.

Mueller, John Theodore. *Christian Dogmatics*. St. Louis, MO: Concordia, 1934.

Mullins, E. Y. *The Christian Religion in its Doctrinal Expression*. 1917. Reprint. Eugene, OR: Wipf & Stock, 2000.

Oden, Thomas C. *Classic Christianity: A Systematic Theology*. San Francisco: HarperOne, 2009.

_____. *Systematic Theology*. 3 vols. Peabody, MA: Hendrickson, 2006.

Ott, Ludwig. *Fundamentals of Catholic Dogma*. James Canon Bastible, ed. Patrick Lynch, trans. St Louis, MO: Herder, 1955.

Packer, J. I. *Concise Theology: A Guide to Historic Christian Beliefs*. Wheaton, IL: Tyndale House, 1993.

Peckham, John C. *God With Us: An Introduction to Adventist Theology*. Berrien Springs, MI: Adventist University, 2023.

Pieper, Francis. *Christian Dogmatics*. 4 vols. St. Louis, MO: Concordia, 1950–57.

Pope, William Burt. *A Compendium of Christian Theology: Being Analytical Outlines of a Course of Theological Study, Biblical, Dogmatic, Historical*. 2nd ed. 3 vols. 1875–76. Reprint. New York: Phillip and Hunt, n.d.

Purkiser, W. T., ed. *Exploring Our Christian Faith*. Kansas City, MO: Beacon Hill, 1960.

Raymond, Miner. *Systematic Theology*. 3 vols. Cincinnati, OH: Hitchcock and Walden, 1877–79.

Reymond, Robert L. *A New Systematic Theology of the Christian Faith*. Nashville, TN: Thomas Nelson, 1998.

Ryrie, Charles C. *Basic Theology: A Popular Systematic Guide to Understanding Biblical Truth*. Wheaton, IL: Victor Books, 1986.

Shedd, William G. T. *Dogmatic Theology*, 3rd ed. Alan W. Gomes, ed. Phillipsburg, NJ: Presbyterian and Reformed, 2003.

Smith, Morton H. *Systematic Theology*. 2 vols. Eugene, OR: Wipf and Stock, 2019.

Spykman, Gordon J. *Reformational Theology: A New Paradigm for Doing Dogmatics*. Grand Rapids, MI: Eerdmans, 1992.

Strong, A. H. *Systematic Theology: A Compendium Designed for the Use of Theological Students*. Rev. ed. New York: Revell, 1907.

Swindoll, Charles R. and Roy B. Zuck, eds. *Understanding Christian Theology*. Nashville, TN: Thomas Nelson, 2003.

Thielicke, Helmut. *The Evangelical Faith*. 3 vols. Trans. Geoffrey W. Bromiley. Grand Rapids, MI: Eerdmans, 1974.

Thiessen, Henry Clarence. *Lectures in Systematic Theology*. Rev ed. Vernon D. Doerksen, ed. 1979. Reprint. Grand Rapids, MI: Eerdmans, 1990.

Thiselton, Anthony C. *Systematic Theology*. Grand Rapids, MI: Eerdmans, 2015.

Thomas, W. H. Griffith. *The Principles of Theology: An Introduction to the Thirty–Nine Articles*. 5th ed. London: Church Book Room Press, 1956.

Turretin, Francis. *Institutes of Elenctic Theology*. 3 vols. George Musgrave Giger, trans. James T. Dennison, Jr., ed. Phillipsburg, NJ: P&R, 1992–97.

Van Genderen, Jan, and Willem H. Velema. *Concise Reformed Dogmatics*. Gerritt Bilkes and Ed M. van der Maas, trans. Phillipsburg, NJ: Presbyterian and Reformed, 2008.

Wakefield, Samuel. *A Complete System of Christian Theology; or, a Concise, Comprehensive, and Systematic View of the Evidences, Doctrines, Morals, and Institutions of Christianity*. New York: Carlton & Porter, 1862.

Watson, Richard. *Theological Institutes*. 3 vols. New York, NY: G. Lane and P. Sanford, 1843.

Wiley, H. Orton. *Christian Theology*. 3 vols. Kansas City, MO: Nazarene, 1940–43.

Williams, Ernest S., *Systematic Theology*. 3 vols. Springfield, MO: Gospel Publishing House, 1953.

Williams, J. Rodman. *Renewal Theology: Systematic Theology from a Charismatic Perspective*. 3 vols. Grand Rapids, MI: Zondervan, 1988–92.

Zuber, Kevin D. *The Essential Scriptures: A Handbook of the Biblical Texts for Key Doctrines*. Chicago, IL: Moody, 2021.

Articles and Chapters

Allen, Michael. "Systematic Theology and Biblical Theology—Part One." *Journal of Reformed Theology* 14.1–2. Mar. 27, 2020. 52–72.

_____. "Systematic Theology and Biblical Theology—Part Two." *Journal of Reformed Theology* 14.4. Dec. 1, 2020. 344–57.

Anckeren, G. F. van. "Theology," in *New Catholic Encyclopedia.* 17 vols. W. J. McDonald, ed. Washington, DC: Catholic University of America, 1967–79. 14:39–49.

Bray, Gerald. "Systematic Theology, History of," in *New Dictionary of Theology.* Sinclair B. Ferguson, David F. Wright, and J. I. Packer, eds. Downers Grove, IL: IVP, 1988. 671–72.

Bromiley, Geoffrey W. "History of Theology," in *New Dictionary of Theology.* Sinclair B. Ferguson, David F. Wright, and J. I. Packer, eds. Downers Grove, IL: InterVarsity, 1988. 309–12.

_____. "Theology," in *Wycliffe Dictionary of Theology.* Everett F. Harrison Geoffrey W. Bromiley, and Carl F. H. Henry, eds. Reprint. Peabody, MA: Hendrickson, 2004. 518–20.

Conn, Harvie M. "Theological Systems," in *Evangelical Dictionary of World Missions*. A. Scott Moreau, Harold Netland, and Charles Van Engen, eds. Grand Rapids, MI: Baker, 2000. 947–49.

Couch, Mal. "What is Systematic Theology?" *Conservative Theological Journal* 8.23. Mar. 2004. 10–28.

Daane, James. "Theology," in *International Standard Bible Encyclopedia*. 4 vols. Geoffrey W. Bromiley, ed. Grand Rapids, MI: Eerdmans, 1988. 4:826–27

Demarest, Bruce A. "Systematic Theology," in *Evangelical Dictionary of Theology*. Walter A. Elwell, ed. Grand Rapids, MI: Baker, 1984. 1064–66.

Engen, Charles Van. "Systematic Theology," in *Evangelical Dictionary of World Missions*. A. Scott Moreau, Harold Netland, and Charles Van Engen, eds. Grand Rapids, MI: Baker, 2000. 925–26.

Fackre, Gabriel. "The Revival of Systematic Theology: An Overview." *Interpretation* 49.3. 1995. 229–41.

Fulkerson, Mary McClintlock. "Systematic Theology," in *The Wiley–Blackwell Companion to Practical Theology*. Bonnie J. Miller-McLemore, ed. Malden, MA: Blackwell, 2012. 357–66.

Garrett, James Leo, Jr. "Why Systematic Theology?" *Criswell Theological Review* 3.2. 1989. 259–81.

Gundry, Stanley. "Evangelical Theology: Where *Should* We Be Going?" *Journal of the Evangelical Theological Society* 22.1. March 1979. 3–13.

Gunton, Colin. "A Rose by Any Other Name? From 'Christian Doctrine' to 'Systematic Theology.'" *International Journal of Systematic Theology* 1. 1999. 4–23.

Healy, Nicholas M. "What is Systematic Theology?" *International Journal of Systematic Theology* 11.1. January 2009. 24–39.

Hefling, Charles. "What Is Systematic Theology?" *Theological Studies* 67. 2006. 894–95.

Henry, Carl F. H. "Where Is Modern Theology Going?" *Journal of the Evangelical Theological Society* 11.1. Winter 1968. 3–12.

Killen, R. Allen. "Theology," in *Wycliffe Bible Dictionary*. Charles F. Pfeiffer, Howard F. Vos, and John Rea, eds. Reprint. Peabody, MA: Hendrickson, n.d. 1690–96.

Lacoste, Jean–Yves. "Theology," in *Encyclopedia of Christian Theology*. Jean–Yves Lacoste, ed. New York: Routledge, 2005. 1554–62.

Markham, Ian. "Theology," in *The Blackwell Companion to the Study of Religion*. Robert A. Segal, ed. Malden, MA: Blackwell. 193–210.

_____. "Doctrine," in *Dictionary for Theological Interpretation of the Bible*. Kevin J. Vanhoozer, ed. Grand Rapids, MI: Baker Academic, 2005. 177–80.

McClendon, James William. "Systematic Theology: Doctrine." *Pro Ecclesia A Journal of Catholic and Evangelical Theology* 6.3. Aug. 1997. 366–68.

Moloney, Raymond. "What is Systematic Theology?" *Irish Theological Quarterly* 72. 2007. 105–06.

Moltmann, Jürgen. "What is Christian theology?" *Theological Review* 29. 2008. 31–44.

Morrow, T. W. "Systematic Theology," in *New Dictionary of Theology*. Sinclair B. Ferguson, David F. Wright, and J. I. Packer, eds. Downers Grove, IL: IVP, 1988. 671.

Murray, John. "Systematic Theology," in *Collected Writings of John Murray*, vol. 4: *Systematic Theology*. Edinburgh: Banner of Truth, 1982. 4:1–21.

Nicole, Roger R. "A Postscript on Theology," in *Basic Christian Doctrines*. Carl F. H. Henry, ed. 1962. Reprint. Dallas, TX: Digital Publications, 2002. 264–68.

Ormerod, Neil. "What is the Goal of Systematic Theology?" *Irish Theological Quarterly* 74. 2009. 38–52.

Pannenberg, Wolfhart. "Systematic Theology." *Pro Ecclesia: A Journal of Catholic and Evangelical Theology* 9.1. Feb. 2000. 108–09.

Peppler, Christopher L. "Systematic Theology," in *A Student's A—Z of Theology: Evangelical Theology in Outline*. Bill Domeris and Kevin Smith, eds. Johannesburg: South African Theological Seminary, 2014. 245–55.

Towns, Elmer L. "The Relationship of Church Growth to Systematic Theology." *Journal of the Evangelical Theological Society* 29.1. 1986. 63–70.

Treier, Daniel J. "Evangelical Theology," in *The Cambridge Dictionary of Christian Theology*. Ian A. McFarland, David Fergusson, Karen Kilby, and Iain R. Torrance, eds. Cambridge: Cambridge University, 2011. 173–76.

Vanhoozer, Kevin J. "From Bible to Theology," in *Theology, Church, and Ministry*. David S. Dockery, ed. Nashville, TN: B&H Academic, 2017. 233–56.

_____. "Systematic theology," in *New Dictionary of Theology: Historical and Systematic*. 2nd ed. Martin Davie, *et al.*, eds. Downers Grove, IL: InterVarsity Academic, 2016. 885–86.

_____. "Systematic Theology," in *Dictionary for Theological Interpretation of the Bible*. Kevin J. Vanhoozer, ed. Grand Rapids, MI: Baker Academic, 2005. 773–79.

Warfield, B. B. "The Indispensableness of Systematic Theology to the Preacher," in *Selected Shorter Writings of Benjamin B. Warfield*.

John E. Meeter, ed. 1897. Reprint. Nutley, NJ: Presbyterian and Reformed, 1973. 2:280–88.

_____. "The Right of Systematic Theology," in *Selected Shorter Writings of Benjamin B. Warfield.* John E. Meeter, ed. 1896. Reprint. Nutley, NJ: Presbyterian and Reformed, 1973. 2:21–279.

Webster, John. "Introduction: Systematic Theology," in *The Oxford Handbook of Systematic Theology.* John Webster, Kathryn Tanner, Iain Torrance, eds. 2007. Reprint. New York: Oxford University, 2010. 13–28.

_____. "Principles of Systematic Theology." *International Journal of Systematic Theology* 11.1. Jan. 2009. 56–71.

_____. "What Makes Theology Theological?" *Journal of Analytic Theology* 3. 2015. 17–28.

Whaling, Frank. "The Development of the Word 'Theology.'" *Scottish Journal of Theology* 34.4. 1981. 289–312.

Williams, A. N. "What is Systematic Theology?" *International Journal of Systematic Theology* 11.1. January 2009. 40–55.

Williams, Michael. "Systematic Theology as a Biblical Discipline," in *All for Jesus: A Celebration of the 50th Anniversary of Covenant Theological Seminary.*R. A. Paterson and S. M. Lucas, eds. Fearn, Ross-shire, Scotland: Christian Focus, 2005.167–96.

Woods, Andy. "The Significance of Systematic Theology." *Conservative Theological Journal* 8.23. Mar. 2004. 301–19.

Yarnell, Malcolm B., III. "Systematic Theology," in *Theology, Church, and Ministry: A Handbook for Theological Education.* David S. Dockery, ed. Nashville, TN: B&H Academic, 2017. 257–80.

_____. "Systematic theology, History of," in *New Dictionary of Theology: Historical and Systematic*. 2nd ed. Martin Davie, *et al.*, eds. Downers Grove, IL: InterVarsity Academic, 2016. 886–89.

Zachhuber, Johannes. "What is Theology? Historical and Systematic Reflections," *International Journal for the Study of the Christian Church* 21.3–4. 2021. 198–211.

MONOGRAPHS

Allison, Gregg R. *Historical Theology: An Introduction to Christian Doctrine*. Grand Rapids, MI: Zondervan, 2011.

Anieor, Uche. *How to Read Theology: Engaging Doctrine Critically and Charitably*. Grand Rapids, MI: Baker Academic, 2018.

Barth, Karl, *Church Dogmatics*, 14 vols. Geoffrey W. Bromiley and Thomas F. Torrance, trans. 1936. Reprint. Peabody, MA: Hendrickson, 2010.

_____. *Protestant Theology in the Nineteenth Century: Its Background and History*. Grand Rapids, MI: Eerdmans, 2002.

Berkhof, Hendrikus. *Introduction to the Study of Dogmatics.* John Vriend, trans. Grand Rapids, MI: Eerdmans, 1985.

Berkof, Louis. *Introductory Volume to Systematic Theology*. 1932. Reprint. Grand Rapids, MI: Baker, 1979.

Blackwell, Ben C., and R. L. Hatchett. *Engaging Theology: A Biblical, Historical, and Practical Introduction.* Grand Rapids, MI: Zondervan, 2019.

Bray, Gerald. *God Has Spoken: A History of Christian Theology*. Wheaton, IL: Crossway 2014.

Briggs, Charles Augustus, and Emilie Grace Briggs. *History of the Study of Theology*. 2 vols. New York: Charles Scribner's Sons, 1916.

Bromiley, Geoffrey W. *Historical Theology: An Introduction*. Grand Rapids, MI: Eerdmans, 1978.

Cameron, Nigel M., ed. *The Challenge of Evangelical Theology: Essays in Approach and Method*. Edinburgh: Rutherford House, 1987.

Cave, Alfred. *An Introduction to Theology*. Edinburgh: T&T Clark, 1886.

Charry, Ellen T. *By the Renewing of Your Minds: The Pastoral Function of Christian Doctrine*. New York: Oxford University, 1997.

Clark, David K. *To Know and Love God: Method for Theology*. Wheaton, IL: Crossway, 2003.

Clark, Gordon H. *In Defense of Theology*. Milford, MI: Mott, 1984.

Cole, Graham A. *Faithful Theology: An Introduction*. Wheaton, IL: Crossway, 2020.

Congar, Yves M. J. *A History of Theology*. Garden City, NY: Doubleday, 1968.

Corduan, Winfried. *Handmaid to Theology: An Essay in Philosophical Prolegomena*. Grand Rapids, MI: Baker, 1981.

Cottrell, Jack. *The Doctrine of God*, vol. 1: *What the Bible Says about God the Creator*. 1983. Reprint. Eugene, OR: Wipf & Stock, 2001.

_____. *The Doctrine of God*, vol. 2: *What the Bible Says about God the Ruler*. 1984. Reprint. Eugene, OR: Wipf & Stock, 2000.

_____. *The Doctrine of God*, vol. 3: *What the Bible Says about God the Redeemer*. 1987. Reprint. Eugene, OR: Wipf & Stock, 2001.

Crisp, Oliver D., and Fred Sanders, eds. *The Task of Dogmatics: Explorations in Theological Method*. Grand Rapids, MI: Zondervan, 2017.

Cunliffe–Jones, Hubert, ed. *A History of Christian Doctrine*. Philadelphia, PA: Fortress, 1978.

Cunningham, William. *Historical Theology: A Review of the Principal Discussions in the Christian Church Since the Apostolic Age*. 2 vols. 1870. Reprint. London: Banner of Truth, 1960.

D'Onofrio, Giulio. *History of Theology,* vol. 2: *The Middle Ages*. Matthew J. O'Connell, trans. Collegeville, MN: Liturgical, 2008.

_____. *History of Theology,* vol. 3: *The Renaissance*. Trans. Matthew J. O'Connell. Collegeville, MN: Liturgical, 1998.

Davis, John Jefferson. *Foundations of Evangelical Theology*. Grand Rapids, MI: Baker, 1984.

_____. *Handbook of Basic Bible Texts: Every Key Passage for the Study of Doctrine and Theology*. Grand Rapids, MI: Zondervan, 1984.

_____. *Theology Primer: Resources of the Theological Student*. Grand Rapids, MI: Baker, 1981.

_____, ed. *The Necessity of Systematic Theology*. Grand Rapids, MI: Baker, 1980.

Dorrien, Gary. *The Remaking of Evangelical Theology*. Louisville, KY: Westminster John Knox, 1998.

Dulles, Avery. *The Craft of Theology: From Symbol to System*. Exp. ed. New York: Crossroad, 1995.

Dunning, H. Ray. *Grace, Faith, and Holiness: A Wesleyan Systematic Theology*. Kansas City, MO: Beacon Hill, 1988.

Ebeling, Gerhard. *The Study of Theology*. Duane A. Priebe, trans. Philadelphia, PA: Fortress, 1978.

Erickson, Millard J. *The Evangelical Left: Encountering Postconservative Evangelical Theology.* Grand Rapids, MI: Baker, 1997.

Evans, G. R. *The Beginnings of Theology as an Academic Discipline.* Oxford: Clarendon, 1980.

_____, ed. *The First Theologians: An Introduction to the Theology of the Early Church*. Oxford: Blackwell, 2004.

_____, ed. *The Medieval Theologians: An Introduction to the Medieval Period.* Oxford: Blackwell, 2005.

Ford, David F. *The Future of Christian Theology.* Sussex: Wiley–Blackwell, 2011.

_____, and Rachel Muers, eds. *The Modern Theologians: An Introduction to the Christian Faith in the Twentieth Century.* 2nd ed. Oxford: Blackwell, 1997.

Frame, John M. *A History of Western Philosophy and Theology.* Phillipsburg, NJ: P&R, 2015.

_____. *Doctrine of the Knowledge of God.* A Theology of Lordship. Phillipsburg, NJ: P&R, 1987.

_____. *On Theology: Explorations and Controversies*. Bellingham, WA: Lexham, 2023.

_____. *Salvation Belongs to the Lord: An Introduction to Systematic Theology*. Phillipsburg, NJ: P&R, 2006.

Franke, John R. *The Character of Theology: An Introduction to its Nature, Task and Purpose: A Postconservative Evangelical Approach.* Grand Rapids, MI: Baker Academic, 2005.

Frei, Hans. *Types of Christian Theology*. George Hunsinger and William C. Placher, eds. New Haven, CT: Yale University, 1992.

González, Justo L. *Out of Every Tribe and Nation: Christian Theology at the Ethnic Roundtable.* Nashville, TN: Abingdon, 1992.

González, Justo L., and Zaida Maldonado Pérez. *An Introduction to Christian Theology*. Nashville, TN: Abingdon, 2002.

Gore, R. J., Jr. *Getting Started: An Introduction to Systematic Theology for Students and Laymen.* Winter Springs, FL: Greater Heritage, 2023.

Greggs, Tom. *Introduction to Christian Theology: A Comprehensive, Systematically and Biblically Based Approach.* London: SPCK, 2024.

_____. *New Perspectives for Evangelical Theology.* New York: Routledge, 2010.

Grenz, Stanley J. *Created for Community: Connecting Christian Belief with Christian Living*. Grand Rapids, MI: Baker, 1998.

_____. *Renewing the Center: Evangelical Theology in a Post–Christian Era.* Grand Rapids, MI: Baker, 2000.

_____. *Revisioning Evangelical Theology: A Fresh Agenda for the 21st Century*. Downers Grove, IL: IVP, 1993.

_____, and Roger E. Olson. *Who Needs Theology? An Invitation to the Study of God.* Downers Grove, IL: IVP, 1996.

Guarino, Thomas G. *Foundations of Systematic Theology.* New York and London: T&T Clark, 2005.

Gundry, Stanley N., and Alan F. Johnson, eds. *Tensions in Contemporary Theology.* Grand Rapids, MI: Baker, 1983.

Hägglund, Bengt. *History of Theology.* 4th rev. ed. Gene J. Lund, trans. St. Louis, MO: Concordia, 2007.

Hart, Trevor. *Faith Thinking*. Downers Grove, IL: IVP, 1996.

Healy, F. G., ed. *What Theologians Do.* Grand Rapids, MI: Eerdmans, 1970.

Hodgson, Peter C., and Robert H. King, eds. *Christian Theology: An Introduction to Its Traditions and Tasks,* 3rd ed. Minneapolis, MN: Augsburg Fortress, 1994.

Holmes, Stanley. *Listening to the Past: The Place of Tradition in Theology.* Grand Rapids, MI: Baker, 2002.

Instone–Brewer, David. *Church Doctrine and the Bible: Theology in Ancient Context.* Scripture in Context Series. Bellingham, WA: Lexham, 2020.

Jamieson, Bobby. *Sound Doctrine: How a Church Grows in the Love and Holiness of God.* Wheaton, IL: Crossway, 2013.

Jenson, Robert W. *Systematic Theology.* 2 vols. New York: Oxford University, 1997–99.

Jinkins, Michael. *Invitation to Theology: A Guide to Study, Conversation, and Practice.* Downers Grove, IL: IVP Academic 2001.

Johnson, Keith L. *Theology as Discipleship.* Downers Grove, IL: IVP, 2015.

Johnston, Derek. *A Brief History of Theology: From the New Testament to Feminist Theology.* New York, NY: Continuum, 2009.

Jones, Beth Felker. *Practicing Christian Doctrine: An Introduction to Thinking and Living Theologically.* Grand Rapids, MI: Baker Academic, 2014.

Kantzer, Kenneth S., and Stanley N. Gundry, eds. *Perspectives on Evangelical Theology.* Grand Rapids, MI: Baker, 1979.

Kapic, Kelly M. *A Little Book for New Theologians: Why and How to Study Theology.* Downers Grove, IL: IVP, 2012.

_____, and Bruce L. McCormack, eds. *Mapping Modern Theology: A Thematic and Historical Introduction.* Grand Rapids, MI: Baker Academic, 2012.

Kasper, Walter. *The Methods of Dogmatic Theology*. Shannon, Ireland: Ecclesia, 1969.

Kelly, J. N. D. *Early Christian Doctrines*. Rev. ed. New York: Harper, 1978.

Kennedy, Philip. *Twentieth-century Theologians: A New Introduction to Christian Thought.* New York, NY: I. B. Tauris, 2010.

Klotsche, E. H. *The History of Christian Doctrine*. Rev. ed. Grand Rapids, MI: Baker, 1979.

Kreider, Glenn R., and Michael J. Svigel. *A Practical Primer on Theological Method.* Grand Rapids, MI: Zondervan, 2019.

Kuyper, Abraham. *Principles of Sacred Theology*. J. H. De Vries, trans. Grand Rapids, MI: Eerdmans, 1968.

La'Porte, Victoria. *An Introduction to Theology*. Edinburgh: Edinburgh University, 2001.

Latourette, Kenneth Scott. *A History of Christianity*. New York: Harper, 1953.

Laurence, John D. *Introduction to Theology*. Boston, MA: Pearson Learning Solutions, 2007.

Lindbeck, George. *The Nature of Doctrine.* Philadelphia, PA: Westminster, 1984.

Lindberg, Carter. *The Reformation Theologians: An Introduction to Theology in the Early Modern Period.* Oxford: Blackwell, 2002.

Lints, Richard. *The Fabric of Theology: Toward an Evangelical Prolegomena.* Grand Rapids, MI: Eerdmans, 1994.

Lohse, Bernhard. *A Short History of Christian Doctrine*. Philadelphia, PA: Fortress, 1966.

Lovin, Robin W., and Joshua Maudlin, eds. *Theology as Interdisciplinary Inquiry*. Grand Rapids, MI: Eerdmans, 2017.

Macchia, Frank. *Introduction to Theology: Declaring the Wonders of God*, Foundations of Spirit–Filled Christianity. Grand Rapids, MI: Baker Academic, 2023.

_____. *Tongues of Fire: A Systematic Theology of the Christian Faith,* Word and Spirit: Pentecostal Investigations on Theology and History. Eugene, OR: Cascade Books, 2023.

Macgregor, Kirk R. *Contemporary Theology: An Introduction,* rev. ed.: *Classical, Evangelical, Philosophical, and Global Perspectives.* Grand Rapids, MI: Zondervan Academic, 2020.

McFarlane, Graham. *A Model for Evangelical Theology: Integrating Scripture, Tradition, Reason, Experience, and Community.* Grand Rapids, MI: Baker Academic, 2020.

McGiffert, A. C. *A History of Christian Thought*. New York: Scribner's, 1946.

McGowan, A. T. B. *Always Reforming: Explorations in Systematic Theology*. Downers Grove, IL: IVP, 2006.

McGrath, Alister E. *Christian Theology: An Introduction*. 3rd ed. Oxford: Blackwell, 2001.

_____. *The Genesis of Doctrine: A Study in the Foundations of Doctrinal Criticism.* Oxford: Basel Blackwell, 1990.

_____. *Historical Theology: an Introduction to the History of Christian Thought*. 2nd ed. Malden, MA: Blackwell, 2013.

_____. *A Scientific Theology*. 3 vols. Grand Rapids, MI: Eerdmans, 2001–03.

_____. *Theology: The Basics*. 4th ed. Oxford: Wiley-Blackwell, 2018.

_____. *What's the Point of Theology? Wisdom, Wellbeing and Wonder*. Grand Rapids, MI: Zondervan Academic, 2022.

McKim, Donald K. *A Down and Dirty Guide to Theology*. Louisville, KY: Westminster John Knox, 2011.

_____. *Theological Turning Points: Major Issues in Christian Thought*. Atlanta: Westminster John Knox, 1988.

Meadors, Gary T., ed. *Four Views on Moving beyond the Bible to Theology*. Grand Rapids, MI: Zondervan, 2009.

Milne, Bruce. *Know the Truth: A Handbook of Christian Belief*. 3rd ed. Downers Grove, IL: InterVarsity, 2009.

Mohler, R. Albert, Jr. *The Pastor as Theologian*. Louisville, KY: Southern Baptist Theological Seminary, 2006.

Montgomery, John Warwick. *The Suicide of Christian Theology*. Minneapolis, MN: Bethany Fellowship, 1970.

Moody, Dale. *The Word of Truth: A Summary of Christian Doctrine Based on Biblical Revelation*. Grand Rapids, MI: Eerdmans, 1981.

Muller, Richard A. *A Post–Reformation Reformed Dogmatics: The Rise and Development of Reformed Orthodoxy, ca. 1510 to 1725*. 2nd ed. 4 vols. Grand Rapids, MI: Baker, 2003.

_____. *The Study of Theology: From Biblical Interpretation to Contemporary Formulation*. Grand Rapids, MI: Zondervan, 1981.

Murray, John. *Collected Writings of John Murray*. 4 vols. Carlisle, PA: Banner of Truth, 1976–82.

Neder, Adam. *Theology as a Way of Life: On Teaching and Learning the Christian Faith.* Grand Rapids, MI: Baker Academic, 2019.

Neilson, Jon. *Knowing God's Truth: An Introduction to Systematic Theology.* Theology Basics. Wheaton, IL: Crossway, 2023.

Neve, J. L. *A History of Christian Thought.* 2 vols. Philadelphia, PA: Muhlenberg, 1946.

Nicholls, William, ed. *Pelican Guide to Theology*, vol. 1: *Systematic and Philosophical.* Harmondsworth, UK: Penguin, 1969.

Oden, Thomas. *The Rebirth of Orthodoxy.* San Francisco, CA: HarperSanFrancisco, 2003.

Ogden, Shubert Miles. *Doing Theology Today.* Valley Forge, PA: Trinity, 1996.

Olson, Arnold T. *This We Believe: The Background and Exposition of the Doctrinal Statement of the Evangelical Free Church of America.* Minneapolis, MN: Free Church Publications, 1961.

Olson, Roger E. *Arminian Theology.* Downers Grove, IL: InterVarsity, 2006.

_____. *The Journey of Modern Theology: From Reconstruction to Deconstruction.* Downers Grove, IL: IVP Academic, 2013.

_____. *Reformed and Always Reforming: The Postconservative Approach to Evangelical Theology.* Grand Rapids, MI: Baker, 2007.

Ortlund, Gavin. *Finding the Right Hills to Die On: The Case for Theological Triage.* Wheaton, IL: Crossway, 2020.

Ottati, Douglas F. *A Theology for the Twenty–first Century.* Grand Rapids, MI: Eerdmans, 2020.

Packer, J. I., and Thomas C. Oden. *One Faith: The Evangelical Consensus.* Downers Grove, IL: InterVarsity, 1999.

Pannenberg, Wolfhart. *Basic Questions in Theology: Collected Essays*. 2 vols. George H. Kehm, trans. Louisville, KY: Westminster John Knox, 1983.

_____. *An Introduction to Systematic Theology*. Grand Rapids, MI: Eerdmans, 1991.

_____. *Systematic Theology*. 2 vols. Geoffrey W. Bromiley, trans. Grand Rapids, MI: Eerdmans, 1991–94.

Pelikan, Jaroslav. *The Vindication of Tradition: The 1983 Jefferson Lecture in the Humanities*. New Haven, CT: Yale University, 1984.

Piper, John. *The Life of the Mind and the Love of God.* Wheaton, IL: Crossway, 2010.

Placher, William C., ed. *Essentials of Christian Theology*. Louisville, KY: Westminster John Knox, 2003.

_____, and Derek R. Nelson. *A History of Christian Theology: An Introduction.* 2nd ed. Louisville: Westminster John Knox, 2013.

Porter, Stanley E., and Steven M. Studebaker, eds. *Evangelical Theological Method: Five Views.* Downers Grove, IL: IVP, 2018.

Poythress, Vern. *Symphonic Theology: The Validity of Multiple Perspectives in Theology*. Grand Rapids, MI: Zondervan, 1987.

Preus, Robert D. *The Theology of Post–Reformation Lutheranism: A Study in Theological Prolegomena. 2 vols.* St. Louis, MO: Concordia, 1970.

Putman, Rhyne R. *In Defense of Doctrine: Evangelicalism, Theology, and Scripture.* Minneapolis, MN: Fortress, 2015.

_____. *The Method of Christian Theology: A Basic Introduction.* Nashville, TN: B&H Academic, 2021.

_____. *When Doctrine Divides the People of God: An Evangelical Approach to Theological Diversity.* Wheaton, IL: Crossway, 2020.

Rahner, Karl. *Foundations of Christian Faith.* William V. Dych, trans. New York: Crossroad, 1989.

Ritschl, Dietrich. *The Logic of Theology: A Brief Account of the Relationship between Basic Concepts in Theology.* Philadelphia, PA: Fortress, 1987.

Sawyer, M. James. *The Survivor's Guide to Theology.* 2006. Reprint. Eugene, OR: Wipf & Stock, 2016.

Schaff, Philip. *The Creeds of Christendom.* 3 vols, 6th ed. Rev. and enl. Grand Rapids, MI: Baker, 1877.

_____. *Theological Propædeutic: A General Introduction to the Study of Theology, Exegetical, Historical, Systematic, and Practical, Including Encyclopædia, Methodology, and Bibliography.* 1894. Reprint. Eugene, OR: Wipf and Stock, 2007.

Shedd, William G. T. *A History of Christian Doctrine.* 2 vols. 1863. Reprint. Minneapolis, MN: Klock & Klock, 1978.

Shults, F. LeRon. *The Postfoundationalist Task of Theology: Wolfhart Pannenberg and the New Theological Rationality.* Grand Rapids, MI: Eerdmans, 1999.

Slavens, Thomas P. *Introduction to Systematic Theology.* Lanham, MD: University Press of America, 1992.

Smart, Ninian and Steve Konstantine. *Christian Systematic Theology in a World Context.* Minneapolis, MN: Fortress, 1992.

Stackhouse, John G., Jr., ed. *Evangelical Futures: A Conversation on Theological Method.* Grand Rapids, MI: Baker, 2000.

Thielicke, Helmut. *A Little Exercise for Young Theologians*. Grand Rapids, MI: Eerdmans, 1962.

Thiselton, Anthony C. *Approaching the Study of Theology: An Introduction to Key Thinkers, Concepts, Methods and Debates*. Downers Grove, IL: IVP Academic, 2018.

Thorsen, Donald A. D. *An Exploration of Christian Theology*. 2nd ed. Grand Rapids, MI: Baker Academic, 2020.

_____. *The Wesleyan Quadrilateral: Scripture, Tradition. Reason, and Experience as a Model of Evangelical Theology*. Grand Rapids, MI: Brazos, 2002.

Torrance, T. F. *The Ground and Grammar of Theology*. Charlottesville, VA: University of Virginia, 1980.

_____. *Theological Science*. New York: Oxford University, 1969.

Towey, Anthony. *An Introduction to Christian Theology: Biblical, Classical, Contemporary*. New York: Bloomsbury, 2013.

Treier, Daniel J. *Introducing Theological Interpretation of Scripture: Recovering a Christian Practice*. Grand Rapids, MI: Baker Academic, 2008.

_____. *Introducing Evangelical Theology*. Grand Rapids, MI: Baker Academic, 2019.

Van Til, Cornelius. *An Introduction to Systematic Theology: Prolegomena and the Doctrines of Revelation, Scripture, and God*. 2nd ed. William Edgar, ed. Phillipsburg, NJ: P&R, 2007.

_____. *In Defense of the Faith*, vol. 5: *An Introduction to Systematic Theology*. Philadelphia: Presbyterian and Reformed, 1976.

Vanhoozer, Kevin J. *The Drama of Doctrine: A Canonical–Linguistic Approach to Christian Theology*. Louisville: Westminster John Knox, 2005.

_____. *Faith Speaking Understanding: Performing the Drama of Doctrine*. Louisville, KY: Westminster John Knox 2014.

_____. *First Theology: God, Scripture, and Hermeneutics*. Downers Grove, IL: InterVarsity, 2002.

Vanhoozer, Kevin J., and Daniel J. Treier. *Theology and the Mirror of Scripture: A Mere Evangelical Account.* Studies in Christian Doctrine and Scripture. Downers Grove, IL: IVP, 2015.

Voekel, R. T. *The Shape of the Theological Task*. Philadelphia: Westminster, 1968.

Veeneman, Mary M. *Introducing Theological Method: A Survey of Contemporary Theologians and Approaches*. Grand Rapids, MI: Baker Academic, 2017.

Volf, Miroslav, and Dorothy C. Bass, eds. *Practicing Theology: Beliefs and Practices in Christian Life*. Grand Rapids, MI: Eerdmans, 2001.

_____, and Matthew Croasmun. *For the Life of the World: Theology That Makes a Difference*. Grand Rapids, MI: Brazos, 2019.

Vos, Geerhardus, *Reformed Dogmatics*. 5 vols. Richard B. Gaffin, Jr., trans. and ed. Grand Rapids, MI: Eerdmans, 2012–16.

Wagner, Richard E. *Strengthened by Grace: A Systematic Theology Handbook.* Larkspur, CO: Grace Acres, 2007.

Wainwright, Geoffrey. *Doxology: The Praise of God in Worship, Doctrine and Life: A Systematic Theology*. New York: Oxford University, 1980.

Ware, Bruce. *Understanding Theology: An Evangelical Understanding of God and His Word*. Camas, WA: BiblicalTraining.org, 2017.

Webster, John B. *The Domain of the Word: Scripture and Theological Reason*. New York: T&T Clark, 2012.

Welker, Michael, and Cynthia A. Jarvis, eds. *Loving God with Our Minds: The Pastor as Theologian*. Grand Rapids, MI: Eerdmans, 2004.

Wells, David F. *No Place for Truth: Or, Whatever Happened to Evangelical Theology?* Grand Rapids, MI: Eerdmans, 1993.

_____, ed. *Toward a Theology for the Future*. Carol Stream, IL: Creation House, 1971.

Wilkin, Jen, and J. T. English. *You Are a Theologian: An Invitation to Know and Love God Well*. Nashville, TN: B&H, 2023.

Williams, A. N. *The Architecture of Theology: Structure, System, and Ratio*. Oxford: Oxford University, 2011.

Woodbridge, John D., and Thomas Edward McComiskey, eds. *Doing Theology in Today's World: Essays in Honor of Kenneth S. Kantzer*. Grand Rapids, MI: Zondervan, 1991.

Yong, Amos. *Learning Theology*. Louisville, KY: Westminster John Knox, 2018.

INDEX

Julian of Norwich, 32, 129
Junod, Éric, 11

Made in the USA
Middletown, DE
10 September 2024

60737854R00192